# NOT
# ALL
# BLACK
# AND
# WHITE

Also by Christopher Edley, Jr.

*Administrative Law*, Yale University Press 1992

# NOT ALL BLACK AND WHITE

## AFFIRMATIVE ACTION AND AMERICAN VALUES

*Christopher Edley, Jr.*

A division of Farrar, Straus & Giroux    New York

Hill and Wang
A division of Farrar, Straus and Giroux
19 Union Square West, New York 10003

Distributed in Canada by Douglas & McIntyre Ltd.
Printed in the United States of America
*Designed by Abby Kagan*
First published in 1996 by Hill and Wang
First paperback edition, 1998

Portions of Chapter 10 are excerpted or adapted from Christopher Edley, Jr.'s "Affirmative Action and the Rights Rhetoric Trap," in Robert K. Fullinwider, Claudia Mills, eds., *The Moral Foundations of Civil Rights* (Totowa, N.J.: Rowman & Littlefield, 1986)

The Library of Congress has catalogued the hardcover edition as follows:
Edley, Christopher F.
    Not all black and white : affirmative action, race, and American
values / Christopher Edley, Jr.
        p.   cm.
    Includes bibliographical references and index.
    ISBN 0-8090-2955-3 (alk. paper)
    1. Affirmative action programs—Law and legislation—United
States.   I. Title.
KF4755.5.E33   1996
342.73'0873—dc20
[347.302873]                                        96-21397

*for*
*Christopher F. Edley III*
*and*
*Christopher F. Edley, Sr.*

*from father to son . . .*

# CONTENTS

# PREFACE

**W**hy yet another book on race? This extended essay is about hard choices and how to think about them, not just about my own conclusions or those of a President for whom I worked. I believe that thoughtful people seeking a deeper understanding of what affirmative action is all about, deciding for themselves how America ought best to achieve racial justice, will profit from a rigorous effort to think about the hard choices and first principles, in much the same way that President Clinton and his advisors did during 1994 and 1995. By thoughtful people, I certainly mean anyone who is reading this book; I also mean people who believe that one need not embrace absolutism in order to be principled, and need not avoid strong value commitments in order to be tolerant.

From classrooms to boardrooms, from dinner tables to Capitol corridors, when our values are in doubt or in conflict, we often shrink from the hard work of understanding each other, of searching for the truth in what each side believes and moving toward something shared. The doubts and conflicts concerning race in America are many and deep. It has ever been so. Still, now and again the earth moves, and then the possibilities of the moment—today's moment—are at once exciting and frightening.

• • •

Consider the drama of Colin Powell. The phenomenon suggests a number of points that concern my general theme:

Colin Powell is a product of affirmative action.* When President Jimmy Carter appointed Clifford Alexander to serve as Secretary of the Army, Alexander was the first African American to hold so high a post in the national security establishment. One of Alexander's heroic accomplishments was to manage the transition of the largest branch of the armed services to an all-volunteer force. Another was to put equal opportunity at the center of the Army's human resources strategy. And he gave personal attention to integrating the senior officer ranks with minorities and women. Colin Powell owes a considerable debt to Cliff Alexander, who looked down a list and singled him out for promotion and advancement. According to Alexander, race was of course a consideration in the decision. Months ago, when I heard the (white) customers at the dry cleaner around the corner from my apartment talking excitedly about the possibility of Powell being a presidential candidate, race was a factor. And it was a factor when I and so many others wondered, nervously, how much special danger from assassins Powell might face in a national campaign, or how much hostility to him the radical right would register, or whether the pack-dog journalism unleashed by the inevitable first whiff of scandal (My Lai?) would be ordinarily color-blind, or rabidly resentful.

The whole thing makes me wonder how much we really understand about race in America. Maybe the central lesson is less about ignorance than about the fluidity and contingency of politics and the social situation. I sense almost overwhelming perils in race relations at the moment, but maybe everything is much more fluid and changeable than I recognize. Things can get better fast.

---

* Based on a conversation with Clifford Alexander, former Secretary of the Army, in which Alexander described efforts to promote equal opportunity in the Army by seeking out qualified minority and women officers for promotion. In his autobiography, General Powell says he opposes "preferences" but favors "affirmative action," which shows him to be a skillful politician. He continues: "I benefited from equal opportunity and affirmative action in the Army, but I was not shown preference." Colin L. Powell, with Joseph E. Persico, *My American Journey* (New York: Random House, 1995), p. 608. This formulation answers, as we will see, none of the difficult questions.

For thirty years I've used the phrase "exception syndrome" to define the application of the "Some of my best friends are Negroes" expression that whites often used (past tense?) to establish their bona fides on racial matters. Not so long ago, the phrase would often be followed by some politely expressed bigotry. In the exception syndrome, one can hold on to a prejudice about a group and treat individual counterexamples as mere exceptions to the rule, possibly exceptions that prove the rule. So, Colin Powell's exceptional qualities leave admirers simultaneously pleased with their personal capacity for racial tolerance while confirmed in their sense that most blacks certainly aren't like Powell. That's what I fear.

More optimistically, the emergence of a widely admired African American as a crossover political leader on the national stage might have a transformative effect, encouraging us toward tolerance, comparable to the effect that John F. Kennedy's presidency had on tolerance for Catholics. Religious denomination has all but disappeared as a factor in polite conversation about political candidates—or at least until the recent rise of the strident radical religious right. Might Colin Powell accomplish a similar transformation? That's what I believe.

Yet modern American political debate is often consigned to a sewer of negativity. The political valence of racial policies—especially affirmative action, the subject of this book—has been heightened in 1996 in two respects. First, there is a battle for the soul of a resurgent GOP. Some GOP strategists see Republican opposition to affirmative action as a way of driving a wedge between conservative and liberal Democrats while cementing the GOP's electoral gains among white male voters. Others want to broaden the party with strategies of inclusion; this group is genuinely thrilled by Colin Powell's decision to join their ranks, not threatened by it. Newt Gingrich seems ambivalent: he echoes an antipreference mantra, but he doesn't want the party of Abe Lincoln to become the party of David Duke. (He wants it to be the party of Newt Gingrich.) Second, battles over legislative and ballot initiatives will challenge the civil rights orthodoxy of the past quarter-century and force candidates and officeholders to declare their views, though many politicians would just as soon avoid or defer those battles.

Beyond politics, there are the frightening portents of sharper division and declining civility in matters of race. The Million Man March, the Simpson verdict, congressional redistricting, a rising incidence of hate crimes at the same time that overall crime declines, the sentencing disparities between the larger number of black defendants in crack cases and the white ones convicted of crimes relating to powder cocaine—every month the United States has faced racial issues that are like Rorschach tests, painfully revealing our national neurosis. For the most part, leaders, analysts, and just plain folks note all this with concern but are unable to prescribe the needed therapy and uncertain about the prognosis for healing.

My focus in this book is on hard choices about race that must be made in our national policies and private practices, and how to think carefully about those choices. My ambition is to face the choices squarely, not make them appear easier than they are. I can't be objective, but I've tried to be as probing and fair as I can without (too often) becoming abstruse. My most important conclusion can be set forth right here: when you think carefully about hard choices, they turn out to be very hard indeed.

People generally fall into two camps: some who are comfortable with complexity, nuance, and qualified propositions, even revel in the play of multifaceted arguments; others who prefer sharp resolution and clear conclusions. It's the intellectual equivalent of the contrast between those whose eyes linger over a wildscape of forest, crag, and brook and those who are drawn to an orderly English countryside of trim fields, prim cottages, and stone walls. The choice between these two intellectual styles is fundamental. There are geniuses and bores in both schools. And each has pitfalls. A taste for complication can lead you to overlook some fundamental, essential truth and the broader understanding to which that leads. The taste for simplicity can lead you to a reductionism that bleaches away inconvenient or confusing details and dissolves the truths that challenge simplification. Both of these pitfalls have snared politicians who face the color question.

In government, I saw plenty of officials and politicians who were loath to make difficult decisions. Sometimes they would sit through a

long meeting, listen to the evidence and the arguments for and against
a proposal, and at the end would ask for more information, and perhaps
another meeting, though the difficulty of the decision had little to do
with missing information. The decision was difficult because the problem was hard. More information wouldn't make the problem easier; it
would just make the list of pros and cons longer. This kind of decision
maker wants to find a way to make hard decisions easier and, if that
doesn't work, to make no decision until a crisis forces one, or the issue
is overtaken by events. But there were other decision makers who made
sure they understood a hard problem on its own terms and, having
satisfied themselves of that, comfortably made a decision and a leap
to action.

My initial instinct was to think of the first kind of decision maker as
analytical and the second as intuitive, or "instinctive." But that is inaccurate. People facing complex decisions use a mix of analysis and intuition which varies from episode to episode and problem to problem. I
suspect it matters how one reacts to messy confusions of competing values, predictions, and goals. This depends not only on an intuitive sense
of the terrain (experience helps) but also on some kind of ineffable aesthetic: if you don't groove on the complexity, you worry the problem to
death or duck it; the more at home you are in the wild policy jungle, the
more likely you are to see and accept a hard choice for what it is, decide,
and then move on, hunting for more big game.

In my aesthetic, the first order of business is not to pick a side and
mobilize arguments in support of it, but rather to investigate why an
important policy debate has the structure that it does and why the
choice is hard. If we can illuminate the empirical propositions and
value commitments underlying the competing points of view, we will
be in a better position to choose sides and participate in the debate.
Sometimes we conclude that the debate is ill conceived, the framework
mistaken, and a fresh way of considering the problem more sensible.
But in any case, the method is to search for the values at stake and at
the same time to avoid turning the disputants into caricatures and their
deep commitments into platitudes.

• • •

Some tensions recur, and they are familiar from countless settings:

*Idealism v. Pragmatism.* One of the great themes in America's race story is the tension between the ideals we preach and those we practice. In the original sin, the Founders wrote "unalienable rights" for all people into the Declaration of Independence while preserving in the Constitution the "peculiar institution" of slavery. From then until now, Americans have been able to sing a hymn of opportunity and equality while living in or near communities where the nation's mythic dreams are fractured by inherited, endemic despair. We have a rich set of social, political, and cognitive strategies for mediating this tension, the most common being ignorance of and indifference to those whom we think of as not really "one of us." But this tension nevertheless is powerful when it comes time to shape public policy.

*Autonomy v. Community.* At the heart of our liberal democratic political culture is a tension between commitments to individual liberty and autonomy on the one hand and collective action through government to advance the commonweal on the other. In race matters, government regulation is a form of interference with personal attitudes and private practices, and the usual range of antistate anxieties and concerns apply: get the government bureaucrats off our backs. Moreover, many remedial measures intended to bring about a measure of racial justice take a form that redistributes opportunity from white men to minorities and women, or at least appears to. It is hard to persuade these white men that they are personally better off as a result of the measures, and an appeal to communal values and needs is often uninspiring, since communal values presuppose community and, as regards race, we don't have it. The complementarity of "rights and responsibilities" becomes dangerously skewed if communal commitments to mutual responsibility wither while strident attachment to personal autonomy flourishes.

*Public v. Private.* A related dichotomy concerns our irrepressible inclination to make a sharp distinction between the spheres of personal or family life and that of civic or public life. Should public schools teach personal *values*? Should public schools instruct children about values of racial tolerance, or evolving models of gender roles, or the original sin of American racism? One way to start on an answer is to ask, "Are schools an extension of the family, or of the state?" Well, yes. Both. When we view them as the former, of course they should teach values. But when we view them as a bureaucratic and potentially threatening extension of the state, we'd rather leave the values instruction to family and mosque, thank you very much. (And what about dysfunctional families and decayed social institutions? Here again is a tension between idealism and pragmatism.) In deciding policies about race relations and community, the sorting-out of the public and private spheres is both critically important and irreducibly complex. In other words, it's hard.

*Nation v. Community.* Much of the complexity in discussing race relations arises from the fact that we are not just Americans. We are members of many groups, and over time and circumstance the strength of our allegiances will vary, whether to country, race, religion, neighborhood, clan, political party, profession, gender, immigrant heritage, sexual orientation, bowling league, gang, sorority, age cohort, economic class. . . . Some people feel powerfully attached to one or two of these communities; many people feel weak attachments to several and strong attachments to none. So there is a potential for "balkanization" when militant membership in one subcommunity becomes a strategy for creating identity and unleashing the power of collective action; but also there is the challenging but rewarding potential for building the "social capital" or connective tissue that makes communities vibrant and productive. Yet these divided, multicentered loyalties confuse public policies on race and other matters when we debate complementary roles for family, community institutions, and governments.

My method will be to identify the various tensions and difficulties embedded in arguments about affirmative action. I find this activity strangely reassuring: the seeming intractability of our disagreements over affirmative action may concern not simply the inherent difficulty of the American neurosis about race but also the many tensions I have mentioned—difficulties familiar to students of any great social problem.

• • •

As regards women and minority groups other than African Americans, my sense is that there are both parallels and distinctions. I focus almost exclusively on the black–white dynamic because that's the set of issues I understand best, and my healthy respect for the complexity of all this makes me more tentative about matters concerning women, Hispanics, Asians, Pacific Islanders, new immigrants, linguistic minorities, HIV victims, the disabled, and homosexuals. Moreover, the black-white tension is the heart, the principal generator, of the minority-rights controversy in national policy argument and in most areas of the country.

I recoil from exercises in comparative oppression. Something of the sort seems necessary, however, so that the justification for affirmative action, in specific contexts, is sensitive to competing moral claims and ethical views, as it should be. For example, the remedial justification for affirmative action asks about the extent of present discrimination, the risk of future discrimination, and the lingering effects from the past. We acknowledge the power and reach of gender bias, and we also see that the present effects of that bias differ markedly from the inherited disadvantages and ghettoization crippling African Americans and, to varying degrees, other racial minorities; moreover, the social distance between men and women is of a different nature and order than that between most whites and most of the African-American community. Just those two observations alone, each deserving extended analysis, have many implications beyond the scope of my work here: the possible function of income-targeted measures, the optimism we might have for "difference-blind" practices, the potential for developing strategies of community-building, the relevance of contrasts between assimilation and identity politics, and much more.

Comparisons with other racial minorities are also difficult, though needed. The circumstances of Asian Americans and new Asian immigrants defy generalization because some of these subgroups share many conditions and are dissimilar in others. Successive waves of Vietnamese immigrants, for example, differed dramatically in their education and training. For most Japanese Americans the World War II internment looms large in their story of America, while immigrants from the Indian subcontinent may consider the internment largely irrelevant to their own group, and those from Southeast Asia may be more concerned with Japanese war crimes of that period or with U.S. participation in the Vietnam War. One can similarly dissect the experiences, conditions, and perspectives of Hispanics. Social science confirms there is still discrimination against all these groups, but slavery has made for important differences and for an important element shared by almost all African Americans.)

Perhaps I can best leave it this way: I hope my readers will better understand why the affirmative action issue, and racial justice debates generally, are so difficult, and will find that answering some of the questions I pose helps to sort things out. And I hope that what I have written provides a helpful starting point for considering related problems (facing, say, women). But beware reckless generalizations. Experiences differ, and in many situations that matters. Beyond that, as the lawyers say, the deponent knoweth not.

# NOT
# ALL
# BLACK
# AND
# WHITE

# INTRODUCTION
# THE WHITE HOUSE REVIEW

*I* have a relative who is a self-described "gun nut." An African-American psychiatrist, he strikes me as borderline paranoid when he talks about the importance of keeping semiautomatic weapons "just in case." Then I think about the Michigan Militia and its sister organizations, some with their militant white supremacy. Suppose the Black Panthers in 1967 had 15,000 armed and trained adherents, as the militias claim today? If they had preached Jesus and religious fundamentalism instead of Maoism and Pan-Africanism? There are reasons why the Panthers' kind of radicalism might not rise again, but there are also reasons why it might, though too few of us appreciate the peril. No one has said it better than James Baldwin with his apocalyptic phrase "The Fire Next Time."

In the past two years I've struggled to understand better that peril which America faces, first working as Special Counsel to President Clinton, managing the White House review of affirmative action, and then writing this book. The peril is that the many sharp differences between the races, expressed along hardened political and social battle lines, may be precursors for an escalating racial conflict and, ultimately, conflagration. This process is already at work, and accelerating. Clever preachers of hate have forever been a threat to free societies, but they are now in the ascendancy in black and white communities throughout the United States, even on the Mall and the steps of our nation's Capitol.

I am very clear in my own mind about the needed response. The peril must be an impetus for self-conscious projects to build bridges among communities. The preachers of hate can be turned out of the temples and replaced by preachers who know that progress comes not from war but from the hard work of building community. Not from isolation and fear but from dreams, hope, and reason. Those are not merely words. They are a prescription for a kind of activism and advocacy that differs from much now practiced on both the left and the right.

So, for me, the agony of observing and living the contemporary problem of race in America is just this: to hold simultaneously the fear of war and the dream of community. Each day's news, each season's book list, every major political campaign, assaults us with upsetting evidence about society's pain and about the gathering storm clouds but brings, too, the glimmerings of something better. Which signs to believe? How to act? And where to find the strength to invest oneself in caring?

### The President's Team Begins

Working on this issue for the President of the United States proved to me what I had previously assumed rather academically: the key to deciding what we believe about affirmative action and other matters of race policy is to understand first the underlying choices about our values and our vision of America, not the details of particular policies or court precedents. This is especially true if we want to have a coherent position that we can explain, defend, and *use as the basis for persuading and leading*.

Some months ago, I was invited to participate in a discussion with a group of minority employees of the Central Intelligence Agency meeting at a covert military facility. I spent about an hour lecturing, and then pressed them to present and defend their own views on affirmative action. I paused to make, lightheartedly, a serious point. "You know,

you folks aren't very good at this. I wouldn't want *any* of you representing my side of this issue in a cocktail party conversation." Even
people intensely concerned about affirmative action, I said—whether
for or against—rarely work hard to understand the arguments on both
sides and to figure out how to persuade others. Instead, we usually talk
about this difficult subject only with like-minded people and avoid the
subject with others. I likened it to being at church and spending all
your energy in choir practice, when what is needed is practice at evan-
gelical missionary work. I'm not very religious, but I know that choir
performances alone do not make converts or create ecumenical understanding.

On July 19, 1995, President Clinton stood in the Great Rotunda of the
National Archives and addressed the nation on the subject of opportunity and affirmative action. Behind him hung replicas of the Constitution
and the Declaration of Independence. Approximately six months had
passed during which he, Vice President Al Gore, and a platoon of aides
had worked to formulate a policy they hoped would, in the fullness of
time, embody a healing vision of progress. I had served as day-to-day
point man on the White House staff for developing that policy—the
chance of a lifetime—and was leader of the President's much bally-
hooed review of the federal government's affirmative action programs.

As the Vice President, two other aides, and I rode in the limousine
with the President to the Archives that Wednesday morning, my heart
was in my throat. I fought back an urge to implore the President to
stop chatting with us and instead to read over the final draft of his long
speech. (His extensive late-night redrafting, plus interruptions from
Bosnia, had made for a mad dash to the finish. As the Vice President
says, "The White House is punctually challenged.") Minutes later,
sitting beside George Stephanopoulos in the second row, my heart was
in my throat again. The President was *into* it, and it was working! The
six-month journey to the speech had been a long, wild ride—always
intellectually stimulating, sometimes politically terrifying, with inter-
mittent moral tribulation. I felt entitled to shed a few tears, and did.

It has become a cliché to note the enduring complexity and pathology of race-related thinking in America—complex in its nature and in the tight weave binding it to other threads of our social and economic fabric, pathological in its dispiriting and sometimes brutal expression. In three tours of duty at the heart of our public policy machinery, I was a witness to and participant in the clash of values, sensibilities, and dreams that occur when color is at issue. As a policy aide in Jimmy Carter's White House, later as the senior policy officer in Michael Dukakis's presidential campaign of 1987–88, and then as a senior budget official for President Clinton, I saw politicians and policy makers struggle to deal with American's color problem, and I did my best to contribute. But it was not until February 1995 that I was thrust directly and centrally into the battle.

I had just resigned as an associate director of the White House Office of Management and Budget, and moved some boxes into an office at the Urban Institute, a Washington think tank that had graciously offered me a decompression chamber before my return to teaching at Harvard Law School. Pleased to escape the roiling cauldron of budgeteering—I felt that I was a tax-and-spend liberal, tragically miscast—I was also guilt-ridden about abandoning one project in particular: some Republicans had just moved the affirmative action issue to the front burner, and George Stephanopoulos had begun a series of meetings of senior policy officials to consider how the administration should respond.

George's title, Senior Advisor to the President for Policy and Strategy, gave only a pale hint of his centrality in any matter he focused on. Now he included me in the affirmative action discussions. We had known each other in the Dukakis campaign; he knew my track record as a policy wonk and as someone who had occasionally committed acts of political judgment, and I was a law professor, to boot. The icing on the cake was that I was the most senior African American in a policy position anywhere within hailing distance of the West Wing. There were more senior blacks in political jobs, yes. (I think, for example, of the enormous talents of Alexis Herman, Assistant to the President in charge of the Office of Public Liaison, and Maggie Williams, the First Lady's chief of staff.) But the dirty little secret was that minorities were few and far between in White House policy positions. George must

surely have calculated that adding some color to these critical deliberations was mandatory.

So, in early February 1995, I went to what was—and was not—
my last meeting before heading off into the sunset. It was held in the
Ward Room—a small dining room on the ground floor of the West
Wing, adjacent to the White House Mess and the super-secure Situation Room. There, a handful of us argued about the strengths and
weaknesses of color-blind and means-tested approaches to social programs, which are the most often cited alternatives to race- and gender-
based affirmative action arrangements. This was neither the first nor
the last such argument, and I once again felt the need to pinch myself:
we were engaging in this hand-to-hand intellectual combat in order to
sharpen the ideas and arguments to be presented to the President and
Vice President, to help them with a decision that might profoundly
affect not only the political fortunes of William Jefferson Clinton and
the Democratic Party but the course of American race relations in the
years ahead; I had arrived where I had always wanted deeply to be. I
said so, and thanked George and my colleagues. I was leaving the
federal payroll, but they and I took comfort in knowing that I would
continue to be involved. My emotions were never more mixed as I
walked across West Executive Avenue (the world's fanciest alley, really) to the massive wedding-cake Executive Office Building and my
farewell party in the ornate Indian Treaty Room.

I had been at the Urban Institute for about three days, much of the
time commuting the dozen blocks back to the White House, when
George insisted that I simply had to move back in as Special Counsel
to the President until the affirmative action issue was settled. I assumed
this meant four or perhaps six weeks. It stretched to six months. (I
abandoned my plans to write, anonymously, a shocking political roman
à clef about White House life.)

During that period, we had several long meetings with President
Clinton and supplied him with many pages of study material. Our goal
was to give him a solid understanding of the underlying facts about
discrimination, exclusion, the design and operation of various federal
programs, and private-sector practices. We considered constitutional
and statutory law, executive orders issued by earlier Presidents, and

key voices from Congress and the statehouses—thoughtful and otherwise. Most important, we reasoned and argued and reasoned some more about the values and dreams that clash in our public and private battles about racial justice. We asked many questions. For example:

- Is discrimination a widespread phenomenon today, as many minorities claim, or is it largely a thing of the past, now broadly condemned? Is the fact that most executive suites are peopled by white males a symptom of wrongful exclusion?
- If we want a society in which opportunities flow in a color-blind manner, should we not adopt that as a principle to guide our public and private actions? What about the argument that such idealism is wildly unrealistic and will fail to create genuine opportunities for everyone?
- When we use race, color, or gender not to burden members of historically disadvantaged groups but benignly to provide them opportunities, must we view it in zero-sum terms as a reduction in the opportunity available to others? And even if it does reduce opportunity for, say, white males, is this redistribution of opportunity *always* wrong? Despite how commonly we impose other redistributive burdens on one another?
- If we are to accept some measure of race- and gender-conscious action, when will it end? How should we define success?
- Critics of affirmative action blame the resentments and frustrations—the "angry white male" phenomenon of popular accounts—on the alleged pervasive structure of racial preferences. Others say the frustrations are generated by economic insecurity and anxiety in an age of corporate restructuring and dangerous global competition. Still others say both explanations are manifestations of racism. Where is the truth in all of this? Is there *one* truth?

Week after week, we worked through hard hypothetical cases and real-life examples:

*[Handwritten margin note, left side, rotated:]* There is no definite answer. We need to creat it, according to our morality, eternal/universal value, and 'ideal/reality.

*Race and Police Promotions.* Despite years of litigation, the Chicago Police Department was still woefully white, utterly unrepresentative of the community it is supposed to serve. Litigants and the courts focused on its hiring policies and promotion examinations; consultants rewrote the exams trying to eliminate their racially disparate effects. But this had only a limited success; Hispanic and African-American scores were still too low. The mayor decided to supplement the list of officer appointees and promotions created solely on the basis of test scores, and made an additional set of "merit promotions" using a more subjective evaluation in which color was a flexible factor. White officers sued. Was it unjust? To whom? What practice would produce the best police department? And is that even the right question?

One reason we focused so closely on this difficult case was that it was raised with the President by Congressman Bill Lipinski (Democrat of Illinois) in an early-spring Cabinet Room meeting with the House of Representatives Democratic Caucus Task Force on Affirmative Action. White House staff members considered Representative Lipinski a good bellwether for the moderate-to-conservative Democrats who were likely to be skeptical of at least some aspects of affirmative action. We knew that whatever the President's final position on the policy, a rigorous policy-making effort and a credible conclusion would have to address the concerns of people like Bill Lipinski. We might not satisfy the Lipinskis of the country, but we had to *engage* them.

*Race and Teacher Layoffs.* A local school board in New Jersey, faced with the need to lay off one teacher in the high school's business-education department, had to choose between two teachers who everyone agreed were identical in seniority, credentials, experience, performance, and all the other ordinary considerations. One teacher was black, the other white. The student body was very largely black, and the school board had had partial success using affirmative action programs to increase the number of minority teachers and administrators. Now, faced with this choice, might the school board use race as a tie-breaking factor? Could diversity be a consideration in making layoff decisions? Did either law or policy require that the school board flip a coin instead? Would the considerations be different for, say, Procter & Gamble? For *The Washington Post*'s reporting staff?

*[handwritten margin note: There are many delicate cases, for that there is no definite standard to measure to what extent it should be done.]*

This example was important because the Civil Rights Division of the Department of Justice had filed court papers defending the Piscataway school board's policy discretion to use its interest in diversity as a factor. Now, in the cold, clear light of a thoroughgoing review of the principles and values at stake in affirmative action broadly, would the President stand by the Justice Department's earlier position? And if so, on what grounds?

*Targeted Scholarships.* The University of Maryland tried for years to bring more minority students to its flagship College Park campus, mindful of the regime of unlawful de jure state-sponsored discrimination that had kept the state's public higher education system segregated as a matter of state law, and then as a matter of practice, well into the 1970s, in the view of federal law enforcement officials in Republican and Democratic administrations alike. The university created the Benjamin Banneker Scholarships—black-only merit scholarships designed to attract highly qualified African-American students who fell just below the grade-and-score-based selection criteria for the university's race-neutral Francis Scott Key Scholars program. Although a small part of its overall financial-aid resources, the program's racial targeting was controversial. When, if ever, are such measures acceptable? Should the principles be different for gender-targeted scholarships? Should it matter if the institution is a public or a private school? Should it matter if the institution has no recent history of actual discrimination, but nevertheless asserts a strong desire to have a more diverse student body? Are the considerations different for scholarships than for admissions?

Here again, federal civil rights enforcers had staked out a position in support of affirmative action, viewing the Banneker program as only the latest step in a fifteen-year-long effort in litigation and negotiations with Maryland. Early in Clinton's administration, Secretary of Education Richard Riley, former South Carolina governor and a good friend of fellow governor Bill Clinton, had promulgated a detailed formal policy statement on race-based scholarships. (The policy, issued in February 1994, clarifies the scope of permissible action under Title VI of the Civil Rights Act of 1964, which prohibits discrimination by recipients of federal funding.) Department of Education officials viewed it

as a pillar of their effort to reconstruct sound sensible civil rights policies from the rubble and disarray that faced them after twelve years
of misadventure and worse under Presidents Reagan and Bush. Would
Riley's policy withstand rigorous reconsideration?

*Entrepreneurship and Government Contracting.* Under the Supreme
Court's June 1995 affirmative action ruling in *Adarand Constructors,
Inc. v. Peña*, the government may use race-conscious measures to ensure that minority-owned businesses participate in government procurement, provided the measure is justified by a "compelling
governmental interest" and is "narrowly tailored" to achieve that purpose—exceedingly vague terms of art to which I will return. If there
is a history of discrimination, with continuing effects, in a given industry and region, what race-conscious measures, if any, are appropriate as remedies? Outreach to see that minority firms know about the
contracting opportunities? Anything more?

There were many more issues, of course, and no shortage of points
of view represented among the participants in the White House meetings. It didn't take a rocket scientist to tell George Stephanopoulos and
me that this was going to be very difficult, and dangerous too. I felt
there was a good chance the assignment would be fatal to my career
in national policy making, and I took great comfort in the security of
my tenured Harvard professorship.


George convened the first serious policy session in the comfortable,
wood-paneled office of White House Counsel Abner Mikva, in the
southwest corner of the West Wing's second floor. (Judge Mikva, who
was out of the building, was a generous soul—in both wise advice and
loans of his office for confidential meetings. He is a former congressman from Chicago and former chief judge of the U.S. Court of Appeals
for the District of Columbia Circuit, the nation's second most powerful
tribunal.) One member of the group was William Galston, the President's deputy domestic policy advisor and a professor of political philosophy on leave from the University of Maryland at College Park. Bill
has been very active in "New Democrat" policy circles allied with the
Democratic Leadership Council as well as with the growing commu-

nitarian movement led by Professor Amitai Etzioni of George Washington University. I always wondered whether part of his intellectual trajectory is a response to the crushing 1984 defeat of presidential candidate Walter Mondale, for whom he had served as national issues director. Many Democrats emerged from that debacle convinced that what they saw as Democratic Party orthodoxy needed complete renovation. Some reached that conclusion as a matter of politics, others as a matter of principled appreciation of the need for better policies, prescriptions, and vision. I've never doubted Bill's principles, which were critical to our deliberations.

Also present was Deval Patrick, Assistant Attorney General for the Justice Department's Civil Rights Division. (He got the job my friend Lani Guinier didn't.) Deval had been a partner in a Boston law firm and before that a very successful staff attorney at the NAACP Legal Defense and Education Fund, our foremost civil rights law outfit. Deval and I had known each other casually since 1982, when he was a student of mine in one of my first courses at Harvard Law School. As fate would have it, the course was entitled "Public Interest Law: Race and Poverty." My senior co-professor, Elizabeth Bartholet, was a veteran civil rights litigator, and we had the overt purpose of encouraging a group of students to pursue public-interest careers by exposing them to various inspiring public-interest lawyers from around the country and to the fascinating doctrinal issues with which those attorneys were struggling. Deval and some of his classmates made it my best teaching experience to date. Now, thirteen years later, here we were at the White House together. *Doing it.*

Gene Sperling, deputy assistant to the President for economic policy, has been a friend since I hired him in 1987 to be an economic policy aide on my issues staff in the Dukakis campaign. ("Hired" is a campaign term meaning "found him a work surface and, months later, lunch money.") Gene was there because of his long-held deep commitment and considerable expertise in civil rights policy. In an internship immediately after Yale Law School, he worked on an important affirmative action case in the Supreme Court, *Wygant v. Jackson Board of Education*, decided in 1986. After the Dukakis campaign, I helped him land a job as an associate in the law practice of my Harvard colleague Laurence Tribe, where he worked on a number of civil rights matters. More important, Gene had a close relationship with George Stephanopoulos from their work together in the Dukakis and Clinton campaigns and innumerable battles together as allies in the Clinton White House. Gene and George share that most precious of qualities— the ability to move effortlessly between the realms of policy analysis, political strategy, and communications tactics and to make star-quality contributions at every turn. Back in 1989, Gene and I together wrote a *Washington Post* essay on race, and I knew very well his values and creativity. Gene was at the White House for a purpose, not for power.

A few things became immediately clear. First, it would not do to write down a list of policy issues and programmatic choices, parcel out assignments to draft the pros and cons, and then just ask the President to check some decision boxes. A considerable amount of thought was needed to figure out precisely what the President needed to decide: certainly not the plumbing details of an Air Force program for hiring construction firms, but more than some general commitment to "equal opportunity," whatever that means.

This problem of deciding what to decide was both a political question and a conceptual one. It was political in that presidential leadership is a matter as much of perception as of action, and we were uncertain how specific we should be—and when—in order for opinion elites and the general public to feel that Bill Clinton was actually leading on this issue. And it was conceptual because when we challenged each other's policy prescriptions by asking "Why?" and played the familiar law school game of Socratic inquiry, hypotheticals, and slippery slopes, it was obvious that answers to problems in one corner of the puzzle had to be consistent with the answers elsewhere—not just consistent in the answer itself but consistent throughout in the underlying values and mode of reasoning.

Conceptual incoherence in any policy would leave it open to the charge that it was developed as an ad hoc product of political calculations—this was the policy-analysis equivalent of situational ethics. In short, even more than we needed a set of discrete policy judgments, we needed a framework of principles from which to derive a host of detailed policy judgments. The framework had to embody Bill Clinton's values and his vision of a better America. It had to be coherent, so that the administration could use it to respond to different problems with reference to that same set of values and that same vision. And so that the American people could understand it, it had to be something he and his surrogates could communicate clearly.

Second, we saw that political analysis alone could not produce clear answers to the affirmative action questions. Each of us could rattle off a detailed analysis of why it was politically necessary to hew close to civil rights orthodoxy in order to bolster the enthusiastic support that minorities, liberals, and activist women gave to the Clinton administration. And we could also construct the "swing voter" argument for moving to some New Democrat position that might significantly restrict affirmative action, perhaps in combination with a new emphasis on race-neutral, class-based ways of looking at programs. It took no time at all to realize there was no end to this debate. *Even if* one were inclined to decide the issue with a wet finger in the air, the gale seemed to blow from all directions. The course would have to be set on coordinates that came from the President's vision of where he wanted to go, not from where the winds seemed likely to carry us.

The so-called character issue, obviously one consideration, reinforced our conclusion that political analysis had to be minor in our work. Any appearance of vagueness or ambivalence would be seized upon by Clinton's opponents as evidence of his trying to have it both ways, of his being unwilling to draw a line in the sand and fight for a principle. Also, sharp criticism of civil rights orthodoxy would be attacked as a craven repudiation of his own record in an effort to curry favor with white male swing voters, while sharp criticism of civil rights revisionism would be attacked as a craven effort to curry favor with traditional minority and liberal supporters on the Democratic left. The conclusion was obvious. The way to win the character issue was to be authentic—to be clear about the values and vision and stand prepared for the political consequences. Brickbats were inevitable, from the left or the right or both. Character meant providing a clear and noble target.

As I recall, just about everyone on the staff agreed on this strategy. Nervously.

A third ground rule emerged. As important as it was to have a framework and ultimate conclusions with respect to key policy issues, it was also important to structure the administration's actions with an eye to advancing a national conversation about race and opportunity. The President would have to give at least one major speech on the subject, but we knew the issue would be around for the 1996 election cycle, and no single speech would either put the issue to rest or bring about significant racial healing. So part of the challenge was to develop a communications strategy that would help to pull Americans together, or at least keep them from splitting further apart. Still another reason to be nervous, I fretted.

### What Is Affirmative Action?

The justification for undertaking affirmative action programs or passing affirmative action laws may be to assure nondiscrimination (i.e., to prevent future discrimination), to give a remedy for current discrimination, to promote diversity, or to do something else. Once the justification is selected and translated into concrete, even measurable social goals, affirmative action is merely one means to achieve a specified end or ends. This raises the age-old question: Do the ends justify the means? As it happens, this is not a fruitful inquiry, because it quickly becomes a battle over definitions. If you let me make the definitions, then I can persuade you to answer the question any way I like.

Some justifications are clearly more persuasive than others: for example, we recognize that it is a right of every American not to be "discriminated" against, while diversity or inclusion in our social or economic life is only a valued aspiration. So, while nondiscrimination is a right, affirmative action is a policy in pursuit of that right *but not itself a right*. Thus, to bring an end to a particular program of affirmative action is not necessarily to dismantle a right. Whether ending it compromises the goal of effectuating the right is an empirical question. President Clinton asked us, "What works, and what doesn't?" However, some measures that "work," that may be effective in the utilitarian sense, are nonetheless impermissible because they violate a deep and honored principle. For example, we might well have more effective law enforcement if we ignored the Fourth Amendment; but we shouldn't.

So in considering affirmative action as a means, we must ask two questions: Does it work? And is it consistent with inviolable principles? In any particular case, one or both of these questions might be answered in the negative. But because affirmative action is a means rather than an end, skepticism about it in such a case is compatible with staunch support for nondiscrimination, at least in the abstract. (A final preliminary point in this regard is that there happen to be very few useful data about "what works," so we quickly come to a value-laden question about how to cope with empirical uncertainty. I will have more to say on these difficulties in later chapters.)

In the first Oval Office meeting I attended with President Clinton on this subject, he said he'd read the stacks of background material—essays, articles, speeches, and so forth, mostly collected by Stephanopoulos. His pithy reaction to his reading was that "most of these people don't know what the hell they're talking about." With a couple of decades of public service, legal study, and civil rights concern under his belt, the President had a well-developed nose for nonsense, and there is certainly a lot of it in the debates over affirmative action. So the first goal he set for the White House review was to produce a document that set the record straight about what affirmative action is and isn't, separating myth and polemic from fact and law.

What *is* affirmative action? In our report to the President, we wrote:

> "Affirmative action" enjoys no clear and widely shared definition. This contributes to the confusion and miscommunication surrounding the issue. We begin, therefore, with a definition:
>
> *For purposes of this review, "affirmative action" is any effort*

> taken to expand opportunity for women or racial, ethnic and
> national origin minorities by using membership in those
> groups that have been subject to discrimination as a consid-
> eration [in decision making or allocation of resources]. Mea-
> sures adopted in court orders or consent decrees, however, were
> outside the scope of the review.

For economy of language, in this document the use of the word "race"
(e.g., "race-targeted scholarship") also refers to membership in an
ethnic group that is disadvantaged because of prejudice and discrimination.

This was embarrassingly infelicitous writing, though perhaps not
by the standards of the government-report genre. I had several specific
goals in mind, however. Affirmative action is a phrase used in a wide
range of contexts, not just about employment and university admissions, which is what most people seem to mention first. Moreover, it is
not a single tool but a family of tools intended to create opportunity
for its beneficiaries. However, it is not *any* opportunity-enhancing measure, only one in which race (or another relevant group characteristic)
is somehow taken into account—precisely how would vary greatly depending on the tool. In short, we wanted to offer for analysis just about
any program or practice that might be challenged morally or politically
by those who advocate "color blindness."

On the other hand, we intended to exclude the judicial realm, since
we thought it inappropriate to take up the independent judiciary's construction or application of statutes, the Constitution, and the courts'
own remedial powers. That seemed too far afield, however interesting
it might be to lawyers. Moreover, we excluded all matters of civil rights
law and enforcement policy, including such issues as whether the current state of employment discrimination law or voting rights law should
be rethought. In this book, I have maintained the same limitations on
scope, with occasional excursions to make broader points about how
we Americans think and fight about race. But while the written report
for the President concerned only programs of the federal government,
our White House discussions encompassed a sweep of moral and policy
questions at issue in public and private race relations, and I attempt
the same sweep in this book.

(The single most pernicious popular misconception about affirmative action is that it means quotas. Polls show that large majorities are opposed to quotas; and the misconception is convenient for unprincipled opponents of affirmative action, who, in fact, fuel the confusion. In truth, quotas—meaning rigid numerical straitjackets—are absolutely illegal under the Constitution and civil rights statutes, except in very unusual and limited court-ordered remedies when a judge finds that a defendant has been uncooperative or defiant and no other solution seems available to remedy a long-standing, proven discrimination. Such measures are so unusual, in fact, that I won't bother to discuss them in any detail; they just aren't part of the picture. *Affirmative action does not mean quotas; quotas are illegal.*)

That is not to say that abuses of affirmative action do not occur. As with almost any policy, there is a right way to do it, but also a wrong way. Or several of them. For example:

- In practice, flexible numerical goals can become rigid numerical straitjackets, or quotas, if the people implementing the affirmative action measure are badly trained, indifferent to the law, or poorly supervised. There is little evidence that this is a widespread problem, but plenty of anecdotes and assertions that it is. Of course, there is no bright line separating flexible from rigid, and this kind of abuse is not just a problem for law enforcement. Like other issues of legal or social obligation—antitrust rules, labor relations, consumer protection, customer service—affirmative action requires good judgment and sound management.

- In practice, flexible consideration of race can become an inflexible emphasis if it sacrifices other objectives inappropriately, the classic complaint being that traditional measures of merit may suffer. This potential abuse deserves careful analysis and attention; I'll have more to say on it.

- It is also an abuse of affirmative action to design a program in a manner that, in the words of judicial doctrine, "unnecessarily trammels" the interests of nonbeneficiaries; i.e., bystanders. The important point here is that the very flexibility of affirmative action, done right, should allow for the interests of all those potentially affected to be addressed. That doesn't mean everyone has to be happy. But, to at least some undefined extent, everyone's interests matter.

- It's an abuse when the design of targeted programs invites fraud. For example, if the premise of a program is that the beneficiaries be minority entrepreneurs who are also economically disadvantaged, it is wrong to operate the program in a way that lets "front" firms participate or that lets participants hide financial assets that in fact make them ineligible.

This partial list should be read as an acknowledgment that affirmative action is a complicated undertaking, and we should have sensible expectations about it. What programs, public or private, are free of abuses? Do we imagine that programs to help family farmers or agribusinesses are abuse-free? What about government programs that give export assistance to manufacturers or tax breaks to passive investors in oil and gas leases or real estate development? Do the owners of muffler shops and grocery stores, appliance dealers, home contractors, and orthopedic surgeons ever commit abuses? Certainly. The questions to ask are how the abuses can be curbed and whether they are tolerable in light of the benefits and costs of the endeavor. Context matters. And we should guard against the tendency, which some critics have, suddenly to be very intolerant of abuse when it occurs in programs involving racial justice.

Two things are true: affirmative action is not perfect; and that is not the standard.)

A second misconception is that affirmative action is one or perhaps two kinds of measure, when in fact there are many contexts and many tools for creating opportunity. Peter Yu, a friend and a White House colleague, developed a matrix to illustrate for President Clinton the variety of affirmative action measures within the federal government. The four rows indicate the contexts: the federal government as an employer itself; various federal benefit or regulatory programs, such as the allocation of broadcast licenses or the sale of foreclosed farmland; the government policies that affect how federal agencies decide which

| | | FEDERAL AFFIRMATIVE | |
| | | *Methods, Spheres of Activity, and* | |
| | OUTREACH, HORTATORY EFFORTS | DISCLOSURE OF DATA | AFFIRMATIVE ACTION PLANS |
|---|---|---|---|
| FEDERAL EMPLOYMENT | military recruitment | head-count reports to Equal Employment Opportunity Commission (EEOC) are required | encouraged by EEOC when appropriate |
| FEDERAL BENEFITS | agencies encouraged to use minority banks; grants encourage states' outreach | Community Reinvestment Act; SBA § 7(a) loan program data from lenders | conditions on certain grants (e.g., Education, Interior) require planning |
| FEDERAL AGENCY PROCUREMENT PRACTICES** | Offices of Small/ Disadvantaged Business (SDB) Utilization in most agencies | SBA monitors and reports on government-wide procurement goals | agencies prepare periodic plans on how they will pursue their contracting goals |
| PRIVATE CONTRACTOR PRACTICES | DOL's awards for Exemplary Voluntary Efforts by contractors | head-count data filed with EEOC | required by Executive Order 11246 when appropriate |

* The FCC program was suspended by the Commission in the weeks following *Adarand*; the rule-of-two program was suspended in October 1995 as part of the Justice Department's review of programs for compliance with *Adarand* and the President's directive on affirmative action. Officials hope to publish

# ACTION EFFORTS

*a Few Illustrative Programs*

| TARGETED TRAINING AND INVESTMENT | GOALS AND TIMETABLES | "SOFT" PREFERENCES | SET-ASIDES |
|---|---|---|---|
| Foreign Service Minority Internships; West Point/ Annapolis prep schools | rare: used by agencies when appropriate | none formally, but many hires and promotions are subjective | none |
| dozens of HHS and education scholarship and faculty programs | SBA § 7(a) district-level loan participation goals | FCC distress sale and tax incentives; some auction-bid price preferences | auctions of foreclosed farmland; auctions of certain FCC licenses* |
| Special Small Business Investment Cos.; SBA § 7(j) technical assistance program | government-wide procurement goals required by statute | up to 10% bid price preference in some cases for SDBs; "evaluation" preferences, too | rule-of-two sheltered competition for SDBs in some cases;* § 8(a) sole-source contracts |
| mentor-protégé programs at DOD | required by EO 11246 to address serious "under-utilization" | none required by federal law | none required by federal law |

the broader proposal for how agencies redesigned SDB contracting programs in the Federal Register eventually.

** SDBs are, by statute and regulations, socially and economically disadvantaged; this presumptively includes minority-owned businesses. See Chapter 8.

private firms they will award contracts to; and the obligations or incentives the government then uses to induce those companies to alter
their own behavior as regards minorities or other groups. The columns
suggest the range of available methods. (Simple outreach and hortatory
efforts are the least controversial, and politically prominent critics of
affirmative action have all voiced approval of them *even though these
measures must by definition pay some attention to race if they are to
have any meaning at all* )(At the other end of the spectrum, there are
preferences that either put a "thumb on the scale" or reserve certain
opportunities for targeted groups, such as a paving contract at an Air
Force base set aside for bidding by minority firms.) (This example is
problematical under the Supreme Court's 1995 decision in the *Adar-
and* case, and the program was suspended by the Defense Department
in October 1995.) Note that the chart does not include quotas, because
quotas are illegal. Contracting and other numerical goals set by statute
and regulation all have escape valves, so that program administrators
are not rigidly required to achieve specific results. The Justice Department is now checking on actual practice.

Although this matrix concerns only federal programs, it gives one
a sense of the richness of the problem in the private and voluntary
sectors. Decision makers have a large toolbox to draw from when they
design affirmative action programs, though in debating affirmative action, we often forget to place it in the larger context of how opportunity
is and can be created in America. Forgetting that context distorts our
appraisal of race-conscious decision making.

Affirmative action suffers when it is asked to meet unreasonable standards for flawless execution, *or* unreasonable standards for what it
might accomplish. On the one hand, some critics believe that the continuing afflictions and deprivations of the poor are evidence that affirmative action is a failure. On the other hand, some advocates seem
single-mindedly to believe that race-conscious policy measures will be
a panacea for all our woes. Both views, and the debating tactics that
caricature them, are deeply wrong. Race is one among several daunting
social and economic problems we face, and indeed several of those
problems are, in origin and likely solution, inextricably bound up with

the matter of color, but neither reason nor experience suggests that the problems of America, or of poor America or black America or poor black America—of *any* America—can be solved by race-conscious measures alone, or even primarily. In particular, the fate of the African-American community depends on public *and* private *and* personal measures that we might call the *opportunity agenda*. Race-conscious government policy is only one of many elements in that agenda. Consider:

- *Public Elements.* Public elements include not only the surviving social welfare programs of the New Deal and the Great Society—Aid to Families with Dependent Children, Social Security, Medicaid and Medicare—but also less familiar public investments in compensatory funding for public K–12 education of the poor, college scholarships, vocational training, subsidized housing, food and nutrition programs, and community economic development. Yet all these programs can only marginally affect the aggregate levels of economic and social opportunity created by more fundamental circumstances subject to government influence: economic growth and overall macroeconomic performance; investments in public infrastructure and regional economic development; public education's baseline level of resources and quality; and conditions of personal and community safety from violence.
- *Private Elements.* The private sector, too, contributes to the opportunity agenda. Firms make decisions about where to locate; how much to invest in training and retraining their workers; what charitable endeavors are worthwhile; whether willingly to comply (or covertly to evade) regulatory norms—about nondiscrimination or environmental protection or collective bargaining; and, of course, whom to hire and promote.
- *Personal Elements.* Often neglected, but of at least equal importance, are elements of the personal agendas we express as individuals, as families, and through affiliative organizations such as churches. The best example of this is the theme of personal responsibility, which regained fashion in the 1980s

by dint of efforts by conservatives. While the danger here is that this theme is emphasized to the exclusion of any discussion about public responsibilities, there is no doubt that effective strategies to tackle our most dire problems require a strong commitment of personal resources. As we shall see, this goes beyond the individual and family to include community institutions. Sermons from the pulpit, a neighborhood's social networks, and the lyrics in a song are all among the resources potentially called to service in the opportunity agenda. (More on this in Chapter 10.)

I risk belaboring the obvious in this very abbreviated inventory, but perhaps I can dramatize the evident foolishness of expecting too much from affirmative action. Imagine parachuting into a harrowing adventure—a sailing voyage turned shipwreck, a military battle somewhere unknown, a stint in a city hospital's emergency room. An irksome interlocutor (a law professor or obnoxious politician or economist) wants to make you pick the single most important tool for what you're doing. The demand is preposterous, because the challenge before you is too difficult and uncertain. Indeed, what is important will shift with the circumstances of the moment. Life is complicated. America is complicated. And race is *really* complicated. How important is the one tool of affirmative action? That is an imponderable question, to which the only correct answer is: "Important enough to think about carefully and debate in earnest."

### Creating a New Debate

To veteran combatants in the national battle about civil rights policy, the right-left debate has many dispiritingly familiar elements. Conservative critics of affirmative action make almost ritual reference to the great legislative and legal victories since *Brown v. Board of Education* in 1954. They do so in part to convey their pride in the ideals represented by those accomplishments, and in part to argue that because we have come so far, liberal and left-wing policy prescriptions are anachronistic, born of hysterical assessments of today's reality. Liberals respond wearily that while we have journeyed far, we have a long way to go. After a difficult decade or more of "wedge" politics, including the frightening deployment of federal resources *against* civil rights in key litigation and policy battles, they are hungry for a politics and language of healing, for a politics grounded in moral vision rather than electoral calculus. The even deeper hunger among civil rights liberals and among minorities is their need to know: Is the cause *safe*? Are *we* safe? At the same time, they also hope for a crack in the orthodoxy— at least in the *expression* of the orthodoxy—because they fear that the old approaches and the old language have stalled our progress and produced a crisis in persuasion.

Civil rights "conservatives," meanwhile, are frustrated because they think the liberal orthodoxy offers no honest assessment of the demerits of affirmative action and the merits of color-blind or disadvantage-only approaches. Liberals, they charge, see no end to racial preferences and acknowledge no inconsistency with traditional values like equal opportunity and merit. It is often difficult to distinguish between those conservatives who want a rollback and those who want continued progress but with new approaches.

The debate over the Civil Rights Act of 1964 showed the nation that controversies still raged over some fundamental issues. Among the most important were whether privately held racial prejudices were to be clearly labeled immoral and un-American and whether behavior arising from such sentiments could be regulated and made illegal. Today, many people have forgotten that the first proposition, concerning morality, was vigorously contested, and not simply by a reactionary fringe but by national leaders in both political parties.

This selective amnesia is understandable, for the new taboo against expressions of racial animus has been very effective, but it is important to appreciate that this taboo is an invention of the modern civil rights revolution of the 1960s, a recent and perhaps, until proven otherwise, tenuous development. Those who argue that the taboo is irreversible seem to ignore not just troubling data about America today but painful national experiences concerning race throughout American history. Racial conflict may be congenital in the human species, but even if it is not, it is a common enough disease with no recent history of extended remission. More, the view of racism and prejudice as moral malady has rarely been either widely held or deeply rooted in America. We should not flatter ourselves by thinking otherwise.

The effective moral argument of the 1960s invoked the sacred text of the Declaration of Independence and, more explicitly, quasi-religious appeals to notions of shared humanity, together with graphically pragmatic illustrations of the tragedies and disgrace of brutal deprivation and dehumanizing incivility to blacks. The reformers sought to frame the issue as a battle to define both the civic and the personal character of Americans.

Beyond the moral standards and ethical aspirations was the still more difficult issue of what the appropriate role of government should be in implementing just civil rights policies. Conservatives and libertarians alike had a second line of defense: even acknowledging that discrimination is wrong, they believed that it was neither feasible nor appropriate to "legislate morality," that laws and governments do not reform hearts. These arguments found ready adherents, for a competing strain in American civic culture is rooted in the philosophical liberalism of the Founders' vision of a limited state, its regulatory ambitions checked lest they lead to tyranny. There is an almost irrebuttable presumption that liberty is best secured by minimizing the role of government. Civil rights reformers trying to use government power through the courts or legislatures to secure liberties for a few were said to be striking at the fundamental safeguards that protect liberties enjoyed by the many. The counterargument, of course, was that there is no legitimate liberty of the many to oppress minorities by denying justice to them.

Again, today most people find the argument peculiar: for example, most people wouldn't agree that while it may be bad for the owner of a luncheonette to refuse to serve minorities, it is wrong for the government to compel him to serve people he does not, for whatever reason, want to serve. Recent books by Dinesh D'Souza and Richard Epstein offer something discomfortingly close to this argument, though I hope it's safe to say their views are extreme. The point is, while extreme, they are also familiar because they are a throwback to a position held by many Americans not so very long ago.

In the end, there was no intellectual reconciliation in 1964 of these two perspectives on the role of government. Both perspectives are formalistic and conclusory, and both appeal to American values that are in inevitable tension. Our history—even the debates among the Framers—is proof enough of that. But there was eventually a political resolution. The Supreme Court made its controversial rulings, and Congress enacted new civil rights laws. The dispute was decided and differences repressed, not resolved. While the moral proposition concerning the wrongfulness of racial prejudice was embodied in a reasonably potent taboo, the political dispute on the regulatory issue has lived on in many judicial and legislative battles. Indeed, there have been serious assaults on the 1964 laws.

For example, consider the long-running debate about whether statistical disparities between racial diversity in the workforce and racial disparity in the available labor pool should constitute proof of illegal discrimination. Embedded in this debate is a disagreement over the proper reach of government. Advocates of limited government and opponents of aggressive antidiscrimination regulation agree that the reach of law should be limited to instances of intentional discrimination, and believe the state should attend only to acts where there is a provable "smoking gun" of racial animus. Despite these recurring political, legislative, and judicial rumblings, however, the settled law is that the employment discrimination statute, Title VII of the 1964 Civil Rights Act, permits plaintiffs to establish a prima facie case of discrimination based on effects rather than requiring proof of intent.

Another telling example is the current interest among congressional conservatives in dismantling the Johnson-Nixon program embodied in Executive Order 11246, which requires large government contractors to develop flexible goals and timetables when there is a manifest imbalance between the diversity of their workforce and the diversity of the relevant pool of qualified labor. Their concern, as we shall see, is that numerical goals and guidelines, flexible in theory, become rigid quotas in practice. (And here they note that although quotas are illegal, the enforcement system fails to detect and correct them. Yet they are often reluctant to acknowledge these same enforcement shortcomings when they concern discrimination against women and minorities.) In addition, both critics of affirmative action and some corporate supporters of it question the executive order because they are generally averse to regulation, period.

In sum, the modern civil rights revolution succeeded in establishing a mainstream taboo against overt prejudice and bigotry, but it was far less successful in creating an enduring consensus about the role of government in combating them. There is no talismanic American ideal that opposes the antidiscrimination principle but, rather, an incurable, congenital American ambivalence about government power and private autonomy. This ambivalence is at least as powerful when it concerns race as anywhere else.

Finally, let us recall Martin Luther King, Jr.'s, observations, toward the end of his life, that the next phase of the civil rights struggle must be to secure the investments in genuine social and economic opportunity for which the laws securing formal civil rights are only a foundation. Jobs and prosperity are inextricably linked with the American dream and with dignity: it was no accident that the civil rights revolution coincided with the Great Society. Nor is it an accident that unresolved tensions in the civil rights paradigm are mirrored in unresolved tensions in America's commitment to the broader opportunity agenda. These tensions have increased to the breaking point, in fits and starts—and in November 1994 contributed very strongly to a Republican-centered counterrevolution. In civil rights, however, the counterrevolution has thus far been less successful, however threatening.


Race has very often been a factor in presidential campaigns, and decidedly so in 1968. George Wallace, the segregationist governor of Alabama, left the Democratic Party and ran as an independent, carrying five states and winning forty-six electoral votes. This success with Southern and blue-collar whites showed how vulnerable the Democratic Party was without these votes, and Republican strategy in that campaign began the process, just now reaching dramatic completion, of capturing the South for a GOP base, which Lyndon Johnson had forecast would be the likely consequence of the Democrats' support of civil rights legislation. First in the campaign and then in his administration, Richard Nixon and his aides criticized court decisions supporting school desegregation and busing of pupils to achieve integration; and Republicans used what liberals called code words, injecting race into the issues of "law and order" and welfare. Political analysts accused the GOP strategists of "playing the race card."

But positioning the party of Lincoln on the conservative side of the race issue was perhaps all but inevitable—a matter of Newtonian politics, as it were. The New Deal coalition had included blacks, and a second generation of blacks had become loyal to the Democratic Party because of its civil rights measures, notwithstanding the harshness of the Dixiecrats and die-hard segregationists in the state parties of the Old South. What accounted for the GOP's resort to the "race card"? Perhaps it was ideas. Perhaps it was the relentless imperative of politics. To many in the civil rights community, the GOP's strategy, focusing on desegregation remedies, smacked of the sentiment expressed in a comment made by an opponent of busing quoted in the title of a report by the U.S. Civil Rights Commission: "It ain't the bus, it's the niggers."

On the other hand, the Nixon administration made important contributions to some items in the civil rights enforcement agenda. President Johnson's executive order prohibiting employment discrimination and requiring "affirmative action" by companies with substantial government contracts had been an important step, but by 1969 observers were disappointed with the results. Led by an African-American assistant secretary in the Labor Department, Arthur Fletcher, Nixon administration officials developed a "goals and timetables" strategy to remedy the foot-dragging of trade unions and employers in the Philadelphia construction trades. In 1970, the resulting "Philadelphia Plan" was codified in new regulations under the executive order. It is no small irony that one of the federal programs under most serious attack by Republicans in 1996 is the requirement for affirmative action goals that Republican administration officials established when they sought to make the promise of the Johnson executive order become reality.

Still, the Nixon administration was decidedly ambivalent about civil rights. (Even adoption of the Philadelphia Plan had mixed motives.) Nixon's Supreme Court appointments have, for the most part, registered either diffidence or revisionism in their votes—and President Reagan's elevation of William Rehnquist to Chief Justice tilts the historical judgment on Nixon's legacy in a decidedly rightward direction. Many of Nixon's political signals were directed at angry white voters, and it is reasonable to assume that this political effect was intended; meanwhile, genuine contributions were made by career civil servants and moderate (by today's standards) political appointees in charge of the enforcement apparatus. These officials, however, were on a tight leash; young Leon Panetta, now Clinton's chief of staff, was fired from his post in the Office for Civil Rights.

Why the ambivalence? The obvious answer is that many different policy and political agendas were represented in the Nixon administration, not just one; in that respect, it was as conflicted as America itself.

In the presidential campaign of 1976, Jimmy Carter squared off against Gerald Ford, the unelected leader following the Nixon administration's mortal wounding in Watergate, who had not been an activist one way or the other during his years in the White House. The general drift of federal activity was alarming to civil rights activists, and they became ever more anxious as years of GOP presidential control rolled by and the activism they perceived as forward progress in the 1960s gave way to a pattern of backward drift. Think of a turbocharged car accelerating up the challenging hill of America's color problem, only to have the foot suddenly removed from the accelerator. Going into the 1976 election, therefore, the mood in the civil rights community can best be described as apprehensive. Gerald Ford was not the devil incarnate but neither was he a great champion. It was a foregone conclusion that Jimmy Carter would win the black vote, but the question remained whether the enthusiasm would be great enough to produce the needed voter turnout on election day.

I became an early Carter supporter when at the urging of a college classmate I studied the very first campaign literature and concluded that Carter was the furthest to the left of the electable Democrats. So, in late winter of 1975—a full year before the New Hampshire primary—I started doing a little work for Carter's campaign efforts in Massachusetts and New Hampshire. In the summer of 1975 I dropped out, however, because of pressing commitments at the *Harvard Law Review*, of which I had just become an editor. Right after the convention in 1976, my friend Rick Hutcheson called to ask if I would move to Atlanta to run the situation room in Carter's national campaign headquarters. I resigned from the *Law Review*, took a leave of absence from law school, and drove south. At that moment, Carter was peaking at about thirty-eight points ahead of Ford, and the campaign headed south too. It was a fairly steady downhill drift all the way to election day, which fortunately came on Tuesday rather than later that week.

Along the way, my front-row seat observing discussions among the senior campaign staff about scheduling, issues development, and communications strategy told me a lot about the matter of race in the top ranks of a Democratic campaign. First, there were the scheduling meetings, where a dozen or so aides would decide which three cities the candidate should visit a week from Friday, say, and what the events and audiences would be. In any campaign, these are among the most important decisions, involving as they do allocation of the most valuable resource—the candidate's time. The fund-raisers argue for fundraising events, the pollsters explain why a certain state needs a "pop," and everyone argues about message and venue. Aides responsible for the care and feeding of particular constituencies (a.k.a. "special interests") lobby for a visit to this convention or that parade as a way of signaling the candidate's devotion. The issues folks say they need a place to roll out a Great Idea—about multilateral trade negotiations, or inner-city housing. Again and again, I saw in the starkest terms the competition between attention to the substantive political concerns of blacks, on the one hand, and to the concerns of organized labor or farmers or "swing white voters," as they were then known, on the other. And again and again I saw this calculation: the black vote has nowhere else to go; invest in the swing or undecided votes; do the bare minimum necessary for blacks; muffle Carter's strong support for the civil rights agenda unless circumstances force him to speak out. The dynamic of scheduling choices was repeated in other campaign functions, such as deciding where to buy campaign ads, which local Democratic candidates to campaign with, or which issue papers to refine. The overall sense I had was that leaders of the Democratic family regarded the black constituency as an embarrassing ne'er-do-well relative, perhaps with some bizarre deformity that made it just as well to keep it out of sight as much as possible.

Second, the short shrift given black America in most campaign councils did not make anyone shy about pressing hard for full mobilization of black voter turnout. Black leaders and black campaign aides serving as liaisons to them argued to white campaign aides that effective get-out-the vote (GOTV) efforts require two kinds of fuel: investments of cash to operate the infrastructure and investments of the candidate's time and ideas to communicate his commitment and to generate voter enthusiasm. But to the white campaign aides, this was just another special-interest plea, just another difficult resource allocation choice. It was about tactics, not racial healing or justice.

Third, the quality of many black staff in national campaigns seemed to me, in those days, problematic. The situation has certainly improved in the twenty years since then, but I had a deep and painful suspicion that the campaign of the Democratic nominee should have been able to do better, that if its white leaders were serious about addressing the needs of black America and mobilizing full-throated support from it, then they should have taken pains to have staff of the highest possible quality working on the problem with plenety of clout. But they didn't. Hiring second-string staff sent a sad and cynical signal which was not lost on observers. (And here is another irony that is not lost on me: the same problem arises in affirmative action programs. Hiring and admissions decisions made with sincere attention to both merit and opportunity will result in the advancement of first-rate people, but if there is a lazy or cynical inclination simply to produce colored folks and achieve numerical goals, the results are painful.)

For both Democrats and Republicans, nothing was to be gained in emphasizing race matters in the 1976 campaign. Gerald Ford was too decent to run on a platform of blatant retrogression; the GOP's established opposition to mandatory school busing was a sufficient signal that not too much gasoline would be "wasted" trying to accelerate the car up the hill. Jimmy Carter, embodiment of the New South, had impeccable center-left credentials on race, and his campaign staff calculated that their great challenge was to communicate his other qualities—qualities more likely to appeal to the elusive swing voters. Carter won, but barely.

The campaign in 1980 was rather different. During the Democratic primaries, black leaders were torn by Senator Edward M. Kennedy's challenge to a sitting President who had a solid, if not inspiring, record on civil rights. Jimmy Carter was not the traditional liberal on economic and social policy that Ted Kennedy and many African-American leaders would have liked. Yet a strong faction among them argued that a primary challenge would weaken Carter and put the election at risk. They were right.

Too late and too faintly, black leaders began to appreciate the risk of Reagan's being elected. There were specific challenges to civil rights orthodoxy in the GOP platform and in campaign pronouncements; clear attacks on the social welfare agenda which black leaders had long considered, as King had, the crucial complement to the agenda of legal rights; and, finally, a clear understanding that aged justices on the U.S. Supreme Court would soon be retiring, and President Carter had not yet had an opportunity to appoint a single one. (He never did.)

All these apprehensions were borne out. Under President Reagan, the smoldering tensions of the civil rights revolution were freely expressed. A critical feature of the Reagan Revolution's success was the ideological consistency and constancy of its appointees in every federal agency and on every policy front. "Reaganauts" had to pass a litmus test, and the more zealous a person was, the better. At the Department of Justice, Attorney General Edwin Meese was an unabashed conservative on civil rights matters, and the Assistant Attorney General for Civil Rights, William Bradford Reynolds, wasted no time setting out to change things. The civil rights community was deeply dismayed, indeed infuriated, by these developments. When Reynolds was nominated for promotion to Associate Attorney General, the third-ranking position in the department, his critics rallied to force a withdrawal of the nomination, and there was more than a little vitriol on both sides of the fight.

Many liberals therefore viewed the campaign of 1988 as crucial. George Bush might be a Gerald Ford-style moderate on civil rights, but there was little expectation that as President he would move forcefully to halt or reverse the ideological course set by the Reaganauts. Michael Dukakis, the Democratic nominee, was surely preferable.

But all was not well within the Dukakis campaign. Having sworn after 1976 never again to work in a presidential campaign, I found myself in March 1987 on his senior campaign staff as national issues director, responsible for policy development, Dukakis's briefings, and all related functions. The same tensions I had seen in Carter's campaign remained a feature of Democratic Party politics three election cycles later, but I don't think I was deluding myself in believing that the balance had shifted somewhat in the direction of greater solicitude and respect for the concerns of African Americans. This was, no doubt, partly due to the Reverend Jesse Jackson's successes in the primaries. Even the most cynical Dukakis operatives understood that failure to challenge Jackson for support in black communities would greatly complicate the task of unifying the Democratic Party for the postconvention general election campaign.

Poison gushed to the surface during the run-up to the convention, however. In late May, with Dukakis's nomination assured, the question of who would be his running mate was at the front of everyone's mind. It was an open secret that Jackson wanted to be asked, and an open secret that the dominant view among white Democratic strategists was that this would make the ill-fated Mondale-Ferraro ticket of 1984 look like a dream team. There was a deeper problem of personality and style, I knew. Both men are brilliant, but one's political style is hot and the other's is cool. Jackson loves to build a powerful emotional connection as he works to *inspire* his audience. Dukakis had a habit of editing out all the hot phrases and applause lines from a speech; at times he seemed uncomfortable with a crowd's emotional energy, as though it interfered with his effort to *persuade* them with a reasoned critique of Republicans and with carefully developed policy prescriptions (which I loved). And Dukakis and Jackson had created campaign organizations in their own images. Given my earlier experiences, I could not imagine any possible way for these two to be effective partners in a campaign, much less in a government.

But notwithstanding the logic, the business of passing over Jackson for the ticket was badly handled. As a result of poor logistics and lousy planning, the press was briefed on Dukakis's selection of Lloyd Bentsen before all the runners-up had been telephoned. Jackson was insulted, and livid; most of Dukakis's senior staff couldn't understand why. I tried to explain. In frustration, I raised it with Dukakis himself in his statehouse office. It was a short discussion. When I said it was a mistake and some serious work would have to be done to repair the damage, he huffily challenged me with a vigorous counterthrust—I was quite used to this combativeness, and actually enjoyed it: why should Dukakis treat Jackson any differently from John Glenn or anyone else? Because, I explained, none of the others won 7 million votes in the primaries, and none of the others had the political power absolutely to guarantee a November defeat. The governor had no parry, but that was never a good enough reason for Mike Dukakis to back away from a position.

At least not at the moment. Eventually (the lag was typical Duke), he and his aides took steps to mend the relationship with Jackson, and the convention was, at least on the surface, a lovefest—thanks in no small measure to Jackson's chief convention negotiator, the amazing Ron Brown, who later became chairman of the Democratic National Committee and then President Clinton's Secretary of Commerce. But the initial episode and the recurring tensions during the general election campaign showed a kind of tone deafness occasionally verging on indifference. Again and again, I had the same sense I had had in 1976: *these folks just don't get it.* Twelve years had meant a lot, but some things, it seemed, never change. There remained a chilling sense for me of differences over dreams and aspirations, frustrations and anxieties, respect and empowerment.

## President Clinton's Speech

As the White House discussions began in early 1995, Gene Sperling and I had a talk. As White House aides, we had both been involved in momentous decisions—Gene far more often than I—yet we agreed that this new undertaking had a special spine-tingling quality, in part because of personal histories and commitments and in part because of what race means to the idea and the experience of America. In those tense days, we had every reason to believe the nation was once again approaching a crossroads on the matter of race. Its course would be determined, perhaps in significant measure, we imagined, by William Jefferson Clinton's decisions in the months ahead.

I was more than concerned, as we struggled though the legal and programmatic trees, that we might lose sight of the forest—especially since we had a surfeit of lawyers: Clinton, Gore, Panetta, Judge Mikva, his deputy Joel Klein, Sperling, Deval Patrick, me (plus other lawyers who I assumed would eventually weigh in—like the First Lady, the Attorney General, Bob Reich, Harold Ickes, and Vernon Jordan). This led me to warn, in one of my earlier memos to the President and his staff, about the dangers of confusing legal analysis with policy principles, and policy analysis with the leadership pulpit. As a glimpse into one aspect of the process, here's what I wrote:

> Perhaps because civil rights discussions are heavily populated with lawyers, we too often debate policy choices within the framework of contested legal doctrines, and even mistakenly believe that most key policy decisions are about what to write in briefs and how to amend a civil rights or set-aside statute. This legalistic conception is a dangerously limited one.
>
> For one thing, it leads people to conflate [sic] *opportunity* into little more than legalistic *antidiscrimination*. But purging the lingering effects of past racial wrongs must go beyond rights-based litigation and legislation in order to address directly the impediments to opportunity. For example, quality K–12 schools, combating teen pregnancy, and the community security agenda must be seen by civil rights traditionalists as absolutely critical measures for saving the

next generation. (To this list one might add voter registration and participation.) The Administration can make that link; a populist and forceful demand that we make progress on that *social policy* agenda will translate for many as a demand for *racial progress*. Which it is.

Similarly, we can make the link between racial progress and democratic participation. When the President exhorts minorities to register and vote, he is simultaneously tapping a fundamentally conservative civic virtue *and* allying himself with the interests of minorities.

Even within the narrower range of conventional civil rights measures, it is a mistake to limit policy debate to the questions presented in litigation. Research is a good example. Government and foundation funding cutbacks, together with the growing "political correctness" of conservative retreat on civil rights matters, jeopardize our intellectual capital. There is too little understanding of effective techniques of outreach, recruitment, affirmative action, conflict management, persuasion and so forth. There is too little basic data about the extent and consequences of continuing discrimination in employment, housing, credit, delivery of public services, etc. (The President's proposed FY 1996 Budget included several proposed investments to help rebuild our capacity, including resources for the Civil Rights Division to use "testers" for research and enforcement purposes, and added funding for the EEOC and the Civil Rights Commission.)

The legalistic perspective misses the point in a more fundamental way, because its focus is on *public policy* rather than *civic virtues* and the *private practices* those virtues engender. It is a cliché to note the President's role as First Preacher and Chief Teacher. That role is often trivialized as First Lobbyist, and it can be dangerously inflated to that of Tiresome Moralist. In between, however, is an honorable role that calls us to our better selves, and recalls the Nation to its deeper meaning. The closing message of Clinton's 1995 State of the Union address was quite explicitly in this vein. The question is how to sustain it in general, and how to apply it specifically in the civil rights arena.

We make the civil rights agenda the domain of political tacticians, career litigators and governance mechanics. But that is the wrong field of battle. Almost without exception, when Bill Clinton has spoken from his soul on civil rights matters he has communicated all the qualities and themes needed to lift the national discourse from the trench warfare over legal doctrine to the vastly more important plane of civic virtues and, where possible, family values.

Communication on this higher plane can and should include a strong personal element, with Bill Clinton speaking about his own experiences and those of his family. His credibility as a leader, and his commitment to racial progress, are most firmly reinforced when he speaks with conviction about how *he* has witnessed the rewards of inclusiveness, and how *he* has come to know the scarring consequences of exclusion.

Gene Sperling, typically, put it perfectly: "Bill Clinton was born to give this speech." Here is how the President concluded it, as we sat and listened in the National Archives:

My fellow Americans, affirmative action has to be made consistent with our highest ideals of personal responsibility and merit, and our urgent need to find common ground, and to prepare all Americans to compete in the global economy of the next century.

Today, I am directing all our agencies to comply with the Supreme Court's *Adarand* decision, and also to apply the four standards of fairness to all our affirmative action programs that I have already articulated. No quotas in theory or practice; no illegal discrimination of any kind, including reverse discrimination; no preference for people who are not qualified for any job or other opportunity; and as soon as a program has succeeded, it must be retired. Any program that doesn't meet these four principles must be eliminated or reformed to meet them.

But let me be clear: Affirmative action has always been good for America. [Applause]

Affirmative action has not always been perfect, and affirmative action should not go on forever. It should be changed now to take care of those things that are wrong, and it should be retired when its job is done. I am resolved that that day will come. But the evidence suggests, indeed screams, that that day has not come.

The job of ending discrimination in this country is not over. That should not be surprising. We had slavery for centuries before the passage of the 13th, 14th and 15th Amendments. We waited another hundred years for civil rights legislation. Women have had the vote less than a hundred years. We have always had difficulty with these things, as most societies do. But we are making more progress than many people.

Based on the evidence, the job is not done. So here is what I think we should do. We should reaffirm the principle of affirmative action and fix the practices. We should have a simple slogan: Mend it, but don't end it. [Applause]

Let me ask all Americans, whether they agree or disagree with what I have said today, to see this issue in the larger context of our times. President Lincoln said we cannot escape our history. We cannot escape our future, either. And that future must be one in which every American has the chance to live up to his or her God-given capacities.

The new technology, the instant communication, the explosion of global commerce have created enormous opportunities and enormous anxieties for Americans. In the last two and a half years, we have seen seven million new jobs, more millionaires and new businesses than ever before, high corporate profits, and a booming stock market. Yet, most Americans are working harder for the same or lower pay. And they feel more insecurity about their jobs, their retirement, their health care, and their children's education. Too many of our children are clearly exposed to poverty and welfare, violence and drugs.

These are the great challenges for our whole country on the home-front at the dawn of the 21st century. We've got to find the wisdom and the will to create family-wage jobs for all the people who want to work; to open the door of college to all Americans; to strengthen families and reduce the awful problems to which our children are exposed; to move poor America from welfare to work.

This is the work of our administration—to give the people the tools they need to make the most of their own lives, to give families and communities the tools they need to solve their own problems. But let us not forget affirmative action didn't cause these problems. It won't solve them. And getting rid of affirmative action certainly won't solve them.

If properly done, affirmative action can help us come together, go forward and grow together. It is in our moral, legal and practical interest to see that every person can make the most of his life. In the fight for the future, we need all hands on deck and some of those hands still need a helping hand.

In our national community we're all different, we're all the same. We want liberty and freedom. We want the embrace of family and community. We want to make the most of our own lives and we're determined to give our children a better one. Today there are voices of division who would say forget all that. Don't you dare. Remember we're still closing the gap between our founders' ideals and our reality. But every step along the way has made us richer, stronger, and better. And the best is yet to come.

Thank you very much. And God bless you.

In this book, I'd like to help readers move in their own direction beyond the traditional debate. The dominant arguments for and criticisms against affirmative action flow from a framework that has produced stalemate and thereby created an opening for the politics of division. The debate is a swirl of themes: opportunity, nondiscrimination, remediation, merit, diversity, inclusion, and so forth. Any sensible position on affirmative action requires one to decide—at least implicitly—which of these themes to emphasize and how strongly. That decision is fundamental. It requires vision. And, if it is to be the basis for healing and coming together, it must be married to a commitment to persuasion, in the highest sense of that term.

**1**

# FACTS AND LAW

$T$o present a coherent, considered policy on affirmative action and related matters to the American people, it was necessary for the President, or any thoughtful person, to consider three preliminary empirical questions: Do the nature and magnitude of continuing economic and social inequality between the races require concerted public and private action, or are natural forces in the economy satisfactorily narrowing the gaps? Do race-based discrimination and exclusion continue to be important factors in American life, affecting the opportunities and welfare of blacks and other minorities, or are they now aberrant and insubstantial? Is affirmative action effective in combating discrimination and exclusion?

Definitive answers depend on staking out some value commitments, but also on some assessment of the available social science evidence. At the White House, we knew that the second and third questions would be especially difficult to get a handle on, but it seemed important at least to give the President a fair assessment of what is known and what is not. This chapter summarizes some of our conclusions, which were based largely on expert sources within the executive branch. As regards the issue of continuing discrimination, we turned to the Council of Economic Advisers, to the Department of Justice, and to statistics compiled by the Equal Employment Opportunity Commission and the Civil Rights Commission. But most important, the Council of Economic Advisers reviewed the empirical literature on inequality and on the effectiveness of affirmative action programs; taking the lead here was a distinguished economist of international repute, Joe Stiglitz, of Stanford University, who as a Council member participated in many White House staff discussions on affirmative action, and continued to do so after he became acting CEA chair (since confirmed), replacing Laura Tyson. Stiglitz and the CEA staff were assisted by the chief economist of the Department of Labor, Alan Krueger, another exceptionally distinguished economist, from Princeton; together, they summarized the literature and assessed the scientific worth of various studies. For example, we all knew that there are substantial methodological problems in measuring the effects of affirmative action as distinct from the effects of basic antidiscrimination efforts. Also, because affirmative action means so many things, it is hard, if not impossible, to be sure—in a statistical sample of workplace affirmative action, say—what any particular employer is actually doing. These academic economists' review of the literature on inequality and the effects of affirmative action was invaluable.

Beyond the social sciences, another area of background information important to policy formulation is the question of legal constraints. As we did for the President, I include some of this background in the second section of this chapter.

### *Social Science Evidence About Inequality, Discrimination, and Affirmative Action*

I won't belabor a point that readers of this book almost certainly believe already: (the pattern of racial disparities in economic and social conditions remains painfully stark. This is not the America we want; the most unrepentant apologist for the status quo cannot dress it up to make an appealing portrait of American justice. For example:

- The black unemployment rate continues to hover at twice that among whites, being the first to rise at the start of recessions and the last to fall as recovery begins. Furthermore, black employment is more volatile than white, so that the effect of recessions is more severe. In the 1981–82 recession, for example, nearly one of every *ten* employed blacks lost his job, while fewer than two of every *hundred* employed whites lost theirs.

- The black-to-white ratio of median income has been stuck in the mid-50 to mid-60 percentage range for two decades, improvement apparently stalled. The median annual income for black males working full-time is 30 percent less than for white males.

- While one in every *seven* white children under the age of six lives below the poverty level, one of every *two* black children does (14.4 percent of whites versus more than 50 percent of blacks and 44 percent of Hispanics). The overall poverty rate for whites is one-third that for blacks: 11.6 versus 33.3 percent.

- According to the 1990 census, only 2.4 percent of the nation's businesses are owned by blacks, and this low number does not express the vastly lower share of sales by or employees in those businesses. For example, 85 percent of black businesses have *no* employees. Recent Commerce Department data suggest that minority business formation accelerated in the late 1980s and early 1990s, but the sales and employee figures continue to lag badly.

- Unequal education is a key variable in creating and sustaining these disparities. Less than 3 percent of college graduates are unemployed (1993 data), but whites are almost twice as likely as blacks to have a college degree.

- White males hold 97 percent of senior management positions in Fortune 1000 industrial and Fortune 500 service corporations. Only 0.6 percent of senior management are African American (0.3 percent are Asian and 0.4 percent are Hispanic.)

- Wealth disparities are even more dramatic than income differences, as shown in the accompanying chart. Net worth measures a household's total assets and liabilities, including equity in home or automobile. The median net worth of black households is only 8 percent that of white households, and the average is 25 percent that of whites. When you exclude home and automobile equity and focus solely on "net financial assets," the situation is even bleaker, for the median black figure is zero—which means that most blacks have no financial assets at all, or are in a net debt position.

The depth and breadth of the disparities is daunting; the examples above are only suggestive. The most troubling aspect of all, however, is the opportunity forecast. Isabel V. Sawhill, of the Urban Institute, has studied the indications that all is not well with America's machinery for generating opportunity:

Sociologists define opportunity as the degree to which the socioeconomic status of adults . . . is independent of the status of their parents. They have found, not surprisingly, that origins matter. According to one respected study, the son of an upper white-collar father is two and a half times as likely as the son of lower blue-collar worker to end up in a professional or managerial job in the United States. But education matters, too. In fact, at first blush, education appears to be about three times as important as parental social class in determining adult success. The problem is that educational opportunities themselves depend on family origins. But even after accounting for this fact, education remains somewhat more important than social background in accounting for where people end up in the social structure.

With respect to trends in social mobility, little good data are available before the 1960s but scholars seem to believe that opportunity increased along with industrialization in the 19th and 20th centuries up until at least the early 1970s.

Such progress is not immutable; indeed, there are disturbing signs that as we enter the 21st century, we can no longer take it for granted. What has captured people's attention most powerfully is data showing that the rich are getting richer, the poor poorer, while the middle class is losing ground. . . . [There] is a widening gap between

| WEALTH AND RACE | | | |
|---|---|---|---|
| RACE | WHITE | BLACK | RATIO B/W |
| MEDIAN INCOME | $25,384 | $15,630 | 62% |
| MEDIAN NET WORTH* | 43,800 | 3,700 | 8% |
| MEAN NET WORTH* | 96,667 | 23,818 | 25% |
| MEDIAN NET FINANCIAL ASSETS** | 6,999 | 0 | — |
| MEAN NET FINANCIAL ASSETS** | 47,347 | 5,209 | 11% |

\* Net worth = all assets, minus debts.
\*\* Net financial assets = all assets excluding equity in a home or vehicle, minus debts.

those at the bottom and those at the top. . . . The postwar baby boom generation is the first to have not done better than their parents. More specifically, young men are earning less than their fathers did at a comparable age. And . . . the prospects for the next century are not encouraging.

Sawhill goes on to explain the role of changes in the economy, the education system, and the family in creating novel difficulties for the production of opportunity in America. Her compelling analysis leaves little doubt in my mind that these difficulties are most threatening to disadvantaged minorities, whose lives and communities are most at risk from the destabilizing changes and entrenched disparities in these three arenas.

The upshot is that the racial differentials we note today not only are old and demonstrably intractable but may well be yet another tragic burden we will bequeath to the next generation. For example, if the bandwagon for thoroughgoing education reform remains stuck in the mud, and is fueled only by a swill of political rhetoric and snake-oil federalism, then inner-city and rural kids will find themselves falling further and further behind their advantaged peers in suburban and elite schools. If the fires of family disintegration and teen pregnancy (both powerful predictors of the impoverishment of children) continue to run all but unchecked, even unchallenged, through community after community, we should not be surprised when the dreams go up in smoke, and then the hope, and then—who knows?

All of this points toward the need for what I call an opportunity agenda, and there is broad agreement that "civil rights" is an element in it. I don't believe the heart of the political difficulty is over how *much* attention to civil rights is needed—like a dispute over budgetary resources for school lunches versus remedial reading. That's ultimately just a dispute about tactics, important as those are. Instead, the heart of the difficulty is in the conception of "civil rights"—whether Martin Luther King, Jr., was right to say both that it includes the challenge of creating genuine economic opportunity, and that race-conscious measures going beyond antidiscrimination are morally and pragmatically justified. (Conservatives often conveniently ignore King's support of race-conscious measures.) This last issue raises directly the question of how race figures in public and private attitudes and decision making today.

I think of America's attitudes and behaviors about race as being akin to a deep, somewhat debilitating neurosis, a mental disorder or illness. What is the state of the patient today? As close to cure as many critics of affirmative action seem to believe? One cannot construct a coherent view on affirmative action without positing an answer to this question, no matter how incomplete the data.

As it happens, the data are about as clear as one could want. The federal government alone continues to receive more than 90,000 complaints of employment discrimination (race and gender) every year, and thousands of other individuals file complaints alleging discrimination in housing, credit, voting, and public accommodations. Justice Department officials testifying before Congress have reported that incidents of racially motivated violence are on the rise, even as the rates for violent crime are declining. According to Dr. Mary Frances Berry, chairwoman of the U.S. Civil Rights Commission, in the filings and level of enforcement activities nationwide by federal, state, and local civil rights enforcement agencies over the past two decades, there has been no downward trend that would suggest that the underlying problems of racial discrimination are abating. And with respect to that particular kind of bias termed "reverse discrimination," the data simply don't make the case that the phenomenon is widespread. EEOC filings have been minimal, as have reverse-bias claims against federal contractors who are obliged to use affirmative action.

Some of the most compelling evidence of continuing discrimination comes from an innovative "tester," or "audit," methodology, in which two individuals are matched in all relevant characteristics, different only in their race or gender or ethnicity, depending on the form of discrimination being studied; they are then sent out to apply for a job, an apartment, a bank loan, or whatever. (Much of this methodological work was pioneered by the Urban Institute.) In contrast to the faceless econometric statistics that show discriminatory patterns, these tester studies offer not just statistics but powerful, illustrative anecdotes and even videotape. Among the early dramatic results were tester studies conducted by the Fair Employment Council of Greater Washington during 1990–92. Blacks were treated worse than equally qualified whites 24 percent of the time and Latinos were treated worse 22 percent of the time. Our report to the President included these examples:

- Two pairs of male testers visited the offices of a nationally franchised employment agency on two different days. The black tester in each pair received no job referrals, while the white testers who appeared minutes later were interviewed by the agency, coached on interviewing techniques, and referred to and offered jobs (as switchboard operators).
- An African-American tester asked about an ad for a sales position at a Maryland car dealership, but was told that the entry-level job was one washing cars, while the white applicant with identical credentials was immediately interviewed for the sales job.
- A black female tester applied for employment at a major hotel chain in Virginia and was told she would be called if they wished to pursue her application. No call ever came. Meanwhile, her equally qualified white counterpart, who appeared a few minutes later, was told of a vacancy for a front-desk clerk, later interviewed, and offered the job.
- A black tester applied for an advertised position as typist/receptionist, was interviewed, and heard nothing further. An identically qualified white tester was interviewed, offered a better position that paid more than the receptionist job, and given tuition assistance. The firm did not respond to the black tester's follow-up telephone calls, even though the white tester refused the job offer.

Similar results were reported in the Urban Institute's *Employment and Housing Discrimination Studies*, in 1991. The white tester advanced further in the hiring process than equally qualified blacks 20 percent of the time. The fact that this blatant discrimination occurs in every level blue-collar jobs strikes me as an especially critical piece of evidence, for the first rung of the ladder is the most important.

As for housing, the Urban Institute's research demonstrated that black and Hispanic testers faced discrimination in roughly half of their contacts with real estate agents. The Justice Department has also conducted its own tester research, documenting numerous instances in which realtors tell black testers that no apartments are available and then show available units to equally qualified whites. Similar research has replicated these results around the country.

In the overall picture—from the Glass Ceiling Commission to testers, from litigation data to anecdotes about professional black men unable to hail a taxicab—the compilation of incidents is somehow swamped in emotional significance by the drama of racially related murders, or police brutality, or gang violence. There are continuing episodes of what can only be termed community terrorism, designed to force out minorities so that neighborhoods remain all white. The Justice Department prosecuted thirty-two individuals for burning crosses in 1994 alone—from Maine to Washington State. Recently the news media reported that a series of black churches across three Southern states had been torched by arson that federal and state authorities agreed was racially motivated. A steady drumbeat of news accounts report on skinhead and neo-Nazi groups, with Klanwatch and other organizations issuing increasingly dire warnings about the rising tide of venom. Again, from the White House Report:

> Earlier [in 1995], a grand jury in Alabama indicted a white man for trying to force several African American families out of town by mailing them threatening letters, which read in part:
>
> "[This] is an ALL WHITE CITY! Get out while you can . . . We are organized and determined to send all Niggers to Africa, ONE WAY OR ANOTHER! SO GET THE [expletive] OUT OF THIS NEIGHBORHOOD.
>
> "GO HOME TO AFRICA YOU NIGGER! Start packing your bags you NIGGER APE BABOON BASTARD! You are going back to Africa, ONE WAY OR ANOTHER! . . . Maybe we will use . . . a NIGGER RESERVATION when the White Race wins the RACE WAR. How about a NIGGER GRAVEYARD. GO TO HELL YOU NIGGER APE BASTARD."

White supremacist activity in the armed forces, investigated by the Secretary of the Army in the Winter of 1995-96, and allegations about such sympathies within the Federal Bureau of Alcohol, Tobacco, and Firearms merely serve to underscore that while the sentiments quoted above no doubt strike many readers as aberrant and extreme, the extreme is closer to home—very much closer—than casual observers realize. But professionals in civil rights enforcement at the Justice Department and elsewhere know that virulent bigotry is alive and well. So this policy battle is about moral and policy subtleties, but also about outright discrimination and a virulent strain of resistant racism, gut-pure and simple as sin.

President Clinton had no doubt that problems of racial exclusion and discrimination are still too severe for us to declare victory in the struggle for racial justice. But we are not writing on a clean slate. It makes sense also to ask what we know about the effectiveness of affirmative action programs or laws thus far. Have they helped to close opportunity gaps and prevent discrimination?

During the early stages of the White House review, we were surprised by how little serious social science has been devoted to this question. Using the expertise of the Council of Economic Advisers and the Department of Labor, we could glean from the literature the summary conclusion that affirmative action has indeed had a modest effect on employment of minorities. The improvement was greater in the 1970s than in the 1980s, which may be explained by the drop in enforcement activity during the Reagan administration, and the overall chill (as affirmative action proponents would put it) which that administration created for civil rights enforcement around the nation.

As I've said, the great difficulty faced by researchers is that it is almost impossible, in observing employment patterns, to separate the effects of pure *antidiscrimination* norms from the effects of the *additional* measures commonly thought of as "affirmative action." Indeed, civil rights liberals are quick to argue that affirmative action is itself a form of antidiscrimination, inasmuch as it encompasses a set of tools or actions designed to *prevent* future discrimination as well as to remedy past discrimination and its continuing effects. Imagine looking at the employment of blacks at a warehouse over the years 1968–75 and seeing that the percentage of blacks in entry-level jobs grows from 1 to perhaps 5. To what extent is that improvement due to the employer's ending his discriminatory practices and to what extent is it due to affirmative action?

Several studies have compared statistics about general employment in the private sector with those that show employment trends in comparable firms that do business with the federal government and are therefore required, under Executive Order 11246, to engage in both nondiscrimination *and* affirmative action. The theory is that the nondiscrimination requirement applies to essentially *all* employers through Title VII of the 1964 Civil Rights Act, while affirmative action is required only of firms subject to the executive order (these firms employ roughly one-quarter of America's workforce). But even firms not subject to the executive order may engage in considerable voluntary "affirmative action," even if they don't call it that, and I would expect that as private-sector employers increasingly accept both nondiscrimination and affirmative action, it becomes harder and harder to disaggregate the effects for study.

In any case, the weight of academic opinion—not unanimity, but certainly the generally accepted view—finds that affirmative action has had a modest positive effect on employment.

In education, the same methodological problems exist. It is clear that the numbers of minorities who attended college increased dramatically during and after the modern civil rights revolution. But that progress has since stalled and even been somewhat reversed: some of the gains may be tenuous, especially as other economic and social difficulties make it harder to reach the first rung of the opportunity ladder. (One thinks, for example, of recent data on rates of black male incarceration; the widening quality gap between inner-city and suburban schools; and the secular growth, thankfully reversed in the last handful of years, in black teen pregnancy rates.) In many elite settings, such as newsrooms and boardrooms, the best that can be said is that affirmative action has often helped to break the color barrier, while not fully accomplishing the hoped-for integration.

Is the glass half full or half empty? Are we racial optimists or racial pessimists? I return to this in Chapter 9, but for now, the key is that civil rights liberals take it as an article of faith that affirmative action and antidiscrimination go hand in hand. Without affirmative action, nondiscrimination can be a hollow formality that results in little actual change in people's lives. The Nixon administration introduced affirmative action goals and timetables in the executive order program precisely because the nondiscrimination command alone had not changed job patterns at firms with federal contracts. Those who dismiss this as ancient history must explain today's discrimination data.

In a sense, the methodological difficulty social scientists face when they try to measure the effects of affirmative action is mirrored by, and arises from, the conceptual relationship between nondiscrimination and affirmative efforts. It takes an affirmative effort to break a comfortable old habit, no matter the decibel level of the lip service paid in acknowledgments that the habit is bad.

## Antidiscrimination Law and Constraints on Public and Private Policy

In considering law in civil rights and affirmative action, let's start with four fundamental truths about the nature of the American legal system.

First, our politico-legal system is *liberal* in the sense of traditional political philosophy. It emphasizes private and personal autonomy and, particularly, freedom from intrusions by the state. The practical consequence is that we expect that whatever the law says about civil rights or affirmative action, substantial scope will remain for private, unregulated decision making and behavior. It would be a classic lawyer's error to focus exclusively, or even primarily, on the law—as it is or as it should be. The struggle to define civic norms and values is far broader than that.

Second, our legal system is *constitutional*, meaning not only that government is limited as required by classic liberalism but also that the structure of and limits to government are shaped substantially by a written Constitution. The national government is limited in its powers to those enumerated in the (admittedly flexible) language of the Constitution; our state governments have plenary power, but all state constitutions limit state government power in ways that more or less parallel the limits imposed by the national constitution on the federal government. The practical consequences for my topic are that governmental power to legislate on matters of race must find a source of authority in the text of the Constitution, *and* that when government does act, it must not violate any limits on governmental power found in the Constitution. Important limits include the ones in the First Amendment, prohibiting Congress from abridging the freedom of "speech" and "assembly," and the guarantees in the Fifth Amendment that no person can be "deprived of life, liberty, or property, without due process of law" and in the Fourteenth Amendment that no *state* can deprive anyone "of life, liberty, or property, without due process of law" or deny anyone "within its jurisdiction the equal protection of the laws."

The Founders conceived of the national government as having limited scope, but the Constitution's grants of legislative authority are framed in general terms. Over the generations, this vagueness has permitted Congress and the President to respond to the evolving needs for national authority—or, if not needs, then at least evolving ambitions of the American people for what they wish to accomplish through collective action, using democratic government. When the Founders wrote, in Article I, that Congress has the power to regulate "commerce with foreign nations, and among the several States," they of course could not foresee a world in which economic forces move almost instantaneously not just across state lines but around the world, in which the income of Texas rice farmers is affected by the monsoon season in South Asia, the demand from cereal processors in Michigan and Pennsylvania, and the marketing decisions of supermarkets in Seattle. And the Founders certainly would not have contemplated that, in the name of regulating interstate commerce, the private owner of a motel would be required by law to serve colored folks whom she hated. (Asks a Founder, "What's a 'motel,' and is it proper for a woman to own it?") Nevertheless, thankfully, congressional authority so to act is settled constitutional doctrine. Since the New Deal the Supreme Court has been generous in interpreting the commerce clause. Moreover, the

Fourteenth Amendment contains, in Section 5, a grant of power to Congress to "enforce, by appropriate legislation, the provisions" of the equal protection clause. While the scope of Congress's authority are uncertain, today the political climate is more a constraint than is the actual issue of legislative authority.

Still, the issue of constitutional liberties and the limits on government's exercise of that legislative authority is complicated. For our purposes, the key provisions are the Fifth Amendment, part of the original Bill of Rights, and the equal protection clause of the Fourteenth Amendment, which was adopted in the aftermath of the Civil War, along with the Thirteenth Amendment abolishing slavery and the Fifteenth Amendment prohibiting denial of the vote on the basis on race (gender had to wait another fifty years for the Nineteenth Amendment). Here are the key passages:

## FIFTH AMENDMENT

No person shall be held to answer for a capital, or otherwise infamous crime, unless on a presentment or indictment of a grand jury, except in cases arising in the land or naval forces, or in the militia, when in actual service in time of war or public danger; nor shall any person be subject for the same offense to be twice put in jeopardy of life or limb; nor shall be compelled in any criminal case to be a witness against himself, *nor be deprived of life, liberty, or property, without due process of law;* nor shall private property be taken for public use without just compensation.

## FOURTEENTH AMENDMENT

[passed by Congress June 16, 1866; ratified July 23, 1868]

Section 1. All persons born or naturalized in the United States, and subject to the jurisdiction thereof, are citizens of the United States and of the State wherein they reside. No State shall make or enforce any law which shall abridge the privileges or immunities of citizens of the United States; *nor shall any State deprive any person of life, liberty, or property, without due process of law; nor deny to any person within its jurisdiction the equal protection of the laws.*

Section 2. Representatives shall be apportioned among the several States according to their respective numbers, counting the whole number of persons in each State, excluding Indians not taxed. . . .

Section 5. The Congress shall have power to enforce, by appropriate legislation, the provisions of this article.

One can see that the Fifth Amendment has civil liberties limitations on what the national government can do, while the Fourteenth Amendment prohibits *state governments* from denying any person due process or equal protection of the laws. (This distinction evidences the Founding Fathers' general assumption that the national government was the thing being created, and it was to have limited powers, whereas the sovereign states were already in place and their powers were not central to the political accommodation represented by the Bill of Rights.) But in the 1954 case of *Bolling v. Sharpe*, the Supreme Court held that the limits on racial discrimination applicable to the states under the Fourteenth Amendment's equal protection clause are also applicable to the federal government, using the interpretative device of "incorporating" its equal protection guarantees into the Fifth Amendment's due-process guarantee. So we loosely speak of the equal protection guarantee as protecting individuals from misdeeds not only of state governments (and their instrumentalities, local governments) but also of the national government.

Third, in the American system of *federalism*, state and local governments are responsible for most lawmaking and law enforcement. In the area of race, there are several levels of law to consider:

- Congress has used its constitutional grants of authority to "regulate" certain private behavior. The most prominent example of this is the Civil Rights Act of 1964, which prohibits discrimination in employment and in "public accommodations." In addition, Congress has enacted a variety of laws intended to remedy or prevent discrimination and its effects, such as racially targeted education and procurement efforts. (I will consider some of these in Chapter 8.)
- State and local governments have likewise adopted statutes and ordinances prohibiting discrimination, as well as pro-

grams intended to help remedy discrimination and race-related disadvantage. These generally follow the pattern of the federal measures, with occasional noteworthy differences. For example, a state may enact antidiscrimination measures in employment or housing that are more protective of victims than any federal law; victims might then seek enforcement in state rather than federal courts. Or, as is debated in California, a state might decide *not* to adopt putatively remedial measures, such as pro-diversity preferences at public colleges, that are permitted or even encouraged under federal law.

- The Fourteenth Amendment prohibits states (including their local creations) from depriving any person of "equal protection," and, as we have seen, this prohibition has been applied to the federal government through the Fifth Amendment.

- Every state has a provision in its state constitution that mirrors the equal protection guarantee in the federal Constitution. These would be superfluous, except that state courts sometimes give them a slightly different (i.e., more protective) reading than federal courts have given the parallel provision in the U.S. Constitution, and the very existence of such a state statute or constitutional provision encourages plaintiffs to proceed in state rather than federal court.

- In federal law, various civil rights statutes require federal agencies to issue detailed regulations spelling out precisely what their legal obligations are. For example, the U.S. Department of Education regulations interpret the nondiscrimination provisions of the civil rights statutes it administers, including Title VI of the Civil Rights Act of 1964, which prohibits discrimination by institutions receiving federal funds, such as universities. Regulations generally have the force of law.

- Lastly, the federal government imposes nondiscrimination and affirmative action obligations on large companies with which it has contracts. Rather than a law, the central mechanism for this is Executive Order 11246, issued by President Lyndon Johnson, and substantially strengthened by the Nixon administration, which added requirements for goals and timetables (*not quotas*). (I discuss this in detail in Chapter 8.)

The Supreme Court's infamous 1896 ruling in *Plessy v. Ferguson* that "separate but equal" did not constitute unconstitutional discrimination gutted the equal protection clause's promise. The resulting network of Jim Crow laws and institutions—America's version of apartheid—survived in important respects well into the 1960s. The significance of *Brown v. Board of Education of Topeka*, in 1954, was that the Supreme Court began dismantling this separate-but-equal doctrine and instead held that the equal protection clause subjects state-sponsored discrimination to "strict scrutiny." The Supreme Court and lower federal courts tolerated years and years of delay in implementing the desegregation imperative of *Brown*; what some saw as revolution, others saw as slow-footed moderation, and still others as a new betrayal.

The cases leading up to and following *Brown* all concerned state or federal laws that were challenged because they seemed to deny the asserted rights of racial minorities or put discriminatory burdens on them. For nearly a quarter of a century after *Brown*, the Supreme Court did not rule on whether state actions that draw racial distinctions burdening the racial *majority* would also be subject to strict scrutiny when challenged under the equal protection clause. Then, in *Regents of the University of California v. Bakke* in 1978, the issue was finally joined. An admissions policy of the UC Davis medical school set aside sixteen places out of an entering class of one hundred that could be filled only by minority applicants. Davis's actions as a public university, an instrumentality of the state, were subject to challenge under the Fourteenth Amendment of the Constitution (a private institution would be subject only to antidiscrimination provisions of relevant *statutes*). The Supreme Court struck down the policy, but in a fractured decision without a majority opinion to provide a consensus rationale.

The swing vote for the majority came from Justice Lewis Powell; his opinion stressed that a diverse student body contributes to a more robust exchange of ideas, which he characterized as both the central mission of higher education and important to First Amendment values in academia. On that point, the dissenters agreed. But the dissenters argued strongly that the core goal of the Fourteenth Amendment was to protect racial minorities, that strict scrutiny of state government actions burdening minorities was therefore appropriate to that purpose, but that the same intensity of judicial scrutiny was not appropriate when a government action burdened the majority for the benign purpose of remedying discrimination against and disadvantage faced by the minority. Justice Powell argued, however, that even when the state government has a benign purpose in relation to minorities, the Fourteenth Amendment will not permit a rigid system such as the UC Davis set-asides; that race can only be used as a *flexible factor* in the admissions process.

Meanwhile, the Supreme Court had held that government action making distinctions on the basis of *gender* were subject to a level of scrutiny more intense than that of a simple test of "mere rationality," which is applicable to most government action, but not so stringent as the "strict scrutiny" applicable to classifications made on the basis of race, religion, or national origin.*

The next significant development was the Supreme Court's 1980 decision in *Fullilove v. Klutznick.* A divided Court upheld a provision in the federal Surface Transportation Act that set a goal that 10 percent of the contract dollars under the program should go to "disadvantaged business enterprises," principally minority-owned companies; the Secretary of Transportation was instructed to devise methods of achieving that goal but was also authorized to abandon the goal when and where impracticable. The implementing regulations included a number of different possible mechanisms. Most important, *Fullilove* applied an "intermediate scrutiny" to this federal race-based affirmative action measure, reasoning that it was remedial in purpose and that Congress has broad power to address the problem of racial discrimination. Under this intermediate standard, the government's categorization of individuals must "serve an *important governmental interest*" and the measure adopted must "be *substantially related*" to that interest. The Court

---

* The Justice Department has asked the Supreme Court to review whether the standard should, instead, be strict scrutiny. The Court may address the question in its decision in the Virginia Military Institute case in the latter part of its 1995–96 term.

noted that Congress had held hearings and made findings about minority business enterprises. The dissenters argued that strict scrutiny should apply; eventually, they would have their day.

*Fullilove* came in the waning days of the Carter administration. The new Reagan administration had quite another view of what the law should be, and the philosophy required of Republican appointees to the federal bench worked just the kind of slow but powerful ideological shift in the federal judiciary that the Founders contemplated, and that makes presidential elections vital to liberty.

By 1986, in *City of Richmond v. J. A. Croson Co.*, the tide had apparently changed. *Croson* involved a white contractor's challenge to an ordinance establishing a target of 30 percent as the proportion of city subcontracts that should be awarded to minority businesses. The Virginia city defended the choice of goal as a compromise between the less than 1 percent of city contracts awarded to blacks and the city's 50 percent black population.

A majority of the Court, in an opinion written by Justice Sandra Day O'Connor, held for the first time that race-based state and local affirmative action measures, like race-based burdens on minorities, are subject to strict scrutiny. The case left open the question of whether *federal* measures might be treated differently.

*Strict scrutiny* has two prongs: the race-based measure must be justified by a "compelling governmental interest" (in this case the purported remediation of discrimination and its lingering present effects); and it must be "narrowly tailored" to achieve that compelling interest. With respect to the *compelling interest*:

- The discrimination to be remedied may be in acts of the government, or it may be in acts of private parties where the government is a "passive participant" and thereby helps to perpetuate a system of exclusion. (The second is often given as the reason for government preference programs.)
- There need not have been a judicial finding of present or past discrimination, but the government must have a "strong basis in evidence" for concluding that present discrimination and/ or lingering effects exist. *Croson* and subsequent cases estab-

lished that statistical disparities can make up the bulk of this showing, provided they are carefully drawn and do more than crudely demonstrate mere underrepresentation. Richmond had statistics which, the Court said, were *not* satisfactory evidence of discrimination in contracting but, at best, evidence of general, "amorphous" societal discrimination. Not good enough.

- The *Croson* ruling requires the government to identify with precision the discrimination to be remedied. Again, general societal discrimination and lack of opportunities are not a sufficient predicate.

- Richmond defended its ordinance on the grounds that it was a *remedial* response to discrimination. The Court therefore did not rule on whether *nonremedial* concerns, such as diversity, might be a "compelling interest." (That issue will soon come to the Court.)

With respect to *narrow tailoring*, the definitive, succinct summary appears in a formal analysis of the Supreme Court's decision in 1995 on *Adarand Constructors, Inc. v. Peña*, which was issued by Assistant Attorney General Walter Dellinger of the Office of Legal Counsel, and included in an appendix to our White House review. Dellinger, a noted constitutional scholar at Duke Law School, first summarized that the purpose of this requirement in strict scrutiny is to ensure that governments adopt race-based measures only after careful deliberation, and only when truly necessary because alternative, less race-conscious measures are unavailable or would likely be ineffective. He continued, distilling scores of court rulings into six factors typically used:

(i) [W]hether the government considered race-neutral alternatives . . . ; (ii) the scope of the affirmative action program, and whether there is a waiver mechanism that facilitates the narrowing of the program's scope; (iii) the manner in which [race] is used, that is, whether race is a factor in determining eligibility for a program or whether race is just one factor in the decisionmaking process; (iv) the comparison of any numerical target to the number of qualified minorities in the relevant sector or industry; (v) the duration of the program and whether it is subject to periodic review; and (vi) the degree and type of burden caused by the program.

Not every factor is relevant in a given case, and it is probably true that a court will not require that a program satisfy every factor. A court's overall decision seems to involve a vague weighing of factors, with a strong showing on one perhaps compensating for weaknesses elsewhere.

Similarly, the Justice Department's analysis also suggests that the two prongs of strict scrutiny "should not necessarily be viewed in isolation": strength in the first may lead a court to be more relaxed in evaluating the second, and vice versa. This interplay has considerable practical importance, because legislators and program administrators may not, when faced with a dramatic problem, take the time and trouble to study the alternatives exhaustively. By the same token, if a race-based measure seems relatively innocuous in operation, a detailed exegesis on the predicate of discrimination may seem unnecessary.

One immediate consequence of *Croson* was that contracting programs adopted by state and local governments around the country were suddenly being sued, or were in danger of suit. Legislatures and consultants went to work: patterns of contracting and hiring were examined in "disparity studies," trying to demonstrate the facts of discrimination or its lingering effects; and policy analysis reshaped the programs in an effort to meet the requirements of narrow tailoring. The Justice Department has collected more than 120 such state and local studies for review, to determine what methodological lessons can be learned for purposes of analyzing federal programs.

Meanwhile, the *Croson* court had left unanswered the question of whether strict scrutiny would apply to affirmative action measures adopted by the federal government. In a 1990 ruling, *Metro Broadcasting, Inc. v. FCC*, the Supreme Court considered congressional measures taken to increase the number of minorities owning broadcast licenses. The central justification for these programs was not that the FCC had once discriminated in awarding licenses or that discrimination existed in private financial markets or was practiced by sellers of licenses. Instead, the case rested on the argument that diversity in ownership would increase the diversity of viewpoints available to Americans who listen to radio and watch television.

A divided Supreme Court upheld the program, 5–4, applying an *intermediate* level of constitutional scrutiny. Justice O'Connor dissented, with three others, arguing for strict scrutiny of federal measures—the same test her majority opinion had applied in *Croson*. She was unimpressed with arguments that greater deference is owed the Congress when it adopts affirmative action than is owed the states. Thus the question of a more generous standard for federal affirmative action hung by one vote.

Then came Justice Clarence Thomas, replacing Thurgood Marshall. (The Clinton appointees, Ruth Ginsburg and Stephen Breyer, have supported affirmative action; they replace justices who were similarly inclined, and therefore have not shifted the balance of the Court back in the direction of *Fullilove* and *Metro Broadcasting*.)

On June 13, 1995, the Supreme Court handed down its long-awaited ruling in *Adarand Constructors, Inc. v. Peña*. At issue was a Department of Transportation (DOT) contracting program with a statutory goal of awarding 5 percent of total contract and subcontract dollars to small firms certified as controlled by "socially and economically disadvantaged" persons. The statute makes African Americans and certain other minorities "presumptively" eligible, but that presumption can be rebutted; the statute also makes it possible for nonminorities to demonstrate that they are eligible. (This is rare in practice.) Under the particular mechanism challenged in *Adarand*, prime contractors get a dollar "bonus" added to their contract if they hire disadvantaged subcontractors; this is meant to compensate them for the technical assistance and other costs they are presumed to incur in subcontracting with disadvantaged firms rather than more established companies. A prime contractor rejected Adarand's low bid in favor of a minority firm presumed to be socially and economically disadvantaged; the prime thereby became eligible for the additional compensation from DOT. A federal district court granted summary judgment upholding the program; the Tenth Circuit Court of Appeals affirmed, applying the "intermediate scrutiny" standard.

The Supreme Court's 5–4 decision, with Justice O'Connor now

writing for the majority, held that the strict scrutiny applied previously in *Croson* to state race-conscious affirmative action must apply also to congressionally authorized programs. In reversing the lower courts, the Court overruled *Fullilove* and *Metro Broadcasting*, insofar as they used the less stringent intermediate scrutiny standard. The four dissenters (Justices Stevens, Souter, Ginsburg, and Breyer) would have reaffirmed the 1990 holding of *Metro Broadcasting*; they argued that there *is* a constitutional distinction between benign and invidious classifications—between a "No Trespassing" sign and a "welcome mat," as Justice Stevens put it. They reasoned, further, that the lesser standard is also appropriate because Congress, unlike state and local governments, has explicit constitutional authority to remedy discrimination against minorities (in Section 5 of the Fourteenth Amendment), and so they concluded that the DOT program should be upheld, citing *Fullilove*.

At 11:30 on the morning *Adarand* was handed down, the White House staff involved on the affirmative action issue huddled in the Roosevelt Room, across the hall from the Oval Office and the Cabinet Room. George Stephanopoulos had also summoned Deval Patrick, John Schmidt, and others from the Justice Department to analyze the opinion and make recommendations for what the President should say. (George and I had both read most of the decision ourselves, but etiquette required that we let Justice Department officials "instruct" us.) Initial reactions around the table ranged from "no big deal" to "disaster," and from "low-key response" to "leadership in a time of crisis."

I alternated among taking notes, doodling, and making interjections to help George keep things moving along constructively. From experience, he and I knew that a meeting this large on a problem this tricky was not going to produce a consensus. Our real purpose was to air things out, let everyone have a chance to give advice, and then take away whatever pearls of wisdom were offered and draft something. Quickly. Serious decisions about tone, nuance, and even policy are best made when you are actually drafting the statement and have it in front of you. Since I felt a strong stake in the outcome, I wanted to be sure that I drew the assignment to write the first draft—not Justice, or White House Counsel, or a wordsmith from the communications shop. I suppose I should have had a draft ready weeks beforehand, since the Court's decision was fairly predictable. I did get control of the pen, since the only people senior enough to pull it away from me—George, White House Counsel Ab Mikva, and Assistant to the President Alexis Herman—were all *too* senior to be able to control their time long enough to write more than three sentences. So, assuming my humble-staffer demeanor, I hustled back to my office to concoct something for our inner circle to chew on.

The key was to make sure that in the rush to prepare something for the White House press corps and the TV networks, we did not miss a substantive nuance or step on a political land mine. By midafternoon I had produced a solid draft and revised it on the basis of George's modest edits. Then I asked other key black staff members to review the draft. Deval Patrick, Maggie Williams, Alexis Herman, and I caucused in Alexis's swell corner office on the second floor of the West Wing. Still determined not to miss a trick, I grabbed Alexis's computer in hopes of maximizing my influence over the editing process. We went around and around, debating phrases and nuances. Alexis drifted in and out; she was juggling some crisis involving Cuba. Assorted other West Wing staff, mostly white, also drifted in and out with substantive and editorial "contributions." Finally we had yet another draft to take downstairs for review by George (again), Leon Panetta, and whoever else would want to stick their spoon in the stew.

Somewhere along the way, momentum developed to strike a few sentences, a deletion that had the effect of subtly shifting the statement in the conservative direction. Most of the second-floor team were not too concerned; it seemed to involve only an obscure subtlety. But to me it was a major sticking point, and I cared enough about it to throw a tantrum. But time was slipping, and I knew that delay could cause us to miss deadlines for the prime-time television news programs. We had only a few minutes to get the President to review and approve the statement. A few senior aides took it in to him, without the sentences I wanted; it was supposed to be a crash session in which they would plow through several decisions on assorted matters in a couple of minutes. I cooled my heels, going into a profound, dramatic funk. I felt that the substantive and political high ground to which we had climbed over the long process of our review was about to be lost by careless staff work done in a hurry. I pondered my inadequacies. (But it felt better to blame others.)

A few minutes later, Alexis and two or three aides finished the quickie session in the Oval Office, and she caught me in the hall outside the Vice President's office. (I visualized the drill. A couple of aides stand around in front of President Clinton's desk as he reads, and everyone talks at him. Sometimes he's reading what you're talking to him about; other times he's "multi-tasking," studying some document from an entirely different policy planet.) She said the President had approved the statement with one change: *he put back in the sentences I had wanted.* This was a victory I needed! In retrospect, I see that it was probably more important to me in its emotional significance than in the actual policy implications, but it felt unbelievably great, and it renewed my confidence that the President was on the right wavelength. The statement was perhaps not quite so critical of the Court as I would have liked, but it was pretty close. And every sentence expressed a carefully considered substantive or political point. Not a bad day's work.

After *Adarand*, we had a practical problem: we had to reshape our report to the President, by then virtually complete. And we had a host of related decisions to make about what to do next—on the Hill, in litigation, and in further legal and policy review of the various federal programs. The Supreme Court had in some respects turned the world upside down, because many matters previously in the realm of policy choice and prudent judgment were now matters of constitutional analysis. For example, the matter of whether the government had a "compelling interest" in the purposes of a health professions development program was related to tough questions we had been asking about justification, though importantly different in two respects. First, as a matter of policy and values, there was a range of possible justifications for the health program that might deserve at least some consideration. But after *Adarand*, the only thing that was clear was that remediation would meet the "compelling interest" prong of strict scrutiny, while

# THE WHITE HOUSE
## *Office of the Press Secretary*

For Immediate Release                                    June 13, 1995

## STATEMENT BY THE PRESIDENT

The Supreme Court's decision sets a new legal standard for judging affirmative action, but it must not set us back in our fight to end discrimination
and create equal opportunity for all.

Despite great progress, discrimination and exclusion on the basis of
race and gender are still facts of life in America. I have always believed
that affirmative action is needed to remedy discrimination and to create a
more inclusive society that truly provides equal opportunity. But I have
also said that affirmative action must be carefully justified and must be
done the right way. The Court's opinion in *Adarand* is not inconsistent with
that view.

It is regrettable that already, with the ink barely dry, many are using
the Court's opinion as a reason to abandon that fight. Exaggerated claims
about the end of affirmative action—whether in celebration or dismay—
do not serve the interest all of us have in a responsible national conversation about how to move forward together and create equal opportunity.

The Supreme Court has raised the hurdle, but it is not insurmountable. Make no mistake: the Court has approved affirmative action that is
narrowly tailored to achieve a compelling interest. The constitutional test
is now tougher than it was, but I am confident that the test can be met in
many cases. We know that from the experience of state and local governments, which have operated under the tougher standard for some years
now.

Some weeks ago, I directed my staff conducting the review of federal
affirmative action programs to ask agencies a number of probing questions
about programs that make race or sex a condition of eligibility for any kind
of benefit. What, concretely, is the justification for this particular program?
Have race- and gender-neutral alternatives been considered? Is the program flexible? Does it avoid quotas, in theory and in practice? Is it transitional and temporary? Is it narrowly drawn? Is it balanced, so that it
avoids concentrating its benefits and its costs? These are tough questions,
but they are the right policy questions and they need answers.

I have instructed the team conducting the Administration's affirmative
action review to include an analysis of the *Adarand* decision and its implications in their report.

the legal significance of nonremedial justifications like diversity was up for grabs. Second, as a practical matter, we had presumed that the policy choices and value conflicts we had wrestled with during our White House review were for ultimate decision by the President and Congress; now the Supreme Court was signaling that federal district court judges all over the country might be getting into the act. In short, this wasn't just about leadership and perhaps legislation. Now it was also going to be about litigation, of a protracted and controversial sort.

There were—and are—three especially important doctrinal questions after *Adarand*. First, it remains to be seen whether lower courts will continue their general practice of permitting governments to introduce evidence of discrimination and lingering effects developed *after* an affirmative action program is adopted by a legislature or agency (the evidence may have been developed for the precise purpose of defending a program in litigation). This issue of post hoc evidence is critical, because many federal programs have been adopted without Congress making detailed evidentiary findings, and relegislating now would be not only burdensome for Congress but politically impossible. (It is true of many programs that the political situation means that it's unlikely Congress will repeal them and also unlikely that Congress will reenact them. The same can be said of a host of laws, including many provisions of the Constitution itself.)

Second, the Court's conclusion that strict scrutiny applies equally to measures benefiting *and* burdening minorities creates a serious anomaly. Equal protection case law has applied intermediate scrutiny to discrimination against women (to the consternation of many in the civil rights movement); that is, the Court has given governments somewhat greater latitude to adopt gender-based classifications than race-based ones, but they must justify them with something more than the "mere rationality" standard used when basing classifications on, say, income or occupation. Most people intuitively sense that affirmative action is easier to justify for racial minorities, but *Adarand* requires that government affirmative action programs benefiting minorities must be subject to the rigorous "strict scrutiny" standard, though actions benefiting women are subject to the less rigorous intermediate standard. In theory, this makes affirmative action for minorities harder to defend legally than similar programs for women, even though our social and moral intuitions point in the opposite direction.

To fix the problem, one of two things must change. Either *Croson* and *Adarand* must be overruled, so that "welcome mat" classifications are subject to a lesser standard of review than "no trespassing" ones, or the Court will have to extend strict scrutiny to apply to all gender classifications, burdensome and beneficent. The White House and the Department of Justice decided to argue the latter position in the Supreme Court, in the appeal concerning sex discrimination at Virginia Military Institute. From the perspective of women's rights, this bold move, if successful, would make sex-based affirmative action more difficult, but in exchange for more rigorous judicial scrutiny of government actions alleged to disadvantage women. The Court's final decision sidestepped the matter, however, and it remains unresolved.

The third major issue left by the Court is whether governmental measures can be justified in contexts apart from remediation of discrimination and its lingering effects. Assistant Attorney General Walter Dellinger's analysis of *Adarand*'s implications put it this way:

> [I]n the wake of *Croson* and *Adarand*, there are substantial questions as to whether and in what settings nonremedial objectives can constitute a compelling interest. (Given the nation's history of discrimination, virtually all affirmative action can be considered remedial in a broad sense. But as *Croson* makes plain, that history, on its own, cannot properly form the basis of a remedial affirmative action measure under strict scrutiny.) To date, there has never been a majority of the Supreme Court that addressed the question. The closest the Court has come in that regard is Justice Powell's separate opinion in *Regents of the University of California v. Bakke*. . . .
>
> In *Metro Broadcasting* [1990], the majority relied on *Bakke* and Justice Stevens' vision of affirmative action to uphold FCC affirmative action programs in the licensing of broadcasters on nonremedial grounds; the Court said that diversification of ownership of broadcast licenses was a permissible objective of affirmative action because it serves the larger goal of exposing the nation to a greater diversity of

perspectives over the nation's radio and television airwaves. . . . The Court reached that conclusion under intermediate scrutiny, however, and thus did not hold that the governmental interest in seeking diversity in broadcasting is "compelling." *Adarand* did not overrule the result in *Metro Broadcasting*—a point not lost on Justice Stevens [a dissenter in *Adarand*].

There can be little doubt that the current Supreme Court, and the many conservative judges in the lower federal courts, will be skeptical about nonremedial justifications for race-based government affirmative action. In the private context, however, where constitutional strict scrutiny does not apply, there may well be considerably more latitude to justify carefully designed race-based measures.

Not all law regulating race-conscious measures is found in the Constitution of the United States or in the substantially similar provisions in every state constitution. The civil rights statutes prohibiting private discrimination must also be considered, since people not benefiting from affirmative action raise claims of "reverse discrimination," cognizable under those statutes. The two principal provisions are in the 1964 Civil Rights Act forbidding discrimination by employers in Title VII and by recipients of federal grants in Title VI.

In a nutshell, the courts have held that the standard for testing whether activities of a state, local, or private entity receiving federal funds violate the nondiscrimination command of Title VI is the same as under the equal protection clause of the Fourteenth Amendment. This applies to "ordinary discrimination." While there is no definitive case law applying this to affirmative action as such—i.e., establishing when such measures constitute illegal *reverse* discrimination—it is reasonable to expect that after *Croson* and *Adarand* the question is whether the entity has a compelling interest and whether the affirmative action measure is narrowly tailored. Even before *Adarand*, for example, the Department of Education in February 1994 issued regulations interpreting Title VI that insist on very much the same kind of measured analysis and justification that the Supreme Court has since required of all government programs under equal protection strict scrutiny.

As for employment, under Title VII voluntary affirmative action has been upheld in many contexts, based on Supreme Court precedents in the 1979 case of *United Steelworkers v. Weber* and the 1987 case of *Johnson v. Transportation Agency of Santa Clara County*. Under the case law, there is somewhat more latitude for private action than there is under either Title VI, applicable to federal grantees, or the equal protection clause, covering the government itself. (Judicial endorsement of voluntary affirmative action is somewhat inevitable. Once the courts concluded in the 1960s that affirmative action was a permissible court-ordered remedy after trials, and after Congress implicitly endorsed those remedies in the 1972 amendments strengthening Title VII, then it would have seriously undermined the notion of voluntary compliance if one denied employers the ability to make good-faith compliance efforts before being sued. And it would not be sensible to require that employers publicly confess past illegal actions, since that would invite stale lawsuits.)

In applying Title VII, the courts have emphasized restrictions on the duration of affirmative action plans, their purposes, their effect on nonminorities, and the means employed to make them work. Most important:

The plan must have a *permissible basis*. The courts have definitively recognized two: (a) to remedy a clear and convincing history of past discrimination by an employer or union; or (b) to correct a *"manifest imbalance"* in a traditionally segregated job category—a showing that need not amount to statistical evidence that would be proof of prior discrimination in a trial. The courts have left open the possibility that there may be other permissible bases for affirmative action. (This is the very issue before the courts in the Piscataway, New Jersey, teachers' case, where diversity is the asserted basis for a school board's policy.)

The plan also must not *"unnecessarily trammel"* the interests of nonbeneficiaries; any use of race as a factor in decision making must be flexible. (For affirmative action plans that are not voluntary—i.e., adopted as court-ordered or court-approved remedies for illegal discrimination—in rare cases courts have ordered extraordinarily recalcitrant defendants to live with numerical straitjackets for a period of time.) Judicial explanations of how one determines whether something "unnecessarily trammels" seem virtually identical to constitutional analyses of "narrow tailoring." The words are different as much by the accident of uncoordinated doctrinal evolution as anything else, but the difference underscores the truth that because Title VII is a mere statute rather than the Constitution, courts are willing to reexamine their approach to it and Congress has full authority to amend or reverse it or modify judicial interpretations that it rejects.

In sum, our White House review concluded, with respect to the basic questions concerning race:

- Economic and social disadvantages remain powerfully linked with color, and this linkage exacts an enormous toll on the perception and reality of opportunity in America.
- Racial discrimination and race-based exclusion remain significant forces.
- Affirmative action has had modest but positive results. It is hard to be precise because of methodological difficulties in measuring separately the effects of nondiscrimination and of affirmative action. The difficulties reflect the close relationship between the two concepts.
- Our laws—the Constitution, the state laws, and various statues—permit affirmative action provided the justification is permissible and the measure appropriately tailored; there are many details and nuances. In general, judge-made doctrine in both constitutional and statutory realms seems designed to ensure that affirmative action will be carefully deliberated and cautiously designed.
- As a matter of law, quotas are illegal and the effect of affirmative action on nonbeneficiaries must be considered. But the courts have rejected flat requirements of color blindness, even in controversies over voluntary governmental affirmative

action; two justices at most on the currently conservative Supreme Court (Antonin Scalia and Clarence Thomas) would be so restrictive.

We also concluded that the hardest work remains to be done, much of it to do with *facts*. An interesting point about facts is that we have so many ways of "finding" them. There is social science research, and there are government agencies that do or commission studies. Trial courts make findings of fact after adversarial combat, and all courts take "judicial notice" of widely accepted facts. Legislatures, too, make findings of fact based on notoriously squirrelly hearings and so-called investigations. All these processes have distinctive strengths and weaknesses, and we should acknowledge that what counts as convincing evidence in one context may be less so in another; what counts as a fatal uncertainty to one species of decision maker may be dismissed as a mere quibble by another.

But the legitimacy of any decision or institution rests on much more than the character of its fact-finding. There is more going on. The Supreme Court, a federal district court, the Richmond city council, a President, a congressional committee, and a reader of a newspaper account (even an accurate one) may all look at the same data and draw very different conclusions about the implications for law and policy.

My various stints in the public sphere—two presidential campaigns, two White House tours of duty, one cabinet officer's personal staff, a big-city mayor's staff—have taught me many compelling lessons about the limits of social science and of law. It doesn't seem much to expect that hard policy choices be made on the basis of the evidence, but experience instructs that it ain't necessarily so. Evidence counts, but doesn't determine. Similarly, law does matter, but often seems far from determinative. Why, then, did it seem so important to lay the foundation of facts and legal background for the President in 1995, and for readers here?

Every "fact" has uncertainties attached to it, and no fact comes with instructions on how much weight it deserves when making tough decisions. We can decide how to grapple with the uncertainty and what weight to give the evidence only when we adopt certain value commitments. And we can make those commitments either in a fuzzy, unexamined and implicit way, or more deliberatively.

Similarly, law is an expression of our value choices—how law is interpreted by courts and others, as well as what goes into the statutes and regulations themselves. But law is only the statement of those few norms we choose to enforce using the power of the state. In a vastly larger domain, we must decide for our private and personal lives what we believe is *right*. Not only does that determine our positions on matters of legal policy but it shapes our behavior toward one another in all those areas of life beyond the practical or even formal reach of regulations, statutes and constitutions.

Facts do matter. Laws do matter. But—Ben Wattenberg stole the best phrase for the title of his 1995 book—*Values Matter Most.*

# 2

# MAKING CHOICES ABOUT VALUES

**N**ow is not the time to minimize our differences, or to make light of the frustrations and anger that separate the combatants. The debate about race in America is *not* simply about disputed facts or varying instrumental calculations about how best to pursue shared goals. It is about these differences and much more: What kinds of risks to assume, what kinds of costs to impose, what kinds of benefits to pursue, and even what kinds of arguments to use in hopes of persuading and leading. None of these questions can be answered without making fundamental decisions about what values are most important, and how tensions among them are to be resolved in the hard cases.

Thoughtful people cannot rest comfortably with an ad hoc set of policy views, using one set of principles and arguments to discuss college admissions and another to consider corporate layoffs or the composition of the federal judiciary. One must have a unifying set of values that provide coherence and permit one to interpolate and extrapolate to new situations and unfamiliar counterarguments. Without such a framework, one has the uneasy sense that one's position is too contingent and perhaps even *un*principled. The antithesis of thoughtfulness is an ideologically driven reductionism, in which much of the complexity is washed away for the political and emotional con-

venience of simplistic formulas and slogans. I doubt that anyone with
such a turn of mind has read this far, because I have nothing to offer
such people besides irritation and the confusion of subtlety.

For my purposes, a "vision" is an encompassing collection of values and ends, of ideals and aspirations for what America should be,
and what the essential qualities of civic and public life should be for
individuals and communities. More, a vision encompasses some assumptions (or conclusions) about factual circumstances and about
means—about how change occurs, and how we should move from
where we are to where we want to be.

But how shall we discover vision, and how shall we link it to the
immediate, pragmatic issues of policy? In the winter of 1995, during
the first White House staff discussions, one or another participant
pressed one or another of three methodological strategies:

- *Inductive Reasoning.* Some argued that the way to build a coherent set of policies for the President was to work through a
  set of decisions about particular examples and hypotheticals,
  initially among ourselves and then with him. By generalizing
  from our conclusions and from the reasoning behind them, we
  would discover the overarching framework of principles upon
  which specific policy choices could be hung. This was an especially attractive approach for the lawyers in the group.
- *Deductive Reasoning.* Others argued that we should begin
  with "first principles," rigorously defining such concepts as
  "equal opportunity," "discrimination," "preference," and
  "remedy." At the same time, we would formulate axioms and
  postulates, such as: *Affirmative action should increase opportunity for benefited individuals without decreasing opportunity
  for others.* Or: *Results are one measure of opportunity, but not
  the only one, so equality of opportunity does not require equality of results.* The social theorists and theorist wannabes liked
  this one.
- *Batch Processing.* Still others, searching in Clintonesque fashion for a "third way," proposed marrying the inductive and
  deductive modes by constructing alternative sets of policy

choices with supporting rationales. Inductive thinkers might view each set as inductively rooted in the specific policy judgments; a deductive thinker could look at the same set as deduced from first principles. The choice between inductive and deductive was, to my mind, a false choice. Go with the flow.

The advantage of this hybrid approach was that it permitted a decision maker—the President then, my reader now—to see the implications of any choice going *upward* to the realm of vision and values and *downward* to the particulars of policy action. If the alternatives are carefully constructed, there will be lots to argue about concerning values and policy, but perhaps fewer surprises because the critical implications will have been predicted and considered.

In the next three chapters, therefore, we consider three alternative visions. The first centers on a conception of "color blindness" combined with enforcement of laws against "discrimination," narrowly defined. The second vision stresses both antidiscrimination and a commitment to "morally equal opportunity." The third goes further to incorporate values of inclusion or diversity. These visions incorporate, I think, the most important schools of thought in public discourse at the moment. This is not to say that all public leaders express one of the three. Many of us talk about affirmative action far less coherently than might be the case if we settled on one or another model. My thesis is that each model is available to a thoughtful person who wants to be *coherent*, to have a unified approach to myriad issues about race. Such coherence is unfortunately an undervalued commodity in the political marketplace—but that is a point for another chapter. And each model can be modified with various bells and whistles. Therefore, along the way we must also consider important crosscutting subthemes— whether to use economic disadvantage instead of race as a basis for preferences, the importance of *merit*, and the question of how to decide what groups should benefit from affirmative action.

• • •

To academics and veteran activists, the affirmative action debate has a familiar, well-rehearsed basic structure. But the structure has an onionlike complexity of layers. A thoughtful person must do the intellectual equivalent of peeling away successive layers of an onion, in search of ever deeper considerations.

Professor Paul Gewirtz of Yale Law School, in a memorandum to President Clinton and others, ably summarized how affirmative action has been explained and defended as necessary, how it is justified as a *race-based* measure, and how it has been attacked as unfair or unnecessary. Affirmative action programs specifying race have been justified as:

... (1) a corrective for the continuing effects of *past* discrimination; (2) a prophylactic against *future* acts of discrimination; and (3) a way to promote diversity, provide role models ... develop competitive advantages in a demographically changing labor market. ... Colorblindness, it is said, either won't achieve the appropriate degree of minority inclusion, or will take too long to achieve it; and, against the backdrop of a terrible history of oppressive color conscious discrimination against minorities, immediate colorblindness would perpetuate exclusion and be unfair.

The longstanding arguments against race-based affirmative action are basically these: (1) that it unfairly discriminates against innocent whites because of their race; (2) that it compromises many good meritocratic standards; (3) that it benefits many groups and individuals that are not sufficiently disadvantaged; (4) that it stigmatizes its purported beneficiaries; and (5) that using race to distribute benefits deepens racial divisions and entrenches racial ways of thinking, instead of moving us toward a more colorblind and united society. In spite of these longstanding concerns, however, race-based affirmative action is now fairly widespread ... —not simply as a court-ordered remedy for proven unlawful discrimination, but as a policy to promote the various objectives noted above.

Some unpacking of these arguments will serve to introduce the subtler moral and policy choices we are discussing.

## Simple Justifications for Affirmative Action

*Correcting the Effects of Past Discrimination.* Stated simply, this seems to skate over a host of controversial issues. What, indeed, constitutes past discrimination? If limited to actions that a court determines to be illegal, then there are enormous practical problems of detection, proof, and excessive litigation in a society that is already too litigious by far. If "discrimination" is not limited to this definition, then where is the stopping point along the spectrum from grievous bigotry to color-correlated social disadvantage?

And what do we mean by "effects" of past discrimination? Specific injury to an identifiable victim traceable to a specific act of illegal discrimination? Or, further down the causal chain, any of a number of possible disadvantages that can be traced to an injustice against someone or their forebears? The underlying moral claim here is one of *remediation*—a duty owed victims by perpetrators or, as a last resort, by society as a whole. But the strength of the claim for remediation naturally enough depends on circumstances, just as it does whenever there are confused culpabilities for broad wrongs done to group interests and individual rights. Intractable problems of causation, compensation, and fairness are familiar in the law—from the sweeping injustices of Japanese-American internment during World War II to the poisoning of communities by a long-forgotten toxic dump, to the gargantuan liabilities of workers exposed to asbestos and condemned to illness and cancer. But, as always, the race issue makes familiar moral and practical conundrums pointedly painful.

*Preventing Future Discrimination.* Fine. But again, what is "discrimination"? For example, with affirmative action programs in place, an employer will voluntarily scrutinize his criteria for employment and promotion to ensure that they do not create unjustified barriers to opportunity for underrepresented groups, and in doing so he can sharply reduce the chance of unwitting discrimination in the future. Affirmative action is a prophylactic here. And employers often mention the defensive benefits of affirmative action, believing it lowers the risk of litigation over alleged discrimination. Remember: the most important civil rights measure concerning employment, Title VII, does not require that a plaintiff prove racist animus; it is often sufficient that the defendant's acts have a discrimination *effect*, and that the acts have no special explanation or justificatory of an overriding sort. A classic example is a job qualification for a police officer or firefighter that establishes a height or strength standard that severely narrows the pool of possible women candidates without any demonstration that the particular standard chosen is related to a police officer's or firefighter's ability to do the job. But are there no limits on such preventive measures? There must be. If opportunity is commonly experienced as a zero-sum situation—and it assuredly is—then too much prevention can be bad, or at least controversial.

*Diversity, or Inclusion.* President-elect Clinton said that he wanted a cabinet that "looks like America," and many colleges and universities assert that a world-class education requires faculty and student diversity. Many institutions have affirmative action programs voluntarily not because they seek to remedy their own or some broader societal discrimination, or because they are altruistically motivated to address disadvantages suffered by members of excluded groups, but because they believe their organization will benefit from diversity.* This justification for using group-based characteristics sometimes seems less thoughtful than it should be, however—perhaps because the arguments were made and decided over two decades ago and people are reluctant to negotiate this difficult terrain again. Often the assumed advantages of diversity go largely unexamined and, therefore, are not defended with serious rigor. Its possible costs—practical and moral— go largely unexamined; therefore, without the airy light of exchange, anxieties pool in dark corners, multiplying and fermenting there like some anaerobic ooze laced with resentment and anger. I have no doubt that much of the desire for diversity and inclusion is justifiable and,

---

* Institutions may decide on the value of diversity as a result of internal strife, such as student protests or employee petitions or, in a few cases, overt external pressure from customers or the public. The fact that a concerted institutional reconsideration of priorities and values has been promoted by pressure does not, ipso facto, make it somehow illegitimate or unreliable as an expression of that organization's needs. Protest may be needed to overcome inertia. Conservative critics and liberal supporters can look at the same history of, say, student protests on a campus, and view the resulting official commitment to a pursuit of diversity either as mere "political correctness" or as improved education policy.

indeed, compelling. But properly crafting affirmative action programs requires a more clear-eyed assessment of what is truly at stake. Central to that assessment must be a very hard look at the concept of "merit" as it applies to the institution in question.

## Simple Justifications for Opposing Affirmative Action

*Reverse Discrimination.* Opponents of affirmative action speak of reverse discrimination as though it were commonplace, but as we have seen, the evidence is quite to the contrary. Still, their argument is a claim that people who are burdened bystanders of affirmative action—the white male, principally—suffer a wrong that, while legally it may not be actionable as reverse discrimination, is surely deserving of some moral consideration. Indeed, the strongest opponents of affirmative action argue that this moral consideration is just as compelling as ordinary discrimination against racial minorities and women. This contention poses perhaps the most fundamental value choice each of us faces.

*Compromised Merit.* Many people believe that having decisions made on the basis of pure personal merit is a matter of right, a form of moral desert; that to violate it by denying it for whatever reason is wrong and, furthermore, ought to be considered discriminatory and hence unlawful. But, as we shall see, notions of merit and desert are complex, and not at all matters of pure individuality. They are often highly contested matters contingent on characteristics of given situations or organizations, not just on an individual. The merit of a given player in an orchestra depends upon the mix of instrumentalists at that moment; merit in a law school class depends similarly on a mix of student backgrounds and aspirations that the teachers believe will "optimize" the learning experience and, ultimately, the legal profession itself. It is not so easy to implement *the* merit principle as its devotees may think.

*Benefits to Those Who Are Not Disadvantaged.* Critics often say that, however strong the justification is for helping a socially and economically disadvantaged African American, surely it is irrelevant for the black son of a successful Pittsburgh neurosurgeon in comparison with the claims of, say, the white daughter of an Appalachian coal miner. There are many variants on this argument: Why should minority business assistance be given to an entrepreneur who owns a $750,000 home and two imported luxury cars or to the junior journalist with Ivy League credentials and country club parents? But the questioners assume that the justification for affirmative action is like the justification for welfare, and principally concerns money; they proceed to criticize the beneficiaries for driving "welfare Cadillacs." Something is clearly missing in the analysis. Income redistribution is *not* the principal rationale offered by most proponents of affirmative action, yet the evidence of continuing disadvantage *is* often cited in loose argument to provide moral justification for the practice. So is the justification based on welfare notions or isn't it?

*Stigmatization.* A growing number of conservative minority and women's voices emphasize that affirmative action stigmatizes all members of the benefited group, because observers may assume that (1) a successful black or Hispanic or woman is a beneficiary of affirmative action and (2) the affirmative action came at the expense of meritocratic standards. My view on this has always been that affirmative action has a cost; that part of the cost is the risk of stigma; but that the stigma I may suffer is a small price compared to the price I would pay if I faced closed doors, or compared to the price paid by crusaders a generation ago who faced vilification, mobs, beatings, and even murder. It is hubris of the most unattractive sort for minorities and women of my generation to complain about our comparatively trivial burdens in carrying progress forward.

*Entrenched Racial Thinking.* Critics of race-based affirmative action believe that by encouraging consideration of racial difference we reinforce its social significance in a negative or destructive way; that we undermine the taboo against difference-based discrimination when we suggest ways in which attention to difference is considered appropriate, even desirable. On the other hand, supporters say that racial difference is a fact of life and we must learn the complicated rules about when and how it has social significance. There are two points of tension here. First, there is a disagreement about predictions: will requiring that people *act* in a color-blind manner hasten the day when people actually *think* in a color-blind way in their socially and economically significant dealings with others? Taboos, such as the one against thinking in a color-coded way, have transformative power. This is a debate in the realm of instrumental calculations, or consequentialism. It assumes that our goal is a color-blind society, whatever that really means. But, second, there is an implicit disagreement about human nature: does human nature compel us to notice differences, and is it only our contingent social conventions that discipline the form that attention takes? Consider history. Consider Bosnia or Rwanda or Coconut Grove or South-Central Los Angeles. Total repression of attention to difference is not possible, not even desirable. So color blindness, as either goal or method, is far from being straightforward.

*Self-defeat.* Finally, some conservatives, among them some prominent black conservatives, argue that affirmative action and preferences generally have become, oxymoronically, a crippling crutch. To the extent that affirmative action compromises bona fide merit, the people who are hired or admitted under its rubric underperform in comparison with nonbeneficiaries. For example, a substantial fraction of black employees in a company are hired or promoted using an affirmative action strategy which "takes a chance" on them, since their job performance may be in the lower range of what is acceptable; observers focused on group performance may then see that *all* the black employees are on average less successful than all the whites. Unless special care is taken, this in turn drives down the expectations of how all blacks will perform, and the lower predictions of black performance limit the future opportunities of blacks who might in fact have been capable of greater achievement (whether or not they were beneficiaries of affirmative action in the first place). Thus a program to give opportunity by bringing people into the workplace or organization may, over time, actually limit opportunity for success and advancement. At the same time, it is argued, blacks who anticipate that they will get preferential treatment have weaker incentives to prepare, compete, and excel to the best of their abilities. This is both a practical problem (the undermining of individual and group achievement) and a moral one (the loss of dignity that flows from fulfillment). "Be all that you can be" is such an emotionally effective marketing phrase for the U.S. Army, and "A mind is a terrible thing to waste" has inspired so many hundreds of millions of dollars in donations to the United Negro College Fund, because those messages express deep values about personhood in our ideal vision of America.

I do not deny that affirmative action comes with risks and costs, but critics overstate them and fail to consider the countervailing truth: *that these practical and moral costs of using affirmative action may be justified by the benefits.* It depends.

Even this brief summary of the structure of justifications commonly offered in support of and in opposition to affirmative action makes clear that this is no simple issue. The familiar, easy arguments do not bear up under even the gentlest of analyses on either side. And the slogan-eering based on simplistic justifications cannot possibly serve thoughtful engagement. So let us now turn to three alternative frameworks within which to consider the conflicting values and judgments at issue in affirmative action. Each has a vision—a set of ideals and aspirations for a better America—and assumptions about how best to achieve it.

# 3

# THE COLOR-BLIND VISION

*C*ritics of race-conscious measures often invoke Martin Luther King, Jr.'s, "content of their character" passage in urging that we hasten the realization of a color-blind society by insisting on color-blind practices *now*: "I have a dream that my four little children will one day live in a nation where they will not be judged by the color of their skin but by the content of their character." The passage remains powerful because the vision is of an America purged not just of discrimination but of racialism, where equality would prevail and color would not matter. The compellingly simple moral force of that goal makes the prescription of color blindness so very powerful. But the phrase can be pushed to extremes. Probably few would argue that all differences of culture should be homogenized into some creamy pink concoction as final proof of Eurocentric hegemony; everyone to the left of the Ku Klux Klan and neo-Nazism seems to recognize that there is at least interest, if not value, in the cultural variety in America. And although much of our history has stressed assimilation—at times to the point of inciting violence and ethnic bigotry—there continues to be an evident tolerance and often celebration of many dimensions of difference. So the shorthand expression "color blindness" is not a prescription for unrelenting homogenization, leaving group membership

*To be born into black, just it accompanys disadvantage in living in the society*

with no cultural or social significance. A more sensible notion is that color should not be a consideration in public or private decisions about important economic and social opportunities.

In June 1995, a month before President Clinton gave his speech, I was on a panel at the National Press Club with the Reverend Jesse Jackson and Congressman Charles Canady (Republican of Florida), among others. When Canady talked about being color-blind, Jackson humorously challenged him: "You don't want to wake up tomorrow morning as a black man. I know you don't." In part this was a point that disadvantage is correlated with blackness because of what has come before and because of continuing problems of discrimination and exclusion today. It was also a subtle point about the desire most of us feel to hold on to a social identity which has our color as one of its elements. (I've always been puzzled—not judgmental—about people who find it comfortable to change the texture or color of their hair, say, as though it were merely ornamental, separate from their essential person, like a brooch or a beret. People draw their personal boundaries in different places. But skin color is surely very close to home, and to the hypothetical question of whether you would change it if you could, few would answer yes. Significantly, this is true even for individuals who firmly believe they suffer net social and economic disadvantage as a result of race discrimination.)

The true meaning of Martin Luther King's message is that we must overcome the hope-crushing, dream-stealing power of prejudice. It is a grotesque distortion of his message to confuse this description of a goal with a prescription for the means of achieving it, and it is sadly manipulative to turn his elegant words against his true meaning. King spoke approvingly of race-conscious affirmative action:

> It is impossible to create a formula for the future which does not take into account that our society has been doing something special *against* the Negro for hundreds of years. How then can he be absorbed into the mainstream of American life if we do not do something special *for* him now, in order to balance the equation and equip him to compete on a just and equal basis?
>
> Whenever this issue of compensatory or preferential treatment

for the Negro is raised, some of our friends recoil in horror. The Negro should be granted equality, they agree; but he should ask for nothing more. On the surface, this appears reasonable, but it is not realistic. For it is obvious that if a man is entered at the starting line in a race three hundred years after another man, the first would have to perform some impossible feat in order to catch up with his fellow runner.

In its pure form, the color-blindness framework would prohibit race-conscious measures in all contexts except as remedies for identified victims of proven acts of specific discrimination. *The central moral tenet is*: race-based decision making is inherently unfair, whether the supposed purpose is benign or invidious. *The central behavioral tenet is*: even if it is possible to isolate circumstances in which race-based decision making is desirable and benign, tolerance of such thinking reinforces racial divisions and tensions, impeding our progress toward a society of true tolerance and equal opportunity. *The central policy prescription is*: race should not be a consideration except in very narrow remedial circumstances, but there should be both vigorous antidiscrimination enforcement *and* race-neutral social investments in equal opportunity programs such as education and training.

Many people are attracted to this color-blind approach but fail to think through its implications. What values are implicit in this framework and what values are implicitly rejected? For example, there is an additional complication if we ask over what period of time the "neutrality" and hence "equality" of social investments is to be measured. Starting today? Or do we acknowledge an accumulated deficit and then use compensatory, targeted investments to right the balance over this longer accounting period? The choice of the measurement period reveals a value choice regarding justice and desert, and no rule of budget arithmetic can turn neutrality (or equality) into an accounting concept rather than a contested proposition about what we will deem to be fair. But those who embrace color blindness, objecting to any race-based targeting, refuse to look back and see that because yesterday was nonneutral, tomorrow must be nonneutral in order to right the balance. There is nothing "neutral" about this choice, and I want to explore what it means and what its moral justification might be.

There is more. Proponents of color blindness often emphasize that enforcement of antidiscrimination laws can be coupled with various public and private investments to enhance opportunity—in other words that the equal opportunity agenda can be attended to with race-neutral educational and other measures, rather than by race-conscious affirmative action programs, including targeting. They argue that these social investments with redistributive consequences are a far better way of correcting race-correlated disadvantages. That this is preferable in the abstract is certainly true. But four underlying presuppositions are more difficult—and controversial: (1) that the working legal meanings of "remedy" and "liability" in the law will appropriately take care of the myriad manifestations of actual discrimination; (2) that even if liability and remedy are narrowly defined, enforcement will be pursued with vigor; (3) that race-neutral and social welfare measures are not merely effective and preferable but are the *only permissible* tools; and (4) that these social welfare tools will in fact be taken up with all the energy and care needed to yield the promised increases in opportunity. We are going to have to think about each of these underlying contentions.

### What Is Antidiscrimination? Violations and Remedies

Advocacy of a color-blind framework goes hand in hand with promises to enforce antidiscrimination laws vigorously, so that the power of law would both reinforce the moral commitment to abjure racial distinctions and, with effective enforcement, eliminate the argument that race-conscious affirmative action is needed as a prophylaxis against future or subtle discrimination.

Proponents of color blindness therefore assert that they stand firmly against race-consciousness—that *all* of it is undesirable, that no legitimate distinction can be drawn between benign and invidious purposes, and that their commitment to vigorous enforcement of anti-discrimination laws shows their willingness to confront any lingering problem of racist bigotry. Within this framework, which clearly excludes voluntary race-conscious measures, can race *ever* be considered in court-ordered remedies? In Justice Antonin Scalia's terms, to force an employer to hire successful minority plaintiffs is not a racial preference, because the race-consciousness is based on their status as victims, rather than their status as minorities.

To put this in context, consider the accompanying chart. We can categorize the circumstances of proof and remedy by distinguishing whether the perpetrator's alleged acts and the victim or victims' identities are established with exacting particularity or only in some more general sense. First, focusing on the defendant-perpetrator's conduct, there is a distinction between identifying specific, purposeful discriminatory acts (which Title VII doctrine calls "disparate treatment" and the Fourteenth Amendment calls simply *intentional* discrimination) and practices that have a "disparate impact" even though no one intended to discriminate. These are the two rows in the chart. The top row requires a smoking gun of specific intent to discriminate, or strong statistical or other evidence that supports an inference of such an intent. The second row considers effects rather than intent, and then asks the defendant for some excuse or justification—like "business necessity."

Second, the columns focus on the alleged victim, or member of the plaintiff class. The distinction is between a specific, identifiable person or persons proved to be personally mistreated by the perpetrator-defendant, and therefore victims in the most traditional sense of common-law injury, and individuals who simply share group status with identifiable victims (if we can find them). In terms of remedy, sometimes the plaintiffs want help for those whom an employer turned away, and other times plaintiffs want the employer ordered to provide opportunities to individuals who never personally had contact with the defendant. The left-hand column has more to do with compensation for specifically wronged people, and the right-hand column seems to add the element of "reforming" the defendant as well as preventing future discrimination.

This two-by-two matrix clarifies some terms of the policy battles. The proposition that full remedies for identifiable victims are consistent with color blindness (it is their status as victims, not as blacks,

| REMEDYING DISCRIMINATION; GENERAL VERSUS PARTICULAR; INTENT, ACTS, AND REMEDIES | | |
|---|---|---|
| | IDENTIFIED VICTIM(S) | GROUP-BASED, UNIDENTIFIED "VICTIMS" |
| SPECIFIC INTENTIONAL ACTS: DISPARATE TREATMENT | [A] defendant specifically discriminated against specific plaintiff(s) | [B] defendant specifically discriminated, but either the victim class is unknowable or the requested relief is cast broadly, based on the group |
| GENERAL ACTS: DISPARATE IMPACT | [C] defendant's general practices have a discriminatory effect, and plaintiff(s) suffered | [D] defendant's practices are general, and the relief sought is broadly based |

*Considerations:*

*Pragmatism:* Can individual victims and intentional acts be discovered and proven? Can subtle forms of discrimination be detected and prevented? Can group-based disparities be discerned, addressed, and phased out—all without resort to proportional representation and implied quotas?

*Social Purposes:* Are we concerned with remedying only intentional acts reflecting racial animus, or are there broader social objectives?

*Moral Philosophy:* Is a consequentialist or utilitarian framework appropriate for debating practical values and policy?

that determines the outcome) suggests that cell A is unobjectionable and that cell C will be too, provided one endorses current law, which makes unexplained disparate impacts illegal in employment. (Justices Scalia and Thomas have opposed this aspect of doctrine, but Congress has clearly endorsed it, most recently in 1991.) Cell A, in other words, is the easy case about which everyone agrees. Adherents of color blindness tend to draw the line there. They would deny group-based relief as in cells B and D, because the people "relieved" are not "victims" in the traditional sense of having a specific injury proximately traceable to the plaintiff's conduct. Also, they reject the kind of liability or fault-finding represented by cells C and D, because defining discrimination to include "mere" statistical disparities is, in their view, tantamount to a legal requirement for proportional representation grounded on race-based nose counting. Even in cell B, where plaintiffs argue there was intentional discrimination, adherents of color blindness strongly resist inferring specific intent to discriminate from statistical evidence, again a more restrictive view than long-standing Supreme Court doctrine.

What is the rebuttal? Let's start with an intuition. I find Justice Scalia's approach unsatisfying, asserting that the beneficiaries of a remedy are somehow accorded preferences based on "victim" status rather than group identity. This seems a clever but disingenuous characterization of what's really going on. It strikes me as far better to say of the color-blind approach that the moral calculation in the court-ordered remedy is simply in a different class because the concreteness and visibility of the wrong demand a greater certainty of societal response and correction than might be the case in other situations, notably voluntary affirmative action, where the truth of discrimination, exclusion, or disadvantage may be clouded. But imagine the case of, say, a mortgage lender or realtor who is found in some definitive way to have discriminated in a broad way against members of a group. Simply to impose a fine and say, "Don't do it again," will not seem an appropriately sure and pointed response. Can we be confident that he would then stop discriminating? Most of us *want* that confidence, and hence find acceptable the more predictably effective remedies. In a color-blind framework, this kind of narrow exception seems justified, yet Scalia's formulation won't reach it.

Under closer inspection, however, our line of thinking turns out to be hopelessly jumbled. It confuses different sorts of moral and empirical issues, mixing apples and baseballs. Here's how.

Proponents of group-based affirmative action often say they support it when there is a proven group-based wrong, even though the individuals who benefit from the remedy may not themselves have been, say, rejected for employment by the defendant company. The difficulty with this is that it leads, eventually, to a battle over values. Proving that the wrongdoer engaged in group-based thinking does not justify a group-based remedy (instead of a pure "don't ever discriminate" injunction) unless you embrace one of these two arguments: first, that only a group-based remedy will effectively undo and prevent the wrongdoer's exclusionary practices, that merely extracting a promise to do better in the future may fail (the pragmatic argument); or, second, that a systematic pattern of group-based thinking has created a systematic form of group-related injury and disadvantage, and that any one lawsuit is an appropriate occasion to strike a blow against it, untilting the playing field, as it were (the social-purpose argument). The first seems a straightforward issue of empirical prediction, but of course it is not straightforward at all because there are no data, because effectiveness is a matter of degree, and because one's view of what is the needed degree of effectiveness inevitably incorporates within it the whole values-laden debate about the costs of discrimination and reverse discrimination. The second, more evidently ambitious, breaks the traditional links of causation and fault passed down through the common-law tradition of civil liability, and takes on the normative trappings of a social welfare argument. Of course, it is not extraordinary for liability and remedial rules in law to be shaped by social welfare considerations or "social engineering," but it is a step outside what is conservative and conventional.

For myself, I find the color-blind objection to group-based remedies, cells B and D in the chart, objectionable for both reasons cited above: the pragmatic one regarding remedies, and also because we need to invoke social purposes in defining "remedy" and "victim" more broadly than traditional common-law principles suggest.

Turning to color-blind objections to a capacious definition of *liability* for discrimination—that represented in cells C and D—we find a twofold complication in defining what kinds of behavior are discriminatory. We have to specify what kind of evidence a plaintiff-complainant must proffer, and what defenses a defendant-respondent may counterpose. As I have noted, civil rights conservatives oppose current law that permits plaintiffs in employment-discrimination suits to make out a prima facie (preliminary, rebuttable) case of discrimination based on a race-related* statistical disparity between a selection device's effect on one group of applicants and its effect on another. They don't like the idea that this "disparate impact analysis" obviates the need for a plaintiff to demonstrate that there was a "smoking gun" of racial or gender animus and intentional action.

As before, we can meet this objection with two rebuttals, one based on pragmatism and the other on social purpose. The pragmatic considerations first. Even though the law gives defendants a chance to rebut the inference of discrimination, conservatives have long argued that, in practice at least, doing so when the focus is on numbers leads inexorably to regimes of quotas and proportional representation, hence to reverse discrimination and the undermining of meritocratic principles. Liberals, on the other hand, view statistical inferences as the only workable means of detecting many forms of subtle discrimination. This disagreement is far from trivial. It has been the subject of major Supreme Court cases, several congressional hearings, and the Civil Rights Act of 1991. But it is more than a practical consideration. Also at issue is an implicit judgment that the practice creating a serious disparity is wrong unless the defendant can otherwise explain it, that no proof of intent or animus is required because the social purpose is to close the opportunity gap, not exclusively to punish the bad character (and associated conduct) of a defendant.

These judgments about what constitutes proof and defense go, really, to the heart of laws prohibiting discrimination. They are impos-

---

* I say "race-related" for simplicity. The same applies to other groups protected by Title VII.

sible to settle without first coming to some basic conclusions about values and vision. My point is that commitment to a color-blind vision plus antidiscrimination enforcement does not answer the question of what discrimination is, or what judicially supervised remedies are permissible. (The exception, again, is that *voluntary* race-based measures are impermissible in the color-blind vision.)

I have presented an analysis of the color-blind perspective on remedies and discrimination and offered rebuttals based on pragmatism and social purpose. But to advance the discussion, we ought to ask a further question: Why do these rebuttals fail to persuade people of good conscience who adhere to the color-blind view? Is there a way to bridge the disagreement?

Consider first the function of arguments about practicality in this debate—the practicality both of remedial "means" and of defined antidiscrimination "ends." Here's the anomaly: If *effectiveness* is a touchstone in deciding whether color-conscious remedies are appropriate for defendants, shouldn't we think that similar considerations of effectiveness likewise make color-conscious measures plausible in at least some contexts far beyond narrow, adjudicated remediation? Put differently, how can people who have conceded that "Discriminate No More" is an ineffective command to a bigot then speak sweepingly about color blindness as not just an end but also an important means to achieve that end? They have acknowledged that it is wanting as a means precisely when it matters most—in the case of narrow remediation. Therefore, faced with fairly compelling evidence that color-blind remedies alone have not been effective, they must reject familiar means-end analysis entirely. They must hold to their impoverished prescription of means based on a moral calculus separate from the pragmatism of a utilitarian or consequentialist framework, which searches for some empirical reconciliation of means and ends. They are unmoved by the counterarguments "*It won't be effective, it doesn't work,*" because they have a different measure of what "works."

To be sure, some advocates of color-blind programs oppose affirmative action because of its alleged bad side effects, such as racial polarization or injury to meritocratic principles. But again, these explanations are couched in familiar cost-benefit consequentialist terms, trying to justify the color-blind vision by changing the accounting of costs. Anyone who has been in the middle of heated debates on this subject knows that empirical evidence about the various costs doesn't persuade people on either side. That's because, at heart, the consequentialist terms don't take account of the value disagreements at stake.

Instead, I think, the core of the color-blind idea must be that race-conscious measures don't "work" because a particular conception of human dignity makes it wrong to treat individuals as ends rather than means; people are not data points in a utilitarian construction of optimal social rules. To give an analogy, pure nonutilitarians would support or oppose the death penalty on moral grounds independent of any social science evidence about its deterrent value or the cost savings compared with lifelong incarceration; whether they were for or against, they would base their view on considerations of the individual's moral relation to the community and the state, the nature of ethical obligations. They might say, "I don't care if the death penalty doesn't deter crime; heinous murders should be punishable by death because it is the morally correct expression of the value we put on human life and on the notion of moral responsibility." Or "I don't care if the death penalty *does* deter crime; it is morally wrong for the state to kill a person because it diminishes our humanity and teaches the wrong lesson about the value of life." What unites the two positions is their disregard for consequentialist calculations of effectiveness.

This is not to say that everyone who takes the color-blind position is a nonutilitarian or that all nonutilitarians embrace color blindness. In fact, moral philosophy determines only what kind of argument tends to be persuasive, not the policy conclusion reached by the arguments. Take, for example, a draft registrant who is considering pacifism; he studies the contrast between the Old Testament "eye for an eye" and the New Testament "turn the other cheek," and quickly sees that he can embrace either the New or the Old as the philosophical framework, or value system, shaping the community; it merely creates the framework for the debate and does not decide the outcome.

I have no doubt that many who adhere to the color-blind vision are indifferent to its comparative ineffectiveness and that in some cases this indifference is malign. But I see a kernel of truth here nonetheless. One might argue that although consequentialist calculations about effectiveness point in one direction, other important considerations sometimes outweigh them. At least, that is the truth I will acknowledge. But they lose me with the extreme view that these other considerations *always* outweigh arguments about effectiveness.

The disagreement over social purpose has a similar problem. (Remember, in what follows, that since we are focusing on the question of the predicate—namely, the behaviors of a defendant that we will term "discrimination" justifying remedy—at issue are the moral justifications for both regulating the defendant and for imposing the burden of remediation on the defendant and bystanders.) In large measure, the argument seems to be about whether the redistribution of opportunities by imposing particular remedies must be predicated on traditional conceptions of personal blameworthiness on the part of the individual "defendant-transferee"—the white male bystander, say. Proponents of affirmative action are likely to see affirmative action as just another form of social or economic regulation in which society transfers something of value from one group to another without blaming the loser for anything. After all, there are the complex sets of winners and losers when a new highway is constructed, or when a tax is imposed to fund a school or museum or homeless shelter. Adherents of the color blind model object to this invocation of ordinary redistributive public policy norms and insist that blameworthy racial animus is the only acceptable grounds for finding genuine "discrimination"—that is, the only acceptable predicate for remediation. Why? The *only* basis I can understand for this objection is an implicit argument that race-based distinctions somehow differ from the distinctions made in the ordinary course of constructing redistributive social and economic measures.

And again, I see a kernel of truth. Yes, race *is* different. That is why we had a civil war, urban riots, and so much more. That is why over the years the Supreme Court has held that race-based classifications made by government must be subject to strict scrutiny under the Constitution's equal protection clause, rather than being subject to the vastly more deferential test of whether they are merely rational. So the color-blind vision, in this most favorable interpretation, is that precisely *because* of the transcendent importance of race, special care must be taken when it is used as the basis for regulation; for many historical, social, and ethical reasons, it is unlike redistribution based on other criteria, such as income or geography or industrial sector or age. Race should not be used for some general social engineering, whether legislated or voluntary—or for any purpose cast in the guise of "social-purpose litigation." With that much I can agree. But advocates of color blindness go further, arguing that race should be used only for the far more limited circumstances of narrow remediation predicated on moral blameworthiness (cell A in the matrix).

How much are we to make of the claim that "race is different"—different in a sense that requires distinct rules about the rightness of policy measures? For me, the point lies not in some consequentialist argument that race is different because tools familiar in other regulatory arenas "won't work" with race; for one thing, the evidence about the effects of affirmative action demonstrates otherwise—to my satisfaction, anyway. No, the argument must be nonutilitarian in some way. For example, we could argue that employers' actions and underlying thought processes should be regulated only when infected with racial animus, because drawing the line there preserves a large sphere of personal autonomy against state intrusion. (Indeed, autonomy would be protected by such a rule in part because violations would be hard to detect.) Or we could argue that the indignity of intentionally imposing a race-based remedial burden on a bystander is morally justified only if the plaintiff has suffered an intentional race-based deprivation that is remediable in no other way.

I don't think of these points of view as crazy, but I disagree strongly with their absolutism. *The kernel of truth is that there is indeed a moral cost to race-based decision making, and this moral cost stands independent of any utilitarian calculations of the effectiveness of antidiscrimination laws.*

I have to take one final step on this branch of the argument. There has been no decisive resolution in moral philosophy between the perspectives of utilitarians and nonutilitarians, except perhaps that probably very few professional philosophers today categorize themselves as pure utilitarians. In our practical lives, we feel pulled by conflicting intuitions, which we can associate with competing schools of moral thought. How do we handle the apparent conflicts between utilitarian and nonutilitarian impulses? Put differently (but it is the same question), how do we mediate the tensions between the values by which we live and the values to which we aspire?

Return to the example of the would-be pacifist comparing Old and New Testament commands and trying to decide which to embrace as both aspiration and daily guide. Few of us are pacifists; most of us, being morally sloppy, might simply distinguish between the practical and the good, and be satisfied to make the former merely approximate the latter as best we can. And we can be sloppy about how fervently we accept the aspiration, or about how seriously we are committed to live by the prescription. But a compulsive analyzer has a tougher time.

With race-based decisions, we are morally sloppy when we give short shrift to evidence that disquietingly undermines our fealty to principle, and we are morally sloppy when we give little respect to the moral claims made by others in the debate. (Neither form of sloppiness is available to the compulsive analyst.) For example, I believe many proponents of color blindness are malignly dismissive of evidence concerning the extent and intractability of continuing job discrimination or of racially motivated police misconduct. In part, this seems to me a way for them to cling to their conviction that *living* the color-blind paradigm will lead to a color-blind world. Call it cognitive dissonance, or repression, or whatever. The point is, filtering out unpleasant data is an effective way to keep from being troubled by the sharp discontinuity between the life you live and the life to which you aspire. I think of it as hanging a "do not disturb" sign on the door to the policy lobe of your brain.

This is not a phenomenon unique to race. We think so often of America's character as embodying a stirring altruism and mutual regard, but this aspiration is at odds with much of our history—certainly with the past twenty years, when disparities in income, wealth, and opportunity have widened while the truly poor often live in cultures that seem far away from the America in our dream. How do we mediate this tension? More often than not, we muddle through by paying scant attention to the unpleasant facts in front of our noses. It's drive-by indifference.

To summarize, in a color-blind framework there is no room for lawsuits or race-conscious measures based on findings of disparate impact or societal discrimination, or on a desire to promote diversity or inclusion. First, none of these entails the level of wrongful intention needed in this framework to justify race-conscious remediation. Second, there is a problem with using statistical disparities to establish a prima facie— i.e., tentative—case of discrimination, inasmuch as moral wrong is seen not in observed disparities but rather in provable instances of bigotry, and opponents of disparate impact analysis refuse to treat manifest numerical imbalances as reliable evidence of bigotry. In the color-blind framework, race can be a factor in decision making only in order to remedy proven cases of discrimination, presumably in court, against identifiable victims. The remedy must not extend beyond the specific victims, and the predicate of specific discrimination is key to the analysis. Instead of group-based remedies, the emphasis is on antidiscrimination enforcement.

A color-blind framework would massively change American statutes and case law, and it would require changes in many practices, both public and private. Senator Phil Gramm and others are correct in asserting that there is much public and private attention paid to race and gender when making decisions, as affirmative action in one form or another has become commonplace (at least in lip service), despite its controversial character. These critics propose not conservative reform but fairly radical revolution. I don't say that disparagingly. But one should choose one's revolutions with care. Theirs is wrong.

### Vigorous Enforcement?

The controversial issue about enforcing antidiscrimination law is not its importance per se but the obvious difficulty of allocating resources to get the job done. During the twelve years of the Reagan and Bush administrations, the budgetary resources of the federal government's principal civil rights enforcement agencies were flat or diminishing in real terms. Meanwhile, all relevant indicators showed a growing enforcement challenge, as backlogs grew and state enforcement agencies struggled unsuccessfully to take up the slack. Under President Clinton, the administration asked Congress for budget increases in most key civil rights enforcement functions, but with only limited success for fiscal years 1994 and 1995. For fiscal year 1996 and beyond, the situation became dire indeed, as Republican congressional leaders pressed for dramatic cuts in domestic discretionary spending. Fair housing efforts at HUD, for example, may not survive at all. So there is little reason to believe that resources will be adequate to meet the enforcement needs. Resources have not been adequate in the past, and the fiscal future is bleaker than ever. One need only consider the difficulty of finding adequate funds to enforce laws directed against violent street crime. Even this far more politically popular mission goes begging at all levels of government. One can expect no better for the controversial mission of enforcing antidiscrimination laws.

There is a closely related point. At various turns in the modern civil rights story, legislative efforts have been made to strengthen enforcement mechanisms by, for example, giving certain government agencies broader remedial powers, giving certain administrative agencies more authority to decide claims rather than merely investigate and conciliate, making greater use of private lawsuits rather than agencies to enforce the laws, or increasing civil penalties for wrongdoing. At every turn, conservatives have been united in opposition, many of them espousing color-blind social and economic programs instead. Viewed most charitably—and this is difficult—there is no logical inconsistency between these past restrictive positions and a rhetorical commitment to vigorous enforcement. Rather, the seeming contradiction indicates that *vigor is in the eye of the speechmaker*; opponents of broader enforcement laws feel free to say that being too activist and responsive in enforcement will tilt the playing field against would-be defendants. Yes, there is a question of bona fides. But putting that to one side, there is a serious difference of opinion about how to strike the balance of burdens between the potential disputants.

Even when resources are available, experience suggests that discrimination and bias are hard for the victim or for enforcement authorities to detect. Unless an employer who rejects my application for a job is a fool, he or she will give a perfectly plausible and respectable explanation, and its truthfulness may be almost impossible for me to discover, even if I am strongly motivated to try. And some decisions—college admissions, faculty hiring, certain promotions in large companies—are made by committees or other collective processes in which the participants may have varied motives; discerning whether one or more is invidious and has impermissibly tainted the whole is difficult both conceptually and practically.

Take it a step further. *Assume* adequate resources. *Assume* detection of the alleged wrongs. Is adjudication of the antidiscrimination claim really going to be effective? For starters, it is conservatives who complain most loudly about the wastefulness of litigation and decry our rush to have the courts resolve all manner of disputes; conservatives lead the way in cutting access to court for the poor by slashing the budget of the Legal Services Corporation, spearhead efforts to "reform" the tort system by decreasing court access and damage awards for everything from medical malpractice to product liability, press for narrowing of the grounds for investor suits under the securities laws, even overriding President Clinton's veto to do so.

So, proponents of color blindness argue that their commitment to fundamental fairness and racial progress is unimpeachable, because they avow staunch support for vigorous enforcement of the antidiscrimination laws. But several crucial points give one pause:

- The resources to enforce antidiscrimination laws haven't come close to keeping up with the need, at least from the perspective of victims or would-be plaintiffs. Conservative proponents of color blindness have generally been indifferent or hostile to the budgetary needs of civil rights enforcement.
- You don't always know whether you've been a victim. Detection can be difficult—which may be reassuring for the imme-

diate self-esteem of a disappointed African American, but the economic and social harm done by discriminatory denials of opportunity is real.

- Even with resources and even with detection, the adjudicatory mechanisms—administrative hearings, court litigation—are costly, time-consuming, and very imperfect.

- And finally, to recapitulate, *the kind of antidiscrimination enforcement that conservatives endorse is unacceptably ineffective, since it wouldn't reach all the behaviors that should be considered impermissible and illegal.*

### A Race-Neutral Opportunity Agenda

Still, we must acknowledge that many people go on urging us to abandon race-based affirmative action in favor of programs based on race-neutral preferences of one sort or another. Indeed, the Supreme Court's decisions now make analysis of such alternatives—we don't know how exacting—a necessary component of the constitutional scrutiny of government programs. But as one might guess, I believe this race-neutral approach has drawbacks.

Preferences based on disadvantage will disproportionately benefit minorities, because minorities are disproportionately poor. But since there is a greater absolute number of poor whites, race-neutral preferences would dilute the concentration of resources on blacks (indeed, that's the point) and slow whatever progress we may be making in closing the opportunity gap between blacks and whites. Are the political and ethical objections to affirmative action powerful and legitimate enough to accept this less effective alternative? In a larger sense, an emphasis on disadvantage is and should be a central focus of America's social and economic agenda, and that agenda is under concerted, partisan attack. Yes, affirmative action is embattled, but programs generally designed to create opportunity and self-sufficiency for the neediest Americans are far from secure.

The pure color-blind framework reminds us of the moral cost in making decisions based on race, but it asserts that the cost is too great to pay, *ever*—or almost ever. Suppose, however, we accept only the more moderate proposition, that there is *some* moral cost to making distinctions based on immutable characteristics. It follows that whenever a race-neutral measure will "substantially" achieve our purposes, we should prefer it. How "substantial" a sacrifice in purpose we are willing to accept depends on how we assess the moral cost we seek to avoid.

Proponents of color blindness, indeed virtually all critics of affirmative action, stress that compensatory education and other social welfare programs can be constructed in a race-neutral manner and be an acceptably effective alternative to racially targeted measures.

Is that really true? Are these alternative social programs at least as effective at offsetting or preventing disadvantage? Do education, training, and similar broad-based government programs actually help minorities, or anyone, to overcome past and present disadvantages? Well, that is the issue that much of the domestic policy struggle is all about. There is certainly a fundamental disagreement between left and right about the appropriate role of government, but apart from small groups of ideological warriors at either end of the spectrum—the extreme right arguing that the welfare state should wither away into a night-watchman state, the far left insisting that social welfare benefits are matters of right and moral desert, not mere policy—Americans seem to approach these social issues with waxing and waning altruism but fairly constant pragmatism. Much conservative opposition seems based less on principle than on a conviction that the programs *don't work*, while much liberal advocacy seems due less to a dedication to statism than to confidence that the programs either do work or *could* work.

Conservatives therefore often say that race-conscious measures should be abandoned in favor of race-neutral social welfare measures, and in the very next breath they attack those same measures for being ineffective and undeserving of fiscal support, if not indeed contrary to some set of principles about the proper role of government. The irony is, then, that proponents of color blindness urge social welfare programs as preferable to affirmative action, and then oppose them anyway as bad policy, while liberal defenders of affirmative action deny that social welfare programs can be an adequate substitute yet in other contexts express great confidence that they either are or could be effective.

For conservatives, the way out of the conundrum is to underscore the public-private distinction, and to argue that the alternative to government-supported race-conscious measures rests not with *government* social welfare programs of dubious quality, but with market-driven and private activities of an improved order—everything from school vouchers to self-help endeavors combating violence and other social toxins, to the dismantling of government programs that they believe only encourage disadvantage by destabilizing family structure. For liberals, the way out is to argue that social welfare programs, which have potential for good on their own terms, are not adequate substitutes for race-targeted measures because they inevitably dilute fiscal and managerial resources that should be focused more sharply on the racial problem. And besides, conservatives won't vote the resources.

*Example*: For several years a consortium of graduate schools of public policy and administration have funded a summer program to prepare minority undergraduates to apply to elite graduate schools. The program emphasizes the quantitative and economic skills in which minority applicants have generally been least well prepared. The organizers report chronic funding shortages; if the program altered to serve *all* students who need additional work of this kind, for example, far fewer minority students would be assisted.

*Example*: The armed services operate very successful remedial preparatory programs to help high school graduates nominated for admission to West Point and the other service academies. The enrollment in those preparatory schools is predominantly African American and Latino. Senior Department of Defense officials acknowledge that the admissions process is "tilted," since the preparatory programs, while not racially exclusive, are designed to support the goal of diversity at the elite service academies.

As these simple examples suggest, the problem is not that race-neutral measures would give no help but that they might not give enough. Affirmative action and race-neutral social welfare measures are not, as a logical matter, mutually exclusive. One can support the latter as preferable but also believe that alone they are limited, especially given the risks of dilution and discrimination.

When adherents to the color-blind vision oppose race-based measures, we see how their opposition stems from a moral position that puts those measures beyond the pale. But when they go further and urge that race-neutral measures are an appropriate substitute, we can have two criticisms. First, any attempt to justify dropping race-based measures because alternatives are equally "effective" puts one back in the consequentialist box, and we know that die-hard color-blind advocates are not moved by empirical arguments about effectiveness, no matter what. In essence, one suspects, they don't really *care* whether the alternatives will be effective but make the claim hoping it will be persuasive to consequentialists who weakly support affirmative action. A cynic might call this debating tactic manipulative, but that's not my point. My point is that since the color-blind critics do not as a moral matter *care* about comparative effectiveness, we have reason to be skeptical about the truth of their claim in this instance—especially since the debate is so polarized that facts and truth have become, uh, flexible.

Second, supporting race-neutral measures while simultaneously trying to gut the budgets of the opportunity agenda raises questions about these critics' bona fides. For example, GOP adherents of the color-blind framework are working in Congress to cut federal investments in education, job training, day care, and welfare. Their budgetary priorities give the lie to their saying that an alternative agenda of equal opportunity investments must be substituted for affirmative action and race-targeted measures. A similar point can be made about the even more fundamental issue of antidiscrimination enforcement. The budget battles over the past several years indicate that many members of Congress are reluctant to increase the resources of the Civil Rights Division of the Department of Justice, the Equal Employment Opportunity Commission, and the Department of Labor's Office of Federal Contract Compliance Programs. Not to put too fine a partisan point on it, much GOP rhetoric about antidiscrimination enforcement and opportunity-enhancing investments rings hollow.

There is, of course, much to recommend an emphasis on "affirmative action" based on need or disadvantage. (Recall, from my list of the basic objections to affirmative action, that many Americans believe that too many people who don't in fact suffer disadvantage are nevertheless benefiting from affirmative action.) But America's commitment to economic redistribution through public policy is itself a deeply and sharply controversial subject in its own right—witness the struggles over welfare reform, or the Great Society's antipoverty programs. Indeed, "antipoverty" is a term so freighted with negative connotations that even devout liberals studiously avoid using it these days. I myself say "opportunity agenda." Redistribution and antipoverty measures look like reasonable public strategies only when held up as alternatives to the even more poisonously controversial stratagems of civil rights and affirmative action. But perhaps the controversy must be faced nonetheless.

We have covered a number of analytical and prescriptive points about the color-blind framework:

- It emphasizes the moral cost of using race as a consideration in decision making, and considers the cost too high outside very narrow, litigated remediation. All voluntary race-based affirmative action is wrong.
- Chief among its claimed practical advantages are fidelity to merit principles and the avoidance of racial balkanization. (I address these subjects in Chapters 6 and 9.)
- It seems incoherent when judged by utilitarian or consequentialist standards. The compelling evidence that "enforcement only" approaches are ineffective can only be trumped by appeal to some supervening moral consideration.
- It does not admit broader definitions of "discrimination" that encompass practices with a disparate impact on minorities. The narrow definitions require a finding of morally blameworthy animus, and reject social purposes that can be stated and measured only in race-conscious terms.
- Nor does it acknowledge nonremedial social purposes, such

as inclusion or diversity, which might be desirable for an organization or for society generally.

The absolutism of this vision creates difficulties, notably its uneasy indifference to arguments about evidence and effectiveness. On the other hand, the absolutism gives ready answers without going through tortured consideration of circumstances and competing goals. I doubt that this clarity should be credited as a plus for a moral framework, but it surely helps with the politics.

# 4

# A SECOND VISION: OPPORTUNITY AND ANTIDISCRIMINATION

*I*n working with President Clinton and Vice President Gore to construct other internally coherent approaches to racial issues, we quickly saw that a more consequentialist commitment to racial progress required a moral framework sharply distinct from color blindness. This second vision, based on genuine opportunity and antidiscrimination, does not demand equality of results, but simply pleads that promises of opportunity be genuine. It is not a demand for quotas or reparations, but rather a plea to understand that "discrimination" today is more than hatefully intended acts of oppression, that it also encompasses practices both overt and subtle that perpetuate the disadvantages historically rooted in our racial caste system.

*The central moral tenet is this*: race-conscious decision making is justified to remedy discrimination; this includes, in at least some limited circumstances, support for targeted efforts against "societal discrimination" that deprives people of effective equal opportunity. But the interests of bystanders cannot be ignored. Race-conscious decision making is not flatly impermissible but neither is it morally costless. *The central behavioral tenet is this*: because a person's opportunities depend both on freedom from discrimination and on economic and social endowments which they inherit—*or which surround them*—genuine equality of opportunity requires not only effective antidiscrimination enforcement in the conventional legal sense, but also social policies to help people overcome disadvantages in social and economic endowments that are the consequence of systemic discrimination, present or past. *And the central policy prescription is this*: race may be one among several factors used flexibly to remedy discrimination and to promote equal opportunity where past or societal discrimination has diminished opportunity. (Note, however, that the Supreme Court has held that, under the Constitution, "societal discrimination" alone does not justify government use of race-based measures.) Care must be taken to minimize the costs imposed on bystanders.

With apologies to readers allergic to platitudes, the starting point for this moral framework was President Clinton's comfortable invocation of the twin principles of "equality of opportunity" and "antidiscrimination." Only moral miscreants object to these principles, stated flatly and without elaboration. What distinguishes them from the "color-blind" approach is, therefore, the additional moral commitment I have been trying to elucidate here: rejection of absolutism, together with a pragmatic concern for effectively closing the opportunity gap between black and white. Our moral calculus and the policies it generates count for little if the consequences for the human condition are trivial.

By introducing the added imperative that we actually get something done, the two mutually reinforcing principles can be slightly recast. We can say it this way: equality of opportunity offers scope for the fullest possible development of individual talents, while antidiscrimination—a more muscular posture than *non*discrimination—guarantees everyone's fair treatment in light of individual talent and effort. (It doesn't guarantee equal results.) But even this requires us to do a bit more unpacking.

### *Another Definition of Antidiscrimination*

Within the first, color-blind vision, we have seen that "discrimination" is limited to a narrow set of circumstances involving proven or provable racial animus and intent. No attention is paid to the pragmatic concern that so restrictive a definition makes it very difficult to detect subtle discrimination and remedy it. The narrow conception of discrimination reflects a narrow social purpose, rooted in a traditional focus on remedying morally blameworthy actions and their proximate consequences. (A different conception of remedying social ills might use a less ethically freighted predicate, like income, for imposing redistributional burdens.)

Within a second, alternative vision emphasizing opportunity and antidiscrimination, "discrimination" encompasses a broader set of actions and maladies. Paying attention to practical, effective measures allows one to use "effects" tests, crafted sensibly, not just "intent" tests. It also means that voluntary remedial measures are permissible, not just measures adopted after costly, time-consuming lawsuits. And it means that we pay heed to manifest imbalances, not merely because we may be able to infer from them a discriminatory intent, but because such imbalances are, absent explanation, problems in and of themselves worthy of voluntary and sometimes legal remediation. In short, we must broaden the range of ills to which we apply the term "discrimination" and also the set of tools we use to detect and prevent it.

Let me dwell for a moment on the matter of "effects" tests, in which numerical disparities become the focus for attention. In theory, it is possible to enforce nondiscrimination. Observers can assess the fairness of hiring rules and the impartiality of their administration, and they can take needed corrective action. But appropriate standards of judgment are not easy to come by. A nondiscriminatory system of choosing individuals from a pool of applicants can produce a wide range of outcomes for different groups, depending on the composition of the pool. If there are gross workforce disparities between blacks and whites in a given industry or firm, notwithstanding a large and diverse pool of eligible employees, a prima facie case of discrimination can be made out—one can infer from the disparity that discrimination is occurring—but the prima facie case can be rebutted with explanations and evidence that something else is going on. So problems arise when rebuttals are ignored or "disparity analyses" are done carelessly.

Consider the following example offered by Stephen Carter of Yale Law School:

> In 1988, . . . members of the Michigan legislature argued that they could tell from the numbers that the Detroit Symphony Orchestra was not doing all it could to attract black classical musicians. Only discrimination, it seems, was a possible explanation for the fact that the orchestra employed only one full-time black performer. Never mind that an entirely blind screening process was used to hire musicians; never mind that out of 5,000 orchestra-bound musicians at the nation's top twenty-five conservatories, only 100 were black, of whom a normal distribution would predict that perhaps a fifth—twenty—were good enough to play in a major orchestra. The Detroit Symphony might have been the most racist institution in the world or the most racially benevolent one, but the statistics do not hold the answer.

There are many possible interpretations of the Detroit Symphony figures, and Carter has it only partially right. First, the fact that a screening process is blind does not mean that it cannot be discriminatory *if* one believes that some disparate *impacts* or *effects* require remedy even in the absence of conscious racial prejudice. Defending the orchestra's results by citing the blindness of the process begs the question of whether certain disparate impacts are, for moral and social policy reasons, appropriate for remedial action. In any case, the only justification for claiming that the demographic figures are relevant here is if the legislature is deciding that the *purposes* of the Detroit Symphony include more than simply creating the best possible music. I was once chosen to sing in an all-state high school chorus which was drawn proportionately from the several regions of my state; the business was as much an exercise in *community* as it was an exercise in culture. The Olympic Games are not for only the best athletes in the world, but for the best athletes from each of many countries. What at least some people in the Michigan legislature may have believed was that the Detroit Symphony is supposed to be an exercise in *community* and in heterogeneous participation in culture as well as in good music making. Carter or any of us may believe that this is a stupid reason for having an orchestra—even a government-funded orchestra—or, alternatively, we may believe that geography is an acceptable consideration in selecting the orchestra members but then *also* believe that race is different and irrelevant. But this is different from saying that there is *no* intelligible principle on which the legislature might base its concern about the racial diversity of the orchestra.

Second, accepting the facts as Carter gives them to us, there's nothing wrong with legislators saying, "We understand there are only a hundred African-American musicians in the qualified pool, but our objection is that the Symphony doesn't seem to be doing anything to expand the pool—to work with promising inner-city kids in hopes that someday a few of them can compete. We think that, in view of the lack of diversity in the orchestra today, such aggressive outreach and training is the civic responsibility of the Symphony our tax dollars support." This approach recognizes that the racial disparity is a function of broader societal patterns—whether one calls it societal discrimination or simply race-correlated socioeconomic disadvantage. The legislators might be saying that the facts create a predicate for strong affirmative action of the outreach and training sort.

Finally, and most obviously, if the legislators did in fact believe that a crude study of the Symphony's demographics established a prima facie case of illegal discrimination, then they were just wrong. As a matter of law and logic, the relevant pool for comparison is the far more limited one Carter describes. The lesson is not that disparate impact analysis is wrong, but that the analysis must be done carefully. Case law, EEOC regulations, and all the legal commentary make that clear.

I have suggested that, within this moral vision stressing opportunity and antidiscrimination, the distinctive attention to pragmatism leads to a conception of discrimination that is broader than the one recognized within the preceding chapter's idealism of "color blindness" we discussed in the last chapter. This broader definition is the result of principled value choices. In addition to the choice of pragmatism, a second commitment is to the idea that "discrimination" is not just about individuals committing moral wrongs, in the model of a common-law tort or crime, but also about racial subjugation in the past and the disadvantages in the present that are the consequences of social and economic forces larger than the sum of individual moral wrongs.

Let us consider a *very* unlikely—you may even think bizarre— analogy. In the Nixon administration, an effort was made to combat inflation by instituting a wage-price freeze. A similar, but less formal, anti-inflation effort was mounted by the Carter administration. In both cases, the idea was to combat a large economic force, inflation, in part by paying exquisite attention to the details of individual transactions. Of course, any one wage contract or wholesale price schedule might seem perfectly justified in its local circumstances and might not significantly contribute to an increase in the consumer price index. Still, the decision was made to regulate (or at least jaw-bone) the individual transactions not because each cost hike was individually unjustified in isolation, but because each was part of a pattern that, in the whole, was pernicious. The big picture justified the regulation, not the blameworthiness of the workers or businessmen in any one transaction. The individual act was problematic less because of its isolated characteristics or motivations than because of its relationship to a larger pattern that had an aggregate effect requiring an equally large response.

Similarly, within a broader conception of discrimination, our attention to racial progress must not be diverted by scattered investigations of isolated cases of provable bigotry. We care, too, about the big picture, the larger forces sustaining racial inequality, and we use a definition we believe will help note those circumstances where intervention will help to blunt or even exorcise those larger forces.

The third, and quite related, value choice implicit in our broader definition is the belief that effective attention to racial division and opportunity is more important than concern about the "heavy hand" of regulation or interference with personal autonomy, by governmental or even private power. Without going to the extreme of libertarianism, there is, of course, a traditional American resistance to state power, and a broader definition of discrimination will broaden the circumstances that might occasion exercises of that power. Within this framework, we duly acknowledge this, *and then we move on*. This point in part explains why traditional ideological conservatives often object to strong formulations of antidiscrimination law, just as they object to aggressive environmental or safety regulations; they believe that while racial justice, clean air, and worker safety are fine ideals, an activist state is dangerous.

A fourth value choice is in many ways the most fundamental one. By attributing a substantial part of observed disparities and disadvantages to racial causes rather than to a host of other possible factors, we are choosing an interpretation of American history and society that acknowledges race as a major current, not a minor eddy. Technically, of course, in a lawsuit this interpretation is subject to empirical proof in court, but empirical methods are imperfect. More important, legislation and voluntary measures need no such rigorous empirical predicate: although they need *some* demonstration, according to the Supreme Court's 1995 *Adarand* decision, just how much evidence a government needs remains very unclear as a matter of constitutional law. ("More than good motives should be required when government seeks to allocate its resources by way of an explicit racial classification system," said the 5–4 Court majority.) Decisions about policy and morality, of course, are informed and in some respects constrained by constitutional doctrine. But there are also important differences.

The fifth and final value choice deserves emphasis. The commitment is to *active* efforts attacking and preventing discrimination, not merely opposing it whenever one happens upon it. This distinction is more than one of mood. It implies concerted, proactive programs. The analogy comes to mind of law enforcement efforts directed at drunk driving or spousal abuse. Years ago, the law enforcement community generally approached these crimes as matters to be dealt with only when and if presented. Today, countless communities have serious public campaigns to prevent and deter both, as well as tougher sentences for offenders. So, too, proponents of affirmative action have always viewed it not only as a remedy in the corrective sense but as a remedy in the prophylactic sense. By engaging in appropriate affirmative action an employer, for example, can help to dismantle the subtle forms of discrimination that occur in ill-conceived recruitment, hiring, and promotion practices—discrimination that might otherwise go undetected or be detected but left unchallenged because of transaction costs and imperfections in the enforcement system.

### Defining "Morally Equal" Opportunity

Here's the opportunity clause of the American credo: *All Americans should have, so far as is possible, a full and equal chance to develop their talents and use them for the betterment of themselves, their families, and their society.* I say "so far as is possible" because social theorists going all the way back to Plato have recognized that parental differences have profound effects on the life chances of their children. Not many folks are prepared to advocate abolishing the family in the name of full equality of opportunity, but it bears mention that some aggressively interventionist strategies for combating social collapse in the inner cities have involved taking kids out of whatever family or nonfamily situation they're in and putting them in boarding schools; this is a de facto removal strategy that would simply strip away many family-based and neighborhood-related environmental disadvantages. A similar point is expressed in the oft-cited African aphorism that "it takes a village to raise a child": education and socialization are both too complex and too important to leave entirely to even a fully functional family unit. What are we to do when *both* family and "village" are dysfunctional? That is a huge, daunting, and very real challenge today. And while race-targeted measures can't do it all, the challenge is sufficiently dire that it seems a cruel folly to cast aside any potentially useful tool.

But I'm getting ahead of myself. What are the determinants of opportunity, and how can they be influenced so as to make opportunity "equal"? I start broadly with three propositions:

1. Your opportunities are a function of what you bring to the game, the nature of that game, and your free will.
2. What you bring to the game depends on your natural

endowments from birth, and on the endowments generated by your environment—family, community, experiences, etc.
3. The nature of the game is itself a function of the fairness of the rules and fairness in how the rules are administered.

The first proposition simply frames our analysis. By separating the issue of endowments—what you bring to the game—from the rules of that game, I am asserting that equality of opportunity between individuals A and B means more than lining them both up to play a nondiscriminatory game. That is, equal opportunity means more than nondiscrimination; it is not just another way of stating the same norm, but is instead an additional social purpose and a supplementary value judgment. President Lyndon Johnson's formulation is the most famous:

> You do not take a person who had been hobbled by chains, liberate him, bring him up to the starting gate of a race and then say, "You are free to compete with all the others," and still justly believe you have been completely fair. . . . It is not enough to open the gates of opportunity. All of our Citizens must have the ability to walk through those gates. . . . Men and women of all races are born with the same range of abilities. But ability is not just the product of birth. Ability is stretched or stunted by the family you live with, . . . the neighborhood . . . the school . . . and the poverty or richness of your surroundings. It is the product of a hundred unseen forces playing upon the infant, the child and the man.

He said this in 1965 when he called the nation to arms to fight the War on Poverty and consolidate the civil rights gains that had so recently been made in the courts and the Congress. This conception of opportunity was certainly distinct from equality of results, as President Johnson himself argued. The central proposition is clear: Genuine opportunity to perform well in the footrace depends on more than the formal rules of the competition, viewed in splendid isolation.

None of this is to gainsay the importance of free will, or *personal responsibility*, in determining the amount of opportunity an individual enjoys. As a professor, I see students with comparable talents and endowments who make different choices about how much effort to invest in their academic work, and these choices in turn are loosely related to the career opportunities they have when they graduate, and often beyond then. Still, it is irksome listening to the party line of many conservatives when you hear the extreme importance they give to this free-will dimension—both to explain what is wrong and to prescribe how progress should be pursued without having the government participate or anyone else make sacrifices. The transparent truth is that people magnify the self-help and personal-responsibility message out of all proportion when for other reasons they want to take themselves off the hook, or want to curb the ambitions and dim the vision of public institutions and progressive political leaders.

What is irksome in general becomes, for me, simply disgusting in the particular case of black conservatives whose celebrity is manufactured by white conservative institutions and ideologues with no bona fide history of affection or even solicitude for African Americans. We are long past the point where trumpeting the personal-responsibility theme can be defended as a useful corrective for an overreliance on government. Among the most obvious features in today's policy environment are the Million Man March and the decimation of means-tested social welfare programs; it is fatuous to argue that social welfare strategies have dominant and exclusive claim on the public's attention. Those who would be responsible participants in the racial justice debate, therefore, must face the question of how to *balance* the strategies of social welfare and personal responsibility.


Let's turn to the second proposition, concerning what you bring to the game. There is little to say concerning *natural* endowments. We know the long, sad history of scientific and pseudoscientific investigation of differences in intelligence said to be inherited and race-linked. The most recent dalliance with this kind of talk, done with considerable subtlety, was *The Bell Curve: Intelligence and Class Structure in American Life*, by Richard Herrnstein and Charles Murray. The subtlety did not fool many reviewers, for criticism of the book from academic and intellectual quarters was overwhelmingly negative and powerful. (The book was nonetheless popular and widely cited.) My point is merely the opposite: I take as a given the mainstream view, which is that the disadvantages we observe disproportionately among blacks or other minorities are *not* caused by race-linked biological differences in cognitive potential, accurately measured.

The story is vastly different for *environmental* endowments. Some aspects of our environment are inherited, though not biologically. We have our parents (or perhaps not), Daddy's trust fund (or perhaps his alcoholism), and a web of family values (or perhaps chaos) which envelops us by accident of birth. In the larger sense, our upbringing makes an enormous difference—family, friends, schools, neighborhood, role models, social habits, language, aspirations—countless forces interact to propel us forward or to trap us. We see this in popular portrayals of the hapless and the heroic alike, nonfictional and fictional.

We do not come to the game with equal environmental endowments, nor could we in an open and diverse society. Differences are inevitable. The central question is this: *Which negative endowments, which disadvantages or handicaps must be remedied in order to give us the moral satisfaction of knowing that opportunity is genuinely equal, and what tools are appropriate to provide those remedies?* I say "moral" satisfaction because, as I shall argue, we are trying to define something that is different in nature from the satisfaction of mere political or policy concerns. I think morality defines the difference between those conditions that most of us would consider essential to a just society and those of an interstitial or perhaps less essential nature, on which we might disagree. We would probably all agree that a just society does not have hordes of homeless children sleeping on steam grates, but we might disagree about whether welfare programs should be designed by federal, state, or local governments; the latter issues seem to be about antipoverty policy, only derivatively about social justice.

Now what about the comparative economic and social disadvantages afflicting the African-American community? Are these concerns of moral justice or merely of social policy? Two factors are telling. First, most Americans would probably agree that poverty and deprivation can reach a level that transcends policy debate and becomes a matter of justice—a matter going to the heart of our conception of the American community. But second, whether the deprivation suffered by African Americans does or doesn't reach that level, a separate consideration weighs on our minds—namely, the linkage between color and the deprivation. Whatever the level of inequality, that inequality takes on a different moral cast if it seems linked or even merely correlated with race. I believe this is a widely shared intuitive judgment. What underlies it?

Fairness depends on both how desperate the woe and how it is distributed. If the pain is heaped on an identifiable group, then the fairness question is whether that woeful group was selected fairly. In the case of African Americans, it was not random, it has not varied from generation to generation, and it is not offset with other peculiar advantages. No, the selection of the descendants of slaves has been anything but fair.

Another way to consider the unjustness of black disadvantage is to ask what kind of national community it creates, what difference it makes to America as a whole to have these divisions and distance, mistrust and fear and hate, these economic and human costs. No observer can fail to smell our disease—from Alexis de Tocqueville 150 years ago to Gunnar Myrdal fifty years ago to Japanese tourists today. One way to understand the injustice is to consider the images in the mirror we prefer to avoid. Averting our eyes confesses our shame.

In my view, all these considerations support a moral claim that socioeconomic disadvantages disproportionately afflicting African Americans amount to a negative endowment that belies the promise of equal opportunity; these disadvantages must somehow be addressed in order to create *morally equal opportunity*. Not an ordinary tragedy of haves and have-nots, but a deeper, historic train of unfairness created race-based disadvantage in the United States. And that unfairness over generations has created a great machine of social and economic laws that tends to propagate the disadvantage as an inheritance from one generation to the next. It flows through time and generations, even more assuredly than that same social machinery transmits the endowments of property and treasure which so advantage the wealthy. The image comes to mind of a huge mechanical loom, weaving threads as long as history—good and stained, beautiful and plain—into a fabric that must be continuous with the fabric that came before. Our original virtues and riches are, unsurprisingly, the source of that fabric's beauty. That the original unfairness—the original sin—stained our American fabric, and still does, is no surprise. We are inheritors of both the good and the bad. Some of this tapestry must be undone, and our interrelationships must be rewoven to create the American fabric we want for today and for the future.

## The Rules of the Game

Equal opportunity depends not only on what you bring to the game, but also on the fairness of the rules—fairness both in the rule book and as practiced. There are three things I want to note in this regard.

Most basically, how fair can it be that the rules allow inherited endowments to determine so much? Can you blame anyone who is underendowed with feeling that the game is rigged? Of course, America's great opportunity engine of upward mobility is supposed to mitigate this unfairness in inheritance, but is the opportunity engine really working? And in particular, is it working for African Americans? The answer is no. As I reviewed in Chapter 1, not only is there a continuing and serious opportunity gap between black and white but there are also important empirical indications that the historically familiar patterns of intergenerational upward mobility and rising real incomes have seriously unraveled in the past twenty years. So the unfair inheritance problem is real, painful, and very much in the minds of African Americans. In this sense, the game really *is* rigged, and interventions are needed to produce morally equal opportunity.

Second, one rule of the game is, obviously, nondiscrimination. I've described how one's very definition of discrimination depends on one's moral framework, and how the definition shifts in moving from a vision based on color blindness to one based on opportunity and antidiscrimination. Thus far, I have discussed only the perspective of the disadvantaged minority, and it may differ from that of an individual who feels victimized by "reverse discrimination." What is the nature of the game in that regard? One possible view of such a person is that affirmative action unfairly saddles him with an inherited debt, based on an original sin which was not his. This perspective may reflect his moral opinion that the redistribution of opportunity away from someone must be predicated on blameworthiness and blameworthiness must be personal, or his view that other bases for redistribution are permissible but not race: "Tax me because I am prosperous, not because I am white." I do not see a *logical* flaw in either view, but I disagree with the implicit value choices. Each view expresses a moral preference for color blindness over equal opportunity, as I would define it.

Third is the issue of merit, about which I shall have more to say in Chapter 6. The point here is that we take it as an article of faith that selection based on merit is fair. (I've already made the point that with a conventional definition of merit, we might consider it "unfair" in certain circumstances to use a rule that gives dispositive weight to the negative endowments representing the continuing harms of racial caste, but forget that quibble.) In affirmative action debates, critics often make the further argument that decisions based on something other than merit are *unfair*. That's problematic for a couple of reasons.

The truth is, most decisions or selections about people aren't made on a strict basis of merit, or not entirely. There are many common counterexamples of selection based on nepotism or cronyism; and random decisions are even more common, or first-come-first-served ones, or ones made on the basis of very little information at all. *And then there are choices we make because of personal preferences having everything to do with taste, comfort, and convenience and nothing to do with efficiency in maximizing profits or with conventional excellence.* I often decide to work with, hire, entertain people because I like them, not because I think they're "best." (It is sophistic to argue that these are decisions in which merit is simply redefined in terms of my personal preferences. That turns the notion of merit on its head, redefining it to mean satisfying my whims, with no regard to recognizable and legitimate business or social purposes.)

Also, a commonsense understanding of "merit" relates a person's qualities or characteristics to the likely contribution he will make to the organization's overall excellence. In many situations, however, we can't tell how much Penelope, say, will contribute unless we know more about the other people and resources available. Perhaps Penelope plays a terrific harp but our orchestra is actually desperate for horn players. Perhaps Penelope speaks Cantonese but what the police department needs are people who can work effectively in the Latino community. In these sorts of situations, merit is defined in relation to both individual and collective qualities; merit-based fairness cannot be based exclusively on individual characteristics and often requires explicit consideration of an organization's broader needs. Penelope may be wonderful, and that isn't always enough.

Does it follow, however, that *race* can be a factor? Within this second vision focusing on opportunity and antidiscrimination, the institution may need to take certain remedial measures, and effectiveness should matter. A comprehensive notion of merit must encompass its need just as it encompasses others. If the remedial purpose is legitimate, conventional understandings of merit can and should be adjusted to reflect the needs. And it seems "fair."

But before using race, one should consider the alternatives. We have acknowledged that while an emphasis on opportunity and antidiscrimination does not rigidly bar race-conscious decision making, such thinking does have a moral cost: the consequences for bystanders. It follows that in adopting measures to bring about greater equality of opportunity, or to remedy discrimination, we must minimize those moral costs by minimizing the need for race-based measures. In constitutional analysis, this is the "narrow tailoring" prong of "strict scrutiny" required by the equal protection clause of the Fourteenth Amendment, as we discussed; in statutory employment discrimination law, it is the "unnecessarily trammels" test to make sure there are no unjustified burdens on those who are not directly benefited.

The broadest criticism of race-based affirmative action is a general injunction favoring other, race-neutral criteria—class or geography. In a phrase: "class, not color; place, not race." I have five key objections to across-the-board substitution of class or geography for race: dilution, overinclusion, underinclusion, the contemporary collapse of the social welfare policy agenda, and the disingenuousness of complex schemes to use race-neutral proxy variables. I explore these in Chapter 6. Taken together, they provide added support for preserving careful explicit attention to race.

Equality of opportunity is traditionally, and correctly, distinguished from equality of result. We have no way of knowing for certain whether or when equality of opportunity for individuals will produce equality of results for groups. There are too many intervening variables. Nevertheless, persistent and dramatic differences in results do need to be explained, and unequal opportunity should be a leading hypothesis or, with an eye to history, a rebuttable presumption.

We have focused, in this chapter, on genuine equal opportunity and nondiscrimination. Genuinely equal opportunity depends on several factors, including not only the fairness of the game but also the inherited and environmental endowments we bring to it, together with our personal choices and will. Those endowments will never be truly equal in a diverse and open society, but some disparities may be morally unacceptable because they are unjust—and then we must remedy them in order to create morally equal opportunity. I argue that the black-white disparities in our society are of this morally unacceptable sort, that the factor of color adds a dimension of genuine injustice to the simple policy claims having to do with poverty. But what remediation is acceptable? Are race-based measures permissible? In this second framework, as I have said, the use of race as a consideration is not flatly impermissible but neither is it morally costless.

By emphasizing practical victories in ensuring opportunity and in combating discrimination, we lose the simple clarity of the color-blind vision. There are definite political liabilities to embracing so complex and imprecise a framework for policy choice and justification. Still, it has the virtue of more nearly corresponding to the moderate, reasonable tendency that most of us have to eschew absolutism and to pay attention to context. When we are loyal to values that compete or conflict, then we have to accept that there's a struggle to make difficult trade-offs and balances. To struggle or not to struggle, that is the question. Then again, why should we expect racial justice to be an easy cause? Just consider our history. And consider our present.

# 5

# A THIRD VISION: REMEDIATION *PLUS* INCLUSION

*It is in my interest and in my family's interest and in my
neighbor's interest, without regard to their race or their background, that every boy and girl in this country grow up to
live to the fullest of their God-given capacity, and that every
man and woman in this country have a chance to contribute
and to do well as far as they can. So I'm hoping that instead
of [this debate] being a bad thing that divides us, we can
turn this thing on its head and take it away from the people
who want to use it for pure politics to get votes out of, and
instead turn it into a conversation about the American family.
I'm going to do my best to do that.*

—President Clinton's radio remarks on the
*Tom Joyner Morning Show*, February 1995

### Remediation, Diversity, and Community

At an Oval Office meeting with the President in the spring of 1995, a
staff member was arguing that one could make a very compelling case
that affirmative action is justified as a remedy and just leave it at that;
that even with a broad conception of "remedy" this was a moral high

ground that the President could take in the ugly debate we feared in the months and years ahead. Many nods all around the room, but I demurred.

"Mr. President," I began, feigning tentativeness, "I'm not so sure that works. Look, during the transition you said you wanted a cabinet that 'looks like America.' Well, did you appoint Ron Brown Secretary of Commerce or Hazel O'Leary Secretary of Energy because you wanted to provide a remedy for discrimination they had suffered, or discrimination practiced by past Presidents in filling cabinet posts? Of course not. You said what you said out of a conviction that by being inclusive and tapping the diversity that is America's strength, the cabinet as a whole would serve you and the American people more effectively. My point is, there are at least *some* circumstances and *some* institutions in which the justification for affirmative action rests on the benefits of inclusion or diversity, rather than on the need to remedy or prevent discrimination. Whether or not one acknowledges this nonremedial justification is one of the major decisions you have to make about the values and moral framework."

We went on to talk about urban police departments, university admissions, and various private-sector employers. Where are the limits of the justification based on inclusion? How does it differ from proportional representation? Is inclusion as weighty a justification as remediation?

Vision I, which I detailed in Chapter 3, is color-blind: in it, no circumstances justify the moral cost associated with race-conscious decision making. Vision II, outlined in Chapter 4, emphasizes antidiscrimination and morally equal opportunity: there are circumstances in which our goals of broader remediation for discrimination and morally unequal opportunity justify certain forms of race-conscious decision making. Vision III, however, moves beyond the remedial justifications.

*The central moral tenet is this:* race-conscious decision making is justified not only in circumstances that suggest remedial purposes but also in contexts where there are substantial benefits to an institution or to society at large from inclusion or diversity. In instrumental terms, diversity is often essential to an organization's effectiveness at its core mission: an urban police department will be more effective if it reflects the diversity of the community it seeks to serve; the armed forces will be more effective if the officer corps and senior enlisted ranks reflect the diversity of the military as a whole, and of the society whose support the armed forces needs to sustain legitimacy. Sometimes inclusion is instrumentally important for broader national or community needs: scientists have been concerned that the United States may face severe human-capital shortfalls in basic research unless more minorities and women develop the interest in and do the training to join the scientists we will need to sustain our fragile preeminence. But there are also noninstrumental reasons. Some have to do with our aspirations to have a more diverse, less balkanized experience of community, and to enjoy its personal and societal benefits; other reasons involve our vision of an America in which every individual is empowered by access to opportunities that enable them to achieve their full potential.

*The central behavioral tenet is this:* exclusion is not solely—or, today, even primarily—the result of present discrimination and racial animus. A large factor is the "birds of a feather" tendency to prefer people like oneself. In hundreds of subtle ways, this tendency pervades American social and economic life, and the aggregate effect is to divide us, starving ourselves and our institutions of the benefits that come from having more diverse and inclusive communities.

*The central policy prescription is this:* just as we need affirmative action in some circumstances as prophylaxsis to prevent discrimination, so too we may need race-conscious measures to lean against that tilt in the playing field that helps those who are familiar to us and hinders those who are different—even when there is no unlawful discrimination. (Dare we seek a renaissance of the *integration* ideal?)

Early on in the White House discussions about affirmative action, I argued for an emphasis on the term "inclusion" rather than "diversity," which carries too much political baggage and for many people means proportional representation. Inclusion, on the other hand, suggests something more active and purposeful, not just a static description of demographics. It suggests a process of opening up, of

*cont next pg.*

relationship building rather than nose counting. Here I shall use the two terms interchangeably, but I believe the more aspirational sense of "inclusion" is critical for our national conversation about race.

Combining the many justifications offered in Vision II and this Vision III, we have the following claims for attention in our moral calculus of racial measures. From Vision II, we have:

- the *remedial* purpose, with a predicate of discrimination or the need to prevent it;
- the broadly remedial, or *curative*, purpose, premised on the need to create morally equal opportunity through measures directly addressing the race-linked disadvantage "inherited" as the lingering effect of pervasive discrimination. We don't like the look of a society with such sharp socioeconomic cleavages along color lines. (And it is dangerous.)

And now, from Vision III, we should add:

- the *empowering* purpose of ensuring disadvantaged individuals access to the critical institutions that provide an opportunity to achieve their full potential;
- the *aspirational* purpose, to create in institutions and in society more generally the reality of tolerant and cohesive community, because such communities will enrich our humanity;
- and the *instrumental* purpose of strengthening organizations and institutions in their core missions, by drawing strength from diversity.

Let's explore these three new elements. The question is whether and when they might be significant enough to provide a nonremedial justification for using race-conscious measures in pursuit of racial justice.

Beyond the narrowly justifiable matters of blame-based cure and remedy, we pursue affirmative action and diversity to *empower* individual beneficiaries and because we have aspirations as a nation to build strength through inclusiveness. These are alternatives to the conceptions and language of blame, guilt, and reparations.

There is more to affirmative action than remedying a proven incident of discrimination with a victim and a perpetrator—what we term the *remedial* context. There is also the general problem of addressing the lingering social and economic effects of past wrongs. As I discussed in Chapter 4, these contribute to the disadvantage suffered by many individually, and disproportionately by African Americans in the aggregate. This is the *curative* context.

Example: White House staff met on February 24, 1995, with a group of minority business leaders who defended the tax preference given to sellers of broadcast properties to minority firms. The central justification they offered was that when the FCC had distributed broadcast licenses in decades past, minorities had not been "at the table," and thus set-asides of various sorts can be defended as a cure now for such systematic denials of access to wealth and the means of accumulating it. There is no proven predicate of identified victims and wrongdoers, but there is a lingering effect of past societal discrimination, or institutional racism. Nor is the notion, strictly speaking, necessarily one of "reparations," in the sense of "compensating" for past wrongs. The focus is on curing today's society of the lingering poisons, and the debate should be over whether the toxins are serious.

But this is not enough. Both "remedy" and "cure" are terms that suggest the moral categories of victim and perpetrator, innocence and fault. They evoke the analytical framework of cause and effect, damages and compensation or, perhaps, reparations. As such, the terms are not politically effective when so many people simply don't believe in the predicate of wrongdoing, or feel that the preference benefits individuals whose own personal link to the wrongdoing is too remote to justify its moral costs. *Indeed, the terms are inherently divisive*, precisely because they invoke the language of blame. This does not mean that this framework is invalid or that we should scrap it, but we have to recognize the limits to its usefulness and the source of those limits.

As an alternative or at least supplementary framework, one could stress the affirmative value of inclusiveness. Inclusion empowers people to realize their full potential and contributes to the well-being of their families and communities. It benefits America as a whole, because our lives are richer as a result of social diversity, and because our communities and our economy are stronger when all of us are full participants in both—carrying a full load of responsibilities and obligations, and a full complement of opportunities. These are unifying themes of empowerment and aspiration. To some, they bespeak a "liberal" persuasion. Can they be reconciled with the more familiar and conservative themes of opportunity and merit?

I believe they can. Opportunity is a value that covers a multitude of agendas. Andrew Johnson invoked equal opportunity to justify his veto of the first post-Civil War civil rights statute, which the Radical Republicans in Congress overrode. Lyndon Johnson put the phrase to better service ninety-nine years later in his commencement address at Howard University. The earlier President Johnson coupled opportunity with a principle of color blindness that was also blind to the shackles of racially determined disadvantage, while the later President Johnson coupled opportunity to affirmative measures. The political logic of emphasizing opportunity is that it gives us active, vigorous antidiscrimination efforts, and strategies for income redistribution, including race-neutral preferences based on disadvantage; both enjoy substantial support. While class-based measures are flawed as substitutes for effective present efforts, this does not mean we should abandon the theme of economic opportunity; like the antidiscrimination principle, it is part of the foundation for whatever else we may construct. But opportunity is both a strategy and a goal. Lyndon Johnson recognized that our goal must be *genuine*, morally equal opportunity. Some race-conscious measures, many argue, are necessary to achieve that goal—not sufficient, but necessary. Advocates on both the left and the right are too often reductionist about this: right-wing critics sometimes debate affirmative action as though its supporters considered it a panacea for all ills, when in fact most supporters readily acknowledge that race-conscious measures are only one of several elements in the opportunity agenda; while on the left, identity politics too often spurs would-be leaders in the black community to focus on the politics of color rather than the wider politics of opportunity. Balance is necessary, for political effectiveness and for sound policy. But this is the subject of Chapter 9, and I'm getting ahead of my story.

There is still another level to the issue of inclusion. Apart from empowering individuals to achieve their full potential, and aspiring to create communities where color no longer divides us, we must tackle the instrumental issue of improving the quality of particular institutions. We now turn to that element.

People sometimes advocate diversity in sweeping terms, with little attention to careful justification for it. This is entirely appropriate when you're trying to decide what restaurant to go to with a group of picky people of widely different tastes. You want a great diversity of items on the menu. And you'd feel the same if you had to pick a restaurant just for yourself at which you'll eat lunch every day for a year. But our focus is on race in the United States, not Chinese food, and because in this third vision there is, still, some moral cost to race-conscious decision making, it is not enough simply to assert that diversity is a good thing. Is it *good enough* to justify the moral costs?

It's also not enough to make purely instrumental arguments about the unarguable benefits—to an organization or to the American economy—of being more inclusive. Saying that we need to include minorities in higher education or in a labor pool in order to increase the gross domestic product sounds, to my African-American ears, like the argument that we have to feed the slaves because otherwise they'll be too weak to pick the cotton and the plantation's bottom line will suffer. In certain respects, stark instrumental justifications for inclusion turn people into objects rather than moral beings. That's not an objection to diversity, merely a caution: Beware of treating people as means rather than ends. The better way to think about (and express) the motivation, I believe, is to understand organizations more as organic communities than as cold factories or economist's production functions, with inputs, technologies, and outputs. If employees are community members rather than mere inputs in the production process, then our concern for inclusion takes on a moral cast quite different from a master's concern for his chattel. In the better view, a community is a collection of talents, relationships, and distinctive perspectives. This is still an instrumental perspective, of course, because the benefits of inclusion refer to the community's mission. Still, this way of expressing it doesn't make my ears burn.

Second, recapitulating the aspirational theme, something else is at stake beyond instrumentalism. Let's return to the restaurant metaphor. In Harvard Square, where I work and live, the restaurants offer a wonderful variety of cuisines, and any local would say this diversity enriches their lives. The stereotypical New York City booster proclaims that the ethnic diversity of Gotham makes living in almost any other American city unthinkable. And visiting someone's home for the first time, I often note whether the book-lined shelves demonstrate a certain flatness of interests and range (like mine) or, instead, a rich set of tastes and experiences. We even put various tchotchkes in fish tanks, convinced that the near-brainless creatures will enjoy their boxed lives more if they have a little variety in their surroundings. To paraphrase President Clinton, the diversity we experience enriches our lives in immeasurable material and immaterial ways, changes who we are and how we develop. This has little to do with instrumentalism and everything to do with wanting completeness in our humanity.

Another way of understanding this is to ask why inclusion should be considered morally superior to the familiar human instinct to prefer the familiar. Why should our civic culture, much less the activities of the state, lean against that human instinct in favor of diversity? (Again, remember that by hypothesis we are outside the realm of discrimination and remediation.) The answer, it seems to me, is that inclusion and diversity correspond to the moral virtue of *tolerance*, which is a fundamental element in American political and civic cultural ideals. Tolerance may well be something we preach more than practice, but the preachments have been consistent for a very long time. For most of us, while indifference to diversity may be barely acceptable, we assume that hostility to it is tantamount to intolerance—as though we cannot conceive of a benign parochialism.

Why is this so? Perhaps most of us take the diversity of America for granted and recognize it as one of our defining *and positive* qualities.

If that is the vision of our nation, then tolerance follows quite naturally and powerfully as an organizing precept. When we observe that important institutions lack diversity, and hear familiar explanations, we cannot dismiss a concern that tolerance needs a booster shot.

### When Is Diversity Compelling?

Because this moral framework acknowledges some moral cost to race-conscious decision making but insists that the cost be weighed in the balance with the benefits to racial justice, it follows that the weight of the inclusion justification depends a great deal on the circumstances—not only as regards the institution and society but perhaps as regards the individual. Recall that, in this vision, the justification for affirmatively including any specific individual does not depend on an argument about that individual having been personally victimized (directly or indirectly); this would be either the familiar remedial or the curative rationale. Instead, it is based on a benefit to the institution or to society at large. But what exactly *is* the benefit? And is it the same if the advantaged individual is, say, an upper-middle-class black? Do the benefits to Harvard Law School of including previously excluded minorities really depend on pigment or, instead, on something for which pigment is merely a proxy? And what about diversity in the cabinet? Is the deeper benefit related, instead, to personal history of disadvantage, or to political and social perspective? And what about retail salesclerks?

*The Rational Decision Maker.* Why might an institution need the extraordinary measure of race-conscious affirmative action at all? Won't rational decision makers adopt the policy of inclusion that makes sense?

In a meeting with President Clinton in mid-July 1995, shortly before he gave his address on affirmative action at the National Archives, several corporate executives expressed strong support for affirmative action. It made sense for them as a "business proposition," they said, citing the advantages of access to a larger pool of human resources, a richer mix of ideas and experiences contributing to marketing and product design and other functions, social harmony in the workforce and with the local communities where the companies operate, and so forth. One of them offered a disclaimer to the idea that they were committed to affirmative action out of some liberal conviction that it was "good for society": while the social benefit is real, he said, the heart of the matter is that it makes good business sense. Strikingly, this disclaimer was identical to the one given during my review of federal programs by the then Deputy Secretary of Defense John Deutch, who explained that the Pentagon's commitment to affirmative action (which they usually call "equal opportunity," apparently to lighten the negative political baggage) was a matter not of doing something socially redemptive and progressive but of effective national security.

Such disclaimers don't square with the fact that there remain throughout society, including parts of the armed forces, plenty of exclusion, glass ceilings, and the like. There are several reasons why we should doubt that rational decision makers will adopt the "optimal" level of inclusion.

Let's personalize the example. Consider a notional CEO. First, he may systematically undervalue the "investment" in diversity—outreach, recruitment, training, retention, mentoring, workforce team building, etc.—because his organization neither sees nor enjoys all the benefits that might flow from it. Economists term this the problem of "externalities," a classic form of market failure that results in economically inefficient, or suboptimal, decision making. It's the single most important explanation for the failure to invest voluntarily in appropriate levels of pollution reduction, say, or worker training. In our case, inclusion of traditionally disadvantaged and excluded groups would substantially benefit society at large, as well as particular families, communities, and other institutions. The executives who met with Clinton and the Pentagon officials disclaiming generous motives are no different than the CEO of a chemical company disclaiming any interest in voluntarily reducing hazardous effluents or waste byproducts except as it would directly improve his bottom line. The fact is, we *want* organizations to internalize both the costs and the benefits their actions generate at large; when they don't, we sometimes think their failure is so serious and costly for society that it warrants governmental regulation of their decision making. In matters concerning the environment, we have a host of statutes and regulations for this purpose. In affirmative action matters, we have no such regimen premised on diversity; the affirmative action obligation that most firms working with the federal government must obey, contained in Executive Order 11246, is premised on the need to remedy and prevent discrimination. *There is no federal regulatory compulsion directed at employers in the name of diversity.*

Second, our CEO may systematically undervalue inclusion because the costs of investing in it are immediate and near, while the benefits seem far in the future. Volumes have been written about the tendency of American managers to make investment decisions for the short term—about managers as a class, if not Americans as a matter of character, not being future-oriented enough. Inattention to the long-term importance of inclusion is on the same footing as inattention to basic research and development or to human capital investments generally.

Third, our CEO may systematically overestimate the risks and uncertainties associated with inclusion. This is the most complex factor. Most fundamentally, this is just "different is risky," an application of the familiar problem that we tend to prefer people like ourselves. The "birds of a feather flock together" bias is not just adaptive biologically but often efficient economically: in hiring, it represents a sensible use of information signals—appearance and résumé—instead of the more cumbersome and costly investigation of or experience with a prospective employee. The difficulty is, our CEO will interpret the information signals in the light of his personal experience, and his experiences contain the biases of a divided society and racial caste. Anyone who has hired someone in a situation that allowed for at least a little subjective judgment has had the experience of looking for some kind of connection with the applicant—some common experience or perspective or temperament, *something*. With black and white communities so separate, such connections are difficult to find. This distortion in the estimates of risks and uncertainties need not result from bigotry or racial animus on the part of the decision maker. It would be an extraordinary person who has wholly escaped the racist toxins flowing through our lives. And in situations where racial prejudice and discrimination are indeed at work, we of course don't even ask whether the rational decision maker underinvested in inclusion; we simply don't trust them.

*The Institutional Inquiry.* What is it about an institution that makes the inclusion of both blacks and whites in it essential, justifying at least some form of race-conscious decision making?

Let's start with the easy case of a police department struggling to serve a diverse and divided city. It is now an article of faith among law enforcement professionals that such a department is far less likely to be effective if an overwhelmingly white organization is facing a minority population. Issues of legitimacy, cooperation, responsiveness (in both directions), and so forth are bound up tightly with the issue of race in such communities. In this context, then, a color-blind aspiration is a profoundly abstract—indeed, academic—ideal. Forget about any history of employment discrimination, or any risk of it for the future. There is an independent justification for affirmative action based on the reasonable belief that inclusion will make the organization better *as a police department.* This is the Pentagon's point about using affirmative action to make the armed forces better *as an instrument of national security.* It is not the entire argument, but it is a compelling start.

Another familiar example concerns higher education. Justice Lewis Powell's opinion in the Supreme Court's *Bakke* decision, in 1978, endorsed the notion that universities have a diversity interest related both to their mission and to First Amendment values. Few leaders in higher education would today dispute this; the debate is over the matter of degree. Nor does anyone contend that racial and gender diversity is all that matter. At selective universities—meaning just about any institution with something less than an "open admissions" policy—the admissions officers may consider everything in a prospective student's background, from alumni connections to athletic prowess to travel abroad to family size. The nature of the academic process is that interaction produces learning and stimulates creativity. The richness of the mix affects the range of each student's possibilities for interchange and growth. Other institutional goals must be served too, of course, and sometimes these are in tension with the goal of racial and other kinds of diversity. For example, a university may feel obliged to focus on state residents, or may want to ensure it has enough students to sustain an engineering department or a baroque wind ensemble or the research work being done in its laboratories.

This is hardly news. The point is that while it is perhaps more difficult to say what makes an effective university than what makes an effective police department (though I admit that my sense of this may simply reflect my own experiences and lack thereof), the justification for inclusion and affirmative action is much the same.

There is an additional consideration. Something about these institutions and their functions in society makes it particularly important to assure their effectiveness in dimensions related to race. We care if a police force is no good at controlling traffic violations or investigating reports of missing persons, but we care more if communities of color are systematically underserved or if there is widespread suspicion of police brutality directed at minorities. Alumni may care when a university lets its athletic program languish or when the reputation of a still-good department is eclipsed by the one in a crosstown rival institution. But its thoughtful leaders would care even more if faculty and students were systematically isolated from exposure to the perspectives, contributions, concerns, and aspirations of an entire segment of our society.

Certain institutions fulfill special social functions: schools socialize individuals and provide the critical mechanism for upward socioeconomic mobility; police departments help to maintain the foundation of community and personal security upon which social and economic stability depend; media organizations give us news and information, as well as entertainment, and these, too, shape our civic culture; banks and other financial institutions are essential intermediaries of economic opportunity and entrepreneurial possibility. It defies logic to suggest that we can overcome America's color legacy and achieve racial justice without ensuring that these and other important institutions "look like America," to use President Clinton's phrase.

*The Individual Inquiry*. Still, that's not the core of the matter. What exactly is it that these organizations actually get by including a given individual? Why does color matter?

When I hear this question, I often just sigh. Deeply. It's almost too basic a question to be answered: "If you don't know the answer, I can't possibly give you an explanation you'd understand." But the need for an explanation is symptomatic of our divisions. What's obvious to those of us on the "providing" end of the diversity transaction may be obscure and theoretical to those whose experience on the "receiving" end is modest—or nil.

I was often the lone person of color in high-level policy discussions in the Carter White House, in the Dukakis presidential campaign, and in the Clinton White House. I was frequently struck by this isolation, and by the sense that I could contribute concerns and views that others could not or would not. For example, in fighting at the White House Office of Management and Budget over the size of the President's budget for urban development and housing funds, I was aware that my racial background had shaped my experiences so as to produce commitments and passions and policy preferences that made my voice different from those of the others around the table—different, even, from (the few) other liberal Democrats there. On the one hand, it is empowering to feel that you have a unique value to add to the discussion and decision; on the other, it is depressing to be constantly reminded that inclusion is still so fragile and even serendipitous. My successor in the White House Office of Management and Budget (white, of course) is not like me. He's outstanding, as I hope I was, but in a different way.

The point is not that there weren't people on my staff or elsewhere in the administration with very similar commitments and passions. There certainly were, and they were of all races. But in that room, in those discussions, with that handful of influential people, the odds of a black voice being heard were markedly advanced because Leon Panetta, when he assembled the senior staff of OMB, thought consciously about the need to be inclusive, and because George Stephanopoulos, when he assembled a team to work on affirmative action, knew that diversity along several dimensions would matter.

It's not a matter of racial determinism in policy views.* If Leon

Panetta had hired a conservative African American after all, the black voice in the discussions would have been quite different from mine. Still, the chances are very good that an African American or Latino on a career trajectory which makes a White House appointment in a Democratic administration conceivable will have a voice that insists on priority attention to the agenda of racial justice. So the race of an applicant for a place in a police force, college, government policy office, or newsroom is perhaps a proxy variable for a set of experiences and perspectives that will add at least one aspect of African-American life. There are, of course, many such aspects. But too many of them remain quite alien to white America, and hence the need for inclusion.

As society becomes more equal in fact, race will become ever more invalid as a proxy, and that will be a measure success. Meanwhile, to the extent that race-neutral inclusion captures many benefits, the principle of narrowly tailoring the design of affirmative action requires that we consider it. So long as the United States is divided, however, there will be generally distinctive experiences and perspectives shared by most African Americans, and that distinctiveness warrants inclusion, within reason. In many settings, inclusion means opportunity and the richness of integration. And in some institutions, especially public and elite ones, visible inclusion also has powerful symbolic value, both political and social. It communicates an openness about the power structure, it commands legitimacy, and it leads traditionally excluded groups to believe, correctly, that the exclusion has softened or perhaps dissolved. It means progress.

---

* Consider the tragic contrast of Thurgood Marshall with Clarence Thomas.

Justice Marshall argued, typically, "It is because of a legacy of unequal treatment that we now must permit the institutions of this society to give consideration to race in making decisions about who will hold the positions of influence, affluence, and prestige in America. For far too long, the doors to those positions have been shut to Negroes. If we are ever to become a fully integrated society, one in which the color of a person's skin will not determine the opportunities available to him or her, we must be willing to take steps to open those doors. Those doors cannot be fully opened without the acceptance of race-conscious remedies." (448 U.S. 448, 522 [1980]).

And from Justice Thomas: "But there can be no doubt that racial paternalism and its unintended consequences can be as poisonous and pernicious as any other form of discrimination. So-called 'benign' discrimination teaches many that because of chronic and apparently immutable handicaps, minorities cannot compete with them without their patronizing indulgence. Inevitably, such programs engender attitudes of superiority or, alternatively, provoke resentment among those who believe that they have been wronged by the government's use of race. These programs stamp minorities with a badge of inferiority and may cause them to develop dependencies or to adopt an attitude that they are 'entitled' to preferences." (*Adarand Constructors, Inc. v. Peña*, 115 S. Ct. 2097, 2119 [1995]).

All these arguments speak to the importance of inclusion in strengthening particular institutions. There is also the empowerment dimension: inclusion to create the opportunities people need to achieve "their full human potential," as President Clinton put it several times. To illustrate this point, let me use again what, in the White House discussions, we called "the coal miner's daughter hypothetical." Imagine a college admissions committee trying to decide between the white daughter of an Appalachian coal miner's family and the African-American son of a successful Pittsburgh neurosurgeon. Why should the black applicant get preference over the white applicant?

My first response to this is always to challenge the premise: it is a wild distortion to conceive of admissions decisions as ever involving this kind of trade-off. The committee may have hundreds of spaces to fill, and there is no reason to imagine a final decision having to be such a choice—rather than, say, between a tennis player and a swimmer, or a tenor and a poet, or a Montanan and a Sri Lankan. Not only is the hypothetical manipulative (law professors make a fine art of that, after all) but it overlooks the fundamental point about preferences: there are many, many types, and the trade-offs among them are *all* conceptually challenging. Race is no different in that respect.

My second response is that both applicants would get preference if I were on the admissions committee, because I think both applicants would add important and different elements of diversity. Their preferences might not have the same weight; after all, the preference any one candidate receives will depend upon the rest of the pool. Are there already a good number of Appalachians, or women, or minorities, or whatever? But in general, I wouldn't give as much preference to the neurosurgeon's son (or my own) as to an African American with far fewer advantages.

My third response takes the bull by the horns. In America, it remains true that even comparatively advantaged minorities face discrimination and disadvantage when compared with similarly situated whites. I and most minorities would, I'm sure, claim this as a moral certainty, even after factoring in whatever benefits may derive from affirmative action. So there is an argument that additional measures are justified to equalize the opportunities. (This sounds in the remedial vein rather than the inclusionary one; the two are difficult to keep separate.) It is certainly possible to conclude, as I would, that the disparity in opportunity between advantaged whites and blacks, say, is genuine but not deserving of a great deal of focused attention, given other problems. Including that of opportunity in Appalachia.

Finally, I have to get personal. In one Oval Office session, as we discussed the coal miner's daughter, I shot my mouth off. "Mr. President, am I less valuable in this conversation, or on your staff, because I am a second-generation graduate of Harvard Law School and never lived in a public housing project?" (The answer should have been: Yes, I was less valuable but still of *some* value. I phrased my statement poorly.) I continued: "How much does Ron Brown's contribution to your cabinet depend on whether he grew up rich or poor? Don't I bring something to this conversation—some benefit from diversity—notwithstanding my relative advantages?" The point of the coal miner's daughter hypothetical, in my view, is that it sharpens our awareness that several important preferences can and should have different weights in our moral calculus. And the justifications of inclusion and remediation are not neatly separable. As we debate the particulars, context matters.

## *How Much Diversity? The Proportional Representation Problem*

Once we advocate inclusion, it is difficult to define success without using numerical tests, which sound like quotas. Supporters of affirmative action generally avoid the question of how much is enough. When will it be done? I return to this in my concluding chapter, but a few points should be made here.

Removing barriers while effectively enforcing antidiscrimination laws, as proposed in the color-blind Vision I, does not entail a commitment to particular results. That has the virtue of making the goals seem achievable, but the indifference to practical effectiveness deprives us of the social and economic benefits to which the inclusion theme speaks. If we give up the results orientation that numerical tests imply, we weaken our chances of securing those benefits. In the private sector, the importance of setting objectives and measuring performance is such a fundamental management principle that all the literature on the topic has for decades focused solely on *how to do it*, not whether it's worth doing. So, is tracking success different when it comes to progress on race and racial diversity?

Well, yes. It differs inasmuch as managing "by the numbers," in most contexts and with respect to most objectives, risks dampening entrepreneurial energy and organizational flexibility, a risk that is understood to be balanced with the benefits of a sound system of performance measurement and accountability. But when it comes to race and diversity, and managing by the numbers makes for numerical strait-jackets, or quotas, more than a matter of commercial efficiency is at stake. The far weightier matter of moral cost requires us to make sure that inclusion does not inevitably lead to quotas. It is consistent with the notion that preferences have costs and must be flexible to say that inclusion is "soft" and must not be translated into quotas. Ever.

That does not mean that numbers and proportions can be dropped altogether. I have pointed out that the federal government's affirmative action regulations under Executive Order 11246 require most firms doing government work to have numerical benchmarks. The touchstone is not whether a specific goal is achieved but whether the company has used "good-faith efforts." The numerical targets are set after analyzing the relevant labor pool, which of course makes sense because the concern is to detect and prevent discrimination.

Is the same approach appropriate when the goal is inclusion rather than remediation? In the abstract, a given organization should, in setting diversity goals, refer to the expected benefits (and costs). But in practice, we haven't a clue how to measure these benefits and costs directly. Indeed, it presses the analytical envelope just to *characterize* the benefits, much less monitor or quantify them. This is not, any more than the risk of quotas, a reason to give up. But it is another reason why race-conscious pursuit of diversity demands caution, and why the inclusion justification itself deserves weight, though not as much as remedial justifications.

• • •

In this third vision we include the remedial and curative justifications of Vision II and add to them a justification based on more aspirational, empowering concerns. We have reviewed the considerations that suggest inclusion be accorded relatively little weight: its benefits vary substantially depending upon the institution or organization and upon who is benefited by the preference applied; working to achieve inclusion carries with it the risk of managing "by the numbers" in a fashion that moves beyond sound principles of accountability to the unacceptable and illegal territory of quotas based on proportional representation; and diversity is not, in and of itself, a moral value in the same sense that nondiscrimination is. But other factors suggest the importance of inclusion: some institutions simply cannot do their work well unless they are inclusive, and diversity will make many others better. When we look at a large corporation or an urban newsroom, a Navy officers' club or police department or college campus, and see a strange picture of a nonexistent white America, most of us recoil, or at least acknowledge that something is amiss. We aspire to have our institutions move toward a reality of *one* America. Beyond this aspiration, we also acknowledge that people have the chance to achieve their full potential in this country if and only if they have access to certain intermediary institutions and services, chief among these being education. Putting a formal end to discrimination, even discrimination broadly understood, will not in and of itself produce a substantial flow of traditionally disadvantaged persons moving through those doors of opportunity. Moreover, inclusion increases the likelihood of interactive experiences that will change everyone's sense of community and values. Without attention to inclusion, the divisions in our society will persist much longer. Inclusion, or diversity, is consistent with (though not identical to) the moral virtue of tolerance.

My conclusion, and President Clinton's conclusion, is that broad rejection of the diversity rationale for affirmative action is wrong as both a practical matter and a moral principle. The sensible ground here is in the difficult realm of studying the context and carefully balancing the competing tensions. Polemics are easy. Justice is hard.

**6**

# MERIT AND NEED

**B**efore concluding our analysis of the alternative moral frameworks for thinking about affirmative action, I want to address in more detail two overarching conceptual issues in debates about race policy. These are the matter of merit and the alternative of focusing affirmative action on some race-neutral criterion of need—"class, not color; place, not race."

## The Merit Principle

The merit principle is an important American value, one of the principles that distinguish us from other societies and cultures, now and historically, where life, liberty, and happiness were contingent on heredity, caste, and privilege. So the affirmative action argument should carefully assess the contending claims regarding merit. So, it bears mention that preferences based on economic disadvantage would also violate the merit principle. The true issues are how we define merit and how we reconcile competing social goals with it.

The debate is simple enough to state. Adherents of the color-blind vision argue that it has the great virtue of being consistent with the merit principle, while race-based preferences are not. More moderate critics assert that, at the least, race-conscious decision making has in practice seriously harmed the merit principle, which helps fuel the substantial backlash against affirmative action. Proponents of affirmative action argue that it is consistent with merit when done properly and that, in any event, institutions usually have illegitimate conceptions of merit and unsatisfactory mechanisms for ascertaining it, paying little attention to it in general.

The core of the moral claim for the merit principle has, I believe, three elements. First, there is an instrumental argument: by emphasizing merit we maximize efficiency and social welfare. Second is a noninstrumental claim: people are entitled to have decisions about them made on the basis of their personal qualities; *individual* desert counts, rather than social or political conventions tied to group identity. The third combines the two: by emphasizing merit at the individual level we align incentives so as to promote and reinforce both autonomy and personal responsibility. Each of these strikes me as substantially true but perhaps academic, given the actual definitions and functions of merit in America today.

*Realities About Merit.* To begin with, there are few places in American society where a conventionally pure form of merit is used to hire or select people. The process is almost never an analytically rigorous optimization based on measured attributes: we look for "qualified" people or firms, and then use something other than merit to make the ultimate decision. We may choose randomly among qualified candidates, or base our decision on convenience, familiarity, or instinct. The fact is, it is usually too time-consuming and expensive to push the analytical approach all the way to determination of the finalist. The marginal gain in quality is rarely worth the effort. Equally important, we may not have confidence in our definition of merit or our ability to measure it anyway, so why make a fetish of it?

Making a final choice among comparably qualified individuals for subjective or even mysterious reasons is natural and unobjectionable, assuming the selection isn't tainted with obvious racial or other invidious prejudice. But we shouldn't confuse this with rigorous systems of pure merit. They are not. Modifying such "fuzzy" systems to include justified, narrowly tailored affirmative action is perhaps not so ethically objectionable as modifying those rare selection mechanisms that are truly based on merit.

In particular, not many hiring decisions are made exclusively on the basis of test scores. There's a lot of discussion and debate about litigation in police and fire department cases in which a civil service examination is thrown out or reduced in significance in order to accommodate the need for remedying discrimination or building a more diverse organization. What's interesting is that those exams were mostly introduced decades ago as a progressive reform intended to eliminate the stranglehold of patronage, cronyism, and nepotism on city bureaucracies. There were never heroic claims that the tests perfectly predicted a person's performance on the job or would overall improve the workforce or the performance of the organization. It is very inaccurate to treat tests as though they were the whole of a carefully honed meritocratic system of hiring or promotion. It is more sensible to view them as one stage in a gradual evolution of selection mechanisms, representing a particular managerial and perhaps ideological response to the social problems of personnel abuses in that day. But challenges change, and selection systems should evolve just as other social institutions must.

*True, Whole Merit—with Reference to the Organization's Needs.* When decision makers purport to make their choices on the basis of merit, how do they define merit? Important cases in employment discrimination law have shown us that once accepted job qualifications (a height requirement for firefighters, for example) had the effect of excluding statutorily protected groups (in the example, women). The employer could, of course, defend the job qualification by demonstrating that it was reasonably related to job performance. But it turned out that many questions about the predictive value of job tests and qualifications had not been asked before and were hard to answer with empirical confidence. To put it more precisely, the screens employers used in many situations could not, upon examination, be shown to be justified by any rigorous connection to what was really required to perform well in the job.

On one level, this is a pretty significant conclusion. For example, we discuss the value of LSAT scores and undergraduate GPA in predicting performance at Harvard Law School. Of course, there isn't much hard evidence that "validates" a Harvard legal education itself. What real proof do we faculty have that what we teach actually makes people better lawyers than they would be with some other preparation? There is ambivalence in the admissions process. Are we selecting applicants who we predict will be good law *students* or good *lawyers*? Can we be sure they're the same? Since decisions must be made, we don't let ourselves be too troubled by these imponderables. Essentially, we do things by habit, despite the absence of any rigorous justification for those habits. (In practice, Harvard empirically "validates" a weighted index of LSAT and institution-adjusted GPA by reference to performance on first-year exams: embarrassing, but true. Then we claim to teach students how to "think like lawyers," when we mostly teach them to think like law professors.)

In private-sector hiring and promotion decisions, much the same seems to be true. Title VII employment discrimination law has warned many big companies not to rely habitually on tests and other selection devices that cannot be justified as job-related. That is a healthy discipline which, ironically, *has served to promote fidelity to the merit principle.* For decades, lots of white men who on the merits would have made perfectly fine police officers or civil servants nevertheless failed exams which tested for things having little to do with likely success on the job; this was unfair to those qualified men. What changed is that Title VII made such unfairness subject to legal scrutiny insofar as the unfairness systematically burdened a group protected by the statute.

All of this goes to the question of whether "merit" is truly defined with reference to what it takes to do the job, rather than something else. And bound up in this is the importance of thinking carefully about what the job really is. For example, there is much talk about the steady transformation of blue-collar manufacturing jobs in ways that will increasingly require workers to cope with complex technology, periodically learn new skills, participate in problem-solving teams, and so

*[margin annotation:]* see case of cheating Aramen (white)

forth. Old ideas about job qualifications must be updated. Even without this kind of sharp transformation, however, hiring habits may simply mistake the nature of the organization's needs.

This is pretty conventional stuff. The larger problem is that in so many situations the attractiveness of an individual applicant depends not only on that person's characteristics but also on the mix of people in the organization and how they contribute collectively to its needs. (The orchestra example.) Merit must be a *whole* concept related both to the context and to the individual. Merit should matter, of course. But it should be true merit, and whole merit.

*Reconciling Race-Conscious and Meritocratic Decision Making.* No doubt some personnel managers hire "by the numbers," converting what should be a flexible policy goal into a numerical straitjacket. When they do so, it is illegal, though perhaps difficult to detect and remedy. (This is the flip side of what I said earlier: that enforcement of antidiscrimination laws is not effective at detecting and remedying discrimination. You have to decide which of the complementary enforcement problems is more troubling, morally and practically.) Hiring by the numbers is also wrong because it is inconsistent with the merit principle. That is, both discrimination and reverse discrimination run afoul of the merit principle.

Still, when affirmative action is done the right way, it is consistent with, and part of, true merit. How so? Both the Constitution and the civil rights statutes, as interpreted by the Supreme Court, require that affirmative action be flexible. That means, among other things, that, except in very narrow court-ordered remedial circumstances of a last-resort nature, any affirmative action program must consider race flexibly, as one of several factors, and numerical goals must be true goals, rather than quotas. The merit principle is protected because the decision makers are able to make judgments about how the organization's affirmative action goals can be made consistent with other needs—i.e., incorporated within the true, whole conception of merit. Indeed, the law *requires* them to decide in this manner.

Race aside, there is nothing unique or even unusual about this process. Companies or universities pursue multiple objectives when they make hiring, promotion, or admissions decisions. The decision maker makes trade-offs designed, in the aggregate, to produce the best portfolio of outcomes. There are few howls about merit when it comes to college preferences for alumni or musicians or would-be social workers. Somehow "merit" can be stretched to encompass those preferences. Race is different, it seems. And by now, the reader knows that the question of *why* race is different is the very heart of the debate. (And a subject for my two final chapters.)

My own view—supported by evidence from sources such as the 1995 Glass Ceiling Commission and the statistics from administrative and judicial litigation—is that organizations and managers all too often fall far short of the good-faith efforts needed for worthwhile affirmative action programs. Yet the very rare cases of abuse—of overly zealous affirmative action—get the attention. How do such abuses arise? Put to one side the (very!) isolated instances when a personnel manager, say, feels so zealously committed to increasing the numbers of minorities that he or she insistently and decisively subordinates all other institutional goals, and merit goes by the board. Of more interest are reasonable managers who believe that the incentive structure they face will reward attention to affirmative action but is unlikely to punish inattention to the other goals. This clearly creates some structural risks of abuse, for incentives must be balanced, and the training of personnel officers and other decision makers must be effective.

We can also look at this from an economic or mathematical perspective, as a colleague and mentor, Richard Zeckhauser of Harvard's Kennedy School of Government, has suggested to me. (And here I lapse into a bit of economics jargon, perhaps unfamiliar to some of my readers.) If we think of an institution's competing desires as elements of an objective function, the trade-offs made to achieve them can be considered in terms of the shadow prices of one variable with respect to others. That is, one can ask how much, at the margin, an additional person with qualities in dimension X will "cost" in terms of sacrificed benefits in dimensions Y and Z. Let's say we're focused (why?) on the median SAT score of an entering freshman class; we might ask how much the median score changes if we admit one more student from Idaho, or from a minority group, or from a coach's "wish list." It makes analytical sense for decision makers to have at least a general sense of the magnitudes of these trade-offs and to ensure that the decision mechanisms are transparent enough to allow the consequences of choices (or priorities or preferences) to be assessed with reference to the multiple goals of the organization, including antidiscrimination and inclusion. If we don't understand the trade-offs—the shadow prices— in at least general terms, then the risks of abuse rise, abuse in the sense of subverting the goal of optimizing the objective function, which is itself the embodiment of a "whole" conception of merit. That's the case for being explicit.

Switching planets again, consider this analogy: tariffs are the traditional prescription of economists and free traders when a nation unwisely *insists* on barriers to competition. The transparency of tariffs makes them an easier target for analysis and policy reform, while a jumble of institutional, regulatory, and other nontariff trade barriers can be inscrutable. The effects on prices and economic efficiency of a tariff, subsidy, or even quota are simpler to evaluate than something like a convoluted wholesale distribution system that mysteriously cuts out competition from foreign goods.

Back in the race context, we can compare different preference mechanisms in a similar way. Set-asides, or reserved slots, are not quite so transparent (as regards their costs to other goals) as an explicitly quantified "thumb on the scale"—a 10 percent contract price bid preference, say, or an SAT "adjustment." On the other hand, a set-aside is more transparent than a vague and subjective decision process in which race is a factor of unspecified weight—unspecified in part because the decision process doesn't operate by attaching "weights" to the variables in the first place. That's the essence of the vagueness, the subjectivity.

This leads us to the tentative conclusion that an organization is more likely to succeed at integrating traditional notions of merit with remediation or diversity if the racial preference is expressed transparently, so that any trade-off—there may be none—can be watched. But I see three very, very large problems here. First, the analytical paradigm has its own dangers: excessive attention to quantification distorts the picture by overemphasizing the factors that are amenable to such calculations, while subtler benefits (and costs) may get short shrift.

Think about college admissions. We have numerical test scores but no numerical measures for the benefits of having a diverse student body or for the postgraduation "success" of different "types" of student. In the rush to "analyze" there are gross simplifications and, perhaps, grotesque distortions. *True* merit suffers.

Second, there is no enthusiasm for this elaborate kind of analysis as a general practice. When we come to affirmative action, the "hassle factor" suddenly goes way up. We don't get books from conservative think tanks about the SAT gap for children of alumni or applicants from the boondocks, though principled economists would say we should. Maybe it's an indication of the American truism that race is different. But there are some unattractive interpretations too.

Third, transparency has social and political *costs*, not just benefits. Free traders want trade barriers reduced to the more understandable character of tariffs not just to analyze their impact but also to stir reform sentiment and focus the terms of trade negotiations. The favored transparency of tariffs is intended as an irritant to the undesirable status quo—and the resulting controversy can be divisive. Ultimately, of course, the status quo may be confirmed and sustained if there is steady majority support. But the controversy has a price, and divisiveness takes its toll. In race matters, the price may be too high to justify the supposed benefits of transparency anyway. I say "too high" because I fear the polarization that would likely accompany any faculty debate on initiating a formal LSAT score "bonus" for disabled women residing in depressed rural counties, say, or for inner-city African Americans. Hard-line opponents of affirmative action might feel differently. One reason: controversial, divisive transparency raises the cost of pursuing affirmative action. It's not a neutral analytical move.

So we have several possibilities for reconciling merit and preferences, some of which can be combined:

- We can reconsider the established notion of merit, and revise it if necessary to reflect the organization's mission and needs completely and accurately.

- We can clarify the factors involved in hiring, promotion, admissions, or other decisions, and indeed have a way within the organization to illuminate the trade-offs and ensure that they express a considered judgment (or consensus, if that is the culture).
- We can make all the elements of the decision process, including, but not only, any race-based preferences, as transparent as possible. *But* such transparency must be pursued with appropriate sensitivity to both benefits and costs, especially the costs of divisiveness.
- In designing an affirmative action program we can have narrowly defined criteria for "short-listing" someone or for choosing among comparably qualified individuals. "Comparably qualified" means just that, and the degree of precision in "comparably" depends on circumstances.
- Qualifications that are sham devices to exclude count for nothing. Qualifications not reasonably related to the work mean nothing. And when "merits" are vague, the selection process highly subjective, and the history suggests exclusion, it is especially important to define "qualified" in an inclusionary way.
- Merit is not an absolute but in every essential sense a social and perhaps political construct. Some writers call it an "ideology," since it has power as an organizing idea and expression of values. In my view, the principle of true, whole merit is indeed valuable and significant, but it stands beside other significant ideas, including the remediation of racial injustices, the achievement of morally equal opportunity, the creation of an inclusive community and nation, and other national ideals as well. None of these should drive out the others; each must be balanced and reconciled. This is not to say, in some mechanically relativist way, that all ideals are equally important. But it makes little sense to suppose that one ideal—be it merit, or even racial justice—dominates all the others in all situations.

Once again, therefore, trying to reason it through has led me to reject absolutes and offer a prescription for balance, for attention to context, and for attention to the process of reflection by which organizations and communities consider value trade-offs.

## *Race-Neutral Affirmative Action*

Only a very rare person opposes absolutely *all* preferences; opposition focuses on *race-conscious* measures. On the other hand, supporters of affirmative action can believe (consistent with either Vision II or Vision III) that the inevitable moral cost to race-conscious decision making should be minimized without allowing unacceptable losses. Therefore, when opponents and proponents search for common ground, they often think they may find it in preferences based on geography or socio-economic class. Hard opponents insist on replacing *all* race-based preferences, while affirmative action supporters acknowledge that in some situations a race-neutral alternative may make sense. After all, we know there is a correlation in the United States between race and measures of poverty, including geographic concentration of poverty. Preferences based on class and place are therefore only seemingly ("racially") neutral with respect to race because, to use Title VII language, they have a decidedly disparate impact. Ironically, some of the same conservatives who oppose using disparate-impact analysis to establish employment or other discrimination (burdening blacks) are willing to *construct* policies with *intentionally* disparate impacts (burdening whites) in order to replace race-based affirmative action. (Supreme Court Justice Robert Jackson, dissenting in a famous administrative law case, said in criticizing a twisted majority opinion: "I give up. Now I realize fully what Mark Twain meant when he said, 'The more you explain it, the more I don't understand it.' " Exactly.)

Discussions of race-neutral measures frequently make one of two errors: the error from the right, neglecting to consider dilution and other issues of effectiveness; and the error from the left, neglecting to consider that sometimes these measures are a sensible, reasonable concession to the moral cost of race-based decision making. The first error bespeaks inattention to, or lack of concern for, the need to effectively close the opportunity gap. The second error bespeaks lack of concern for the moral and political consequences of treating race as though it were no more problematical than geography or income—to me, a patently wrong view.

The advantages of seemingly neutral approaches are obvious. They sharply reduce the moral cost associated with race-based decision making—although an intentionally disparate impact seems to me to carry at least some moral cost, not generally acknowledged. The tensions and conflicts around the scope of remedial justifications are put aside by—well, by ignoring the idea of remedy entirely and focusing instead on the social welfare idea of opportunity-enhancing investments. While social welfare programs have their own political baggage and ideological controversies (for some other book), at least the battles are not so directly about the great problem of race. On the other hand, class- and place-based alternatives share five problems: dilution, over-inclusion, underinclusion, disingenuousness, and the retrenchment in social welfare policy.

*Dilution.* Class-based and geography-based measures intended to narrow the opportunity gap for African Americans would be over-inclusive and would dilute the effectiveness of our limited public resources. True, programs targeted on the poorest classes would disproportionately benefit minorities, but as I have observed before, there are more poor white people than poor black people, and in absolute dollar terms, a fixed amount of resources or opportunities will be available to many fewer blacks if we substitute race-neutral criteria.

This objection is of no serious concern to those who hold to the color-blind framework, because for them pragmatic factors like effectiveness are obliterated by the uncompromising moral view that race-conscious decision making has a moral cost too high to be paid, ever. In the framework focusing on equal opportunity plus antidiscrimination, pragmatic concerns have standing, and so the diminished effectiveness of race-neutral measures must be considered. It isn't all or nothing: in some situations, the loss of effectiveness would be a reasonable price to pay, given the moral and political benefits of avoiding race-conscious measures—it depends on the context, and on the very process by which the measures (race-conscious or otherwise) are developed. As I will argue later, the moral costs associated with any scheme are partly a function of who has had a voice in shaping it and through what process.

*Overinclusion.* A facially race-neutral preference will include people who in some sense don't deserve the preference. (I don't mean nonminorities; the whole point, after all, is to make it extend to nonminorities.) Overinclusiveness comes in at least three varieties. First, the measures of need may be imprecise—in assessing family resources in need-based college admissions, for example. Second, we may want to attend to "need" that comes from some hard-to-define, difficult-to-measure disadvantage, but elusive social or historical considerations may not lend themselves to policy rules. Third, our definition of need may be qualified by moral judgment—liberals sarcastically used the phrase "deserving poor" to disparage the moralistic welfare reformers who believe that aid given to the poor should be contingent on the recipient's worthiness. For example, the themes of personal responsibility and self-help will still make preferences controversial. For all these reasons, if you use "need" as the basis for a preference, you have controversy over definition and implementation.

As for place-based preferences, the obvious difficulty of overinclusion is simply that geography works as a proxy for socioeconomic disadvantage only because the poor tend to be geographically segregated, or concentrated. Indeed, this pattern has been increasing in recent years. But no matter how tight the screen used to select communities, not all the included residents will in fact be disadvantaged.

*Underinclusion.* Race-neutral approaches alone do nothing to address the fact that African Americans outside a targeted class or locale, although better off than those who are poor or living in areas of concentrated poverty, are nonetheless disadvantaged relative to similarly situated whites, and still face various forms of discrimination and exclusion. Many whites in elite or professional circles where strong taboos prohibit overt discrimination or expressions of prejudice, voice disbelief that blacks who have "made it" are still disadvantaged on the basis of race. Sure, they accept the truth of the now familiar stories about professional black men unable to hail taxicabs (yes, me too), but anything more substantial seems to them surprising or even implausible. This is just one sign of the perception gap between whites and blacks. Every black professional I've ever discussed this issue with has felt the burden of race in a host of subtle, intangible ways and also in very pointed, clear ways. Even those of us who readily acknowledge that affirmative action has been beneficial for us have also felt the sting of "otherness" and even of prejudice. The question is not whether someone has "made it." The question is what they might have achieved but for the burden of race.

Putting this problem of a perception gap to one side, one might still discount the argument about underinclusion by saying that the diminution in opportunity suffered by comparatively successful blacks is just not substantial or tragic enough to worry about. That is an understandable conclusion, either morally (the cost of race-based remedies) or politically (why expend limited capital on this particular element of the racial justice agenda). But it is a mistake to reach it without acknowledging it as a *choice*: a choice to discount or dismiss the just claims of a subgroup of Americans in the belief that there are higher priorities and limited resources.

Glenn Loury, of Boston University, is among the prominent conservatives arguing that this choice is more often than not made implicitly by elite blacks who predictably overvalue the justness of their own claims. Loury believes we have squandered a vastly disproportionate amount of political and other resources on affirmative action schemes that benefit this group, while other items on the racial-justice agenda more likely to benefit the underclass have gone begging for attention.

I see a kernel of truth in this, but much of it is wide of the mark. To be sure, the danger of leadership elites setting self-interested priorities is ever present. White folks have the same problem. And certainly there have been serious abuses: I think of meetings I've had over the years with black business leaders who were unabashed in their overt, grasping claims for government assistance and a "fair share," which they simplistically equated with "justice." But most leaders and most organizations have had more complex agendas, and made strategic judgments over time about what to emphasize and what to defend. It paints with too broad a brush to imply that the NAACP agenda should be indistinguishable from that of an antipoverty organization. Agenda setting is more complicated than that.

Taking together the risks of dilution, overinclusion, and underinclusion, I am reminded of an exercise we went through when I served on the White House Domestic Policy Staff in the Carter administration. After the President's comprehensive welfare reform package had been declared dead, we put togher a modest incremental plan which, among other concessions to fiscal and political realities, replaced a job or training "guarantee" for eligible welfare recipients with a thinner, underinclusive program that simply would not cover the number of people for whom we wanted to offer a clear path from the welfare rolls to the job rolls. With the gallows humor of people devoted to a dying cause, we joked about this as a "guaranteed job *opportunity*," in the sense that a lottery ticket is a guaranteed opportunity to win the jackpot. Offering diluted or poorly targeted measures as a dodge is a fiscal concern, but it is a moral concern, too. In many contexts.

*Disingenuousness.* Which brings us to the simple problem of honesty. It might be possible, in some situations, to replace a racial preference with a carefully worded, complex kind of Rube Goldberg preference, race-neutral but narrow enough to be as well targeted as a racial preference. A White House colleague suggested, for example, that the University of Pennsylvania might consider giving undergraduate admissions preference to low-income graduates of Philadelphia public high schools. One objection to such a policy would be its absence of candor in stating and defending its intention to benefit minorities. Everyone is diminished by this lack of candor, as is our civic culture. Apart from substantial legal problems, there are times when it makes sense to tell it like it is, and defend a policy on the basis of the values and vision motivating it.

*Dead-End Welfare Agenda.* There are many important policy justifications for having social welfare and other measures targeted on the basis of class or geography, but most of them have nothing to do with racial justice. I'm all in favor of antipoverty efforts of many sorts, passionately so. But relying on them to close the racial opportunity gap is in large measure exactly what we have done, and it hasn't worked.

Moreover, American politics have shifted away from the altruism of the Great Society, the War on Poverty, and even the New Deal. It would be ahistorical to imagine that this turn away from social welfare liberalism is temporary or out of character. A better reading of American history would reveal that our moments of compassionate public investment have been so noteworthy because they have been so exceptional. We are not so good a people as I would like to believe—another example of the lack of connection between the values we espouse and the values we live.

Another reason to be cautious about class-based social welfare alternatives is that, as conservatives continuously remind us, the record of success or effectiveness is mixed. Their criticisms are usually excessive, for poverty *has* been reduced from what it would otherwise be by Social Security; cuts in Aid to Families with Dependent Children *do* swell the ranks of the homeless; the educational achievements of many Americans *have* grown as a result of Head Start and Title I; infant mortality and morbidity *have* declined as a result of nutrition programs; life expectancy and productivity *have* improved as a result of expanding access to health care; and so on. That said, the isolated success stories—from education to welfare-to-work transitions, to substance abuse programs—have yet to be translated into effective national strategies, broad in scope and deep in reach. If race-based measures have something to contribute, it is certainly needed.

Lastly, the underfunding and unsatisfactory performance of these social welfare programs will hardly be helped by adding "racial justice" to the list of justifications for them. Indeed, quite the contrary, given the politics of race.

Deciding on the seriousness of these five drawbacks depends on the context, of course, and on the weight you accord the various under- and overincluded subgroups. A good way to understand this is to return to the coal miner's daughter: should there be a college admissions preference for the well-to-do black son of a Pittsburgh neurosurgeon as against the white daughter of an Appalachian coal miner? A preference based on place or economic need would not reach the black applicant. How concerned are we about leaving him out? In part your answer turns on whether you agree with most African Americans that the race problem will burden the young man in comparison to comparably situated whites, and that institutions and society will benefit from a broader inclusiveness brought about with the aid of affirmative action. And in part it turns on how important you believe it is to remedy or offset that burden, how weighty the benefits of inclusion to the college are as regards this individual. Instead, suppose we have a race-conscious preference benefiting the black son and excluding the white Appalachian daughter. If race is used as a proxy for need, then it is underinclusive as regards the girl and overinclusive as regards the boy. How we might feel about this depends upon what else is going on. Why isn't there a separate preference for poor people or for residents of distressed regions? How substantial are the diversity benefits from including the black? I believe that while such questions deserve a national conversation, they *require* careful consideration and decision in light of the context, and that careful process must take place in organizations and communities throughout the country.

To sum up, moving to facially race-neutral preferences involves several conclusions:

- We must abandon the remedial goals of affirmative action, since the neutral preferences are not designed to combat or prevent discrimination or its lingering effects.
- We must accept the inevitable dilution of resources, either because we calculate it to be acceptable in the circumstances or because we don't care that much about effectiveness anyway.
- We must accept levels of under- and overinclusion, since we are attaching greater moral or political weights to the groups who are made better off by the "reform" than we do to those who are made worse off.

If these aren't troubling enough, there is a fundamental moral problem for adherents of color blindness who offer race-neutral appeasement. To the extent that we propose and design race-neutral measures to substitute as closely as possible for race-based measures—with demographics and projections to ensure that "enough" benefits continue for minorities—have we not taken on much the same moral burden as race-based measures have? This is certainly true from the absolutist position of the color-blind vision, because we would be considering race as we test the acceptability of the substitute measure. But more generally, *we cannot believe that the ultimate moral calculus is different because motives are unspoken and costs disguised.* Indeed, judges who purport to demand color blindness would be required by their principles to strike down as intentional discrimination any public or private measure, race-neutral on its face, if its designers purposefully used race as even one of several flexible factors just in the design, not even in the actual operation of the scheme. (Thus, perhaps racial diversity could be a goal, but you would be forbidden to take any steps specifically intended to advance that race-based goal, even using proxy variables.) This is unthinkably sweeping, even Kafkaesque. But we come to this only by using a moral and doctrinal framework, the color-blind one, that fails to acknowledge the possibility of distinguishing between benign and invidious attention to race.

If nothing else, this discussion indicates that moving to race-neutral preferences is far from costless, and it is impossible to come to sweeping conclusions about when such preferences make sense. It is not *the* remedy. Unless, of course, you just ignore the hard questions.

As we saw in Chapter 1, the Supreme Court's rulings in *Croson* and *Adarand* require that race-based affirmative action measures taken by federal, state, and local governments must be "narrowly tailored" to achieve a "compelling governmental interest." For private decision makers, the case law interpreting Title VII and other civil rights statutes commands that voluntary affirmative action measures not "unnecessarily trammel" the interests of nonbeneficiaries. Both tests— "narrow tailoring" and "unnecessarily trammel"—ask us to assess whether race-neutral measures would be adequate substitutes for racial preferences; neither requires that these actually be tried and proven unsuccessful. But as litigation develops in the wake of *Adarand*, and if reverse-discrimination plaintiffs are emboldened by the political stirrings of forces opposed to affirmative action, we can expect increasing pressure on those who favor affirmative action to show they've done their homework by analyzing the race-neutral alternatives.

A certain amount of this pressure is healthy, I believe. That is because, in both Visions II and III, we acknowledge that there is some moral cost to race-conscious decision making, and public and private policy makers should make reasonable efforts to minimize it. The difficulty is that several hundred trial judges around the country are charged with applying the tests, and we cannot know how burdensome the evidentiary standards will be. When data are unavailable about the effects of various preference systems, how will judges respond? Will they allow time for research? Will they insist that the proponent of affirmative action persuade the court that the race-neutral measure would be "substantially" inferior? What standards will courts use in making such judgments? There are countless imponderables here, and much—too much—depends on the vagaries of the law. With reason, lawyers themselves often refer to litigation as a lottery.

We would do well, therefore, to put the matter of courts, laws, and litigation to one side. We should focus instead on deciding what we believe to be right, for any given institution and set of circumstances. And that is surely a hard enough undertaking.

# 7

# DESIGNING AFFIRMATIVE ACTION MEASURES

The alternative moral frameworks that support some forms of affirmative action recognize important limiting principles. In practice, how should preferences be designed so as to honor those limiting principles?

## *Careful Justification and Tailoring*

The story thus far has led us to conclude that race-based preferences have a moral cost, and therefore must be (1) carefully justified and (2) tailored in means and duration to fit that justification. In public-sector efforts, the justification must be found in some "compelling governmental interest," and the means chosen must be "narrowly tailored" to the pursuit of that interest—so the Supreme Court has ruled in interpreting the equal protection clause of the Fourteenth Amendment. In the private sector, Title VII of the Civil Rights Act requires that employers using voluntary affirmative action are within the law if the measure can be justified by pointing to a "manifest imbalance" in representation, and the measure adopted does not "unnecessarily trammel" the interests of otherwise unaffected people—i.e., bystanders. Similar legal principles apply in other private contexts.

Now, we must explore not only the subtler implications of the *legal* norms but also the related though not identical norms to which our values and moral considerations might point. These considerations are infra-legal in the sense that they are interior to and more nuanced than sweeping laws; they are meta-legal in the sense that they may suggest the larger influences that shape how we develop and interpret law.

The overarching point is simple enough to state. Because the moderate approaches represented by Visions II and III recognize that there are benefits to affirmative action as well as costs to race-conscious decision making, it follows that our judgment about the acceptability of a particular measure will be somehow affected by a comparison of the nature and magnitude of those benefits and costs. I don't mean that we should do a mechanical cost-benefit analysis of the sort at issue in the great debates over regulatory reform and risk assessment. I simply mean that it is not all black and white. *Context matters* in many systematic ways. If a rather thin justification for a measure offers small benefits in a given context, then the tailoring must be careful enough to keep costs down. Here are some schematic examples:

- A college wants some form of admissions preference so as to have a more diverse student body, which, it believes, will improve the quality of the education it offers. *Versus:* A college wants to have some form of preference so as to purge itself of the present, lingering effects of discrimination in its not too distant past.
- A manufacturer of machine tools wants diversity in its workforce. *Versus:* A city police department wants diversity in its patrol force roughly corresponding to the diversity of the community it seeks to serve.
- A municipality wants to use preferences when it awards contracts to private firms in order to enhance the opportunities for entrepreneurship available to minorities in the community. *Versus:* A municipality wants to use contracting preferences in order to remedy its own history of discrimination in the awarding of contracts.
- The Federal Communications Commission (FCC), citing the

importance of opening up entrepreneurial opportunity to
groups underrepresented in telecommunications, wants to use
preferences to ensure that a racially diverse group of companies will be able to compete to win licenses for so-called personal communications services (PCS) in auctions of newly
available portions of the spectrum. (PCS applications are advanced, nonbroadcast applications for cellular telephone, pag-
ing, and the like.) *Versus:* The FCC, citing First Amendment
values of expression in the marketplace of ideas, wants to use
preferences to ensure that a diverse group of owners hold licenses for radio and television broadcasting.

People will differ about which of these alternatives cross the
threshold of acceptability. My own sense is that, whether one has
adopted Vision I, II, or III, the second example in each pair presents
the weightier justification for affirmative action because of simple intuitions about the nature and magnitude of the benefits.

By the same token, we have certain intuitions concerning tailoring
of specific measures. Consider:

- A mortgage lender offers a favorable package to all minorities
  in the city, regardless of neighborhood or history of previous
  loan application. *Versus:* The same mortgage lender offers a
  special package of favorable loan terms only to blacks whom
  it had turned down under a now abandoned practice verging
  on redlining.
- A college provides an admissions "plus factor" to any academically qualified minority applicant. *Versus:* A college applies a flexible "plus factor" with increased weight for
  minority applicants who come from poor families, or who are
  first-generation college-goers, or who come from hypersegre-
  gated poor communities.
- A city police department with no history of discrimination
  gives a hiring preference to all Latino applicants. *Versus:* The
  department gives preference only to Spanish-speaking Lati-

nos and only for positions that require contact with the public or involve making policy.

- An employer with a manifest imbalance in the makeup of its workforce uses weak preferences to increase and maintain the number of minorities; the preferences apply to recruitment, hiring, promotion, and layoffs. *Versus:* The employer gives preferences only in recruitment and hiring, uses them selectively in promotion, and not in layoffs.

Again, in each pair the costs associated with the second approach seem less, and there may or may not be a substantial difference in the level of benefits. And if the cost is low enough, it may not seem so important to have a strong justification. The examples further suggest the impossibility of imposing flat rules about what kind of tailoring should be required, or even what specific design wrinkles must be analyzed. Having moved away from the stark absolutism of Vision I to embrace the rich interplay of multiple values, the decisions are as complicated as life itself. Still, there may be some themes to guide the weighing of costs and benefits. Let me suggest three possibilities.

*Purpose v. Scope.* We can decide on a rough order of the most compelling justifications for affirmative action and the least costly forms of remedial targeting. The accompanying chart goes from narrow remediation for proven acts of discrimination to a general plan for racial inclusion or diversity. I believe with all my heart that all of them offer substantial benefits that justify both public and private race-conscious affirmative action, and I suspect that people disagreeing with me might nevertheless acknowledge that the ranking makes sense.

Along the horizontal axis the costs of over- and underinclusivity, and of spillovers, seem to increase as the affirmative action measure broadens the class of intended beneficiaries from identifiable victims of discrimination to the larger class of those who stand in the same shoes as the would-be victim, finally to all African Americans—the group membership as a whole. The best place to be on this matrix, other things being equal, is in the upper left corner. The most controversial place is the bottom right corner. (Other considerations would

## TAILORING AFFIRMATIVE ACTION: BENEFITS OF JUSTIFICATION AND COSTS OF REMEDY

| *PURPOSE OR SCOPE* | IDENTIFIED VICTIMS | VICTIM CLASS | OVERALL GROUP |
|---|---|---|---|
| NARROW REMEDIATION | the strongest case: specific wrongful acts and individual victims can be identified | wrongful acts are not clear, but it's not possible to identify all (or any) individual victims; relief given for a class of would-be victims | no causal link; wrongdoer contributes for a general social purpose; beneficiary group is overinclusive as regards remedial goal |
| BROAD REMEDIATION | plenty of evident disparity, and a prima facie case of wrongful conduct or at least manifest imbalance | require opportunities to be open without identified victims; include those hypothetically likely to have suffered; emphasize prevention | no effort to target beyond simple group membership; no "subdifferentiation" regarding risk of discrimination, or disadvantage |
| SOCIAL REMEDIATION AND MORALLY EQUAL OPPORTUNITY | targeted on identified sufferers of race-linked disadvantages—smoking gun required; e.g., graduates of segregated schools, residents of hypersegregated areas | strong focus on those with socioeconomic disadvantage, especially that traceable to discrimination, racial caste, segregated patterns in society | race used as a proxy for dis-advantage in general and overall denial of morally equal opportunity; even successful blacks are comparatively disadvantaged |
| INCLUSION, DIVERSITY | victim status not relevant, because the justification is nonremedial; but diversity is less compelling than remediation | no illegal discrimination, but the underrepresentation of this class—the class that's "out"—weakens the organization | most controversial: race used as proxy for diversity; group-based measures without need-based tailoring; risks overinclusion |

in certain situations encourage me to defend a program in that corner—
for judicial selections, say, or minority elementary school teachers. But
I admit I have more work cut out for me there.)

*Opportunity v. Results.* Another, complementary approach emphasizes the familiar theme of providing opportunity, not guaranteeing
results. That homily ought to have lots of qualifications, including the
conceptual confusion of the distinction itself, but it nevertheless expresses powerful values of our civic culture. Robert Penn Warren, in
his famous interviews with Southerners following *Brown v. Board of
Education*, asked, "What does the Negro want?" A black store owner
suggested, "It's opportunity a man wants. . . . Just to get along and
make out. You know, like anybody."

How does the opportunity-results distinction apply here? As we
worked through the major themes during the White House discussions
on affirmative action, we arrived at a general consensus that programs
in education were the most important and most easily defended, that
policies in government contracting and business opportunities were
less likely to engender broad public support, and that employment
programs were somewhere in between. Intuitively, this ranking seemed
to correspond to the spectrum that runs from programs stressing opportunity to those stressing results:

- Education and investment in it are the very heart of America's opportunity engine—we take that as an article of faith,
  and there is a fair amount of evidence to confirm it. Affirmative action in education expresses and reinforces our commitment to the American opportunity ideal.
- Having a job is certainly the bedrock of economic security for
  families and communities. If being educated opens doors,
  then getting hired is walking through the door. The job is in
  one sense a "result" of what you've already done, but in a
  perhaps more substantial sense, being hired simply gives you
  a new opportunity to prove yourself, to succeed, and to advance. There is no guarantee that you will keep the job or
  move up the ladder of prosperity.
- Finally, to "give" a businessman a $1 million government con-

tract with a 5 percent profit margin is to give him an "opportunity" to become a more successful entrepreneur, but in another sense it is like handing him a sack with $50,000 in it. That's an opportunity to go on and make even more money, but it is also $50,000 of "results."

So, though I don't claim analytical purity for this ordering, the opportunity-results spectrum offers one account for the intuition we have that the justification for affirmative action becomes weightier as one moves from entrepreneurship to employment to education. (We could explore the location of other concerns along the spectrum—access to health care, participation in cultural institutions, and so on. Trying to do so triggers interesting debates about context, and about the determinants of morally equal opportunity.)

The various tools of affirmative action can also be ranked along the opportunity-results spectrum, which we presented to the President in a chart. Outreach and recruitment are at one end, with set-asides and quotas at the other. Quotas, to reiterate, are illegal because of their rigidity and the sharp threat they pose to other values, such as merit. (In contrast, a more flexible system of race-conscious goals might be a means of discovering merit within people whose full talents would otherwise not have an opportunity to develop or be discovered.) But we can also see that a quota is more like a guaranteed result—at least for the group, though not the individual—and measures that fall just short of a quota which have this result-like nature are to varying degrees morally and politically problematical for similar reasons.

Once again, the upper left corner shows us the least controversial programs and the lower right the most controversial ones. Leaving aside the far right column of "quotas," we have the question whether to separate acceptable from unacceptable measures by a vertical line or a diagonal one running from upper right to lower left. I am convinced that much of the political and moral argument over specific affirmative action measures can be understood in terms of his opportunity-results grid; we can then better appreciate the relatively controversial nature of contracting set-asides, say, and the near-universal support for college recruitment programs.

# AFFIRMATIVE ACTION: OPPORTUNITY VERSUS RESULTS FRAMEWORK*

*Comparing the Case for Different Race-Conscious Mechanisms, Across Different Policy Contexts*

"Opportunity" → → → → → → → → → "Results"

| | OPPORTUNITY-ENHANCING ASSISTANCE | ADVANTAGES AND PREFERENCES | SET-ASIDES | QUOTAS (ILLEGAL) |
|---|---|---|---|---|
| **EDUCATION** | compensatory education; outreach and recruitment; historically black colleges and universities [HBCUs] | multifactor college admissions policies | group-based scholarship and training programs; e.g., NIH minority fellows | two-track admissions programs (as struck down in *Bakke*) |
| **EMPLOYMENT** | outreach and recruiting; apprenticeships; "second look" programs, e.g. the military | multifactor hiring; e.g., Clinton judicial nominations; Chicago police | exclusive job listings; anecdotes from university faculty hiring** | race-normed tests to ensure proportional representation |
| **GOVERNMENT CONTRACTING/ PROCUREMENT** | technical assistance; firm-to-firm mentoring; assistance in financing performance bonds | 10% bid price preferences; "subcontractor compensation clause"; *Adarand*-type programs | SBA § 8(a) program of sole-source contracting; "rule-of-two sheltered competition set-asides** | none authorized by statute; practices are under detailed Justice review |

\* Adapted from a chart prepared by Peter Yu.

\*\* These programs present very substantial legal problems, particularly in light of *Adarand*.

*Process and Preciseness.* A third way to think about the interaction of justification and narrow tailoring is to consider the sophistication of the process and the precision of the empiricism that underlie the design decisions. There are several steps in thoughtfully designing an affirmative action program. The following list ranks the considerations for which elaborateness and empirical detail might win special "credit" toward meeting the narrow-tailoring test, with the most important toward the top:

- *Decision Makers.* Who is included in designing and operating an affirmative action measure? Are various types of individuals and the interests included directly or through some sort of "virtual" representation of their concerns? The more inclusive the process, the better its moral attributes—at least, that is the classic lawyerly intuition, and one familiar to admirers of democracy. (I may be peculiar in ranking this so high.)
- *Detailed Costs Analysis.* How precisely do we know the costs of a proposed measure? Do we know who will be adversely affected, and can we measure or estimate the consequences to them? Care in designing affirmative action requires us to understand the interests at stake on all sides. We must be especially (though not exclusively) concerned with legally cognizable interests of so-called bystanders who have benefited personally from earlier patterns of exclusion in only an attenuated way. On the other hand, identifiable victims of illegal discrimination are at the head of the queue, which leads us to . . .
- *Detailed Benefits Analysis.* How precisely do we understand the benefits? Have we committed ourselves to an articulation of the justification, the objectives, of the affirmative action measure, and its intended results? Are we being clear about what the evidence is that leads us to believe there is a problem in the first place?
- *Alternatives.* Have we considered the alternatives carefully?

Have we been able to identify the most important options, and the interests and implications of each? How precisely?

• *Intrusion.* Have we chosen the "least intrusive" measure that holds a reasonable promise of effectiveness? The emphasis on least intrusive methods is fundamental because it acknowledges that there is an ethical cost to racial preferences and that we must judge in each instance whether the cost justifies the hoped-for progress. This doesn't mean we have to implement and exhaust other measures on a list of alternatives before initiating a program or that such exhaustion be a matter for close judicial inquiry. Instead, this principle is to abjure reckless disregard for the interest of "bystanders" by requiring a reasonable estimate or prediction about the efficacy of alternative methods. By favoring the least intrusive method, we minimize the ethical cost and, we hope, the divisive social costs as well. Effectiveness is not an absolute; there is no running away from the balancing implied by this formulation. But facing this in a framework that respects the needs and aspirations of all concerned is the only way out of the mess we are in.

• *Success.* Can we say what our test and measure of success will be? When will we be done? Or is that left for future discussion or decision—and if so, decision by whom, based on what information and considerations?

Not a great deal turns on whether the ordering above is exactly right, and we could debate it. The point is that the various aspects of care and detail are flexible factors because, in a world of incomplete and imperfect information, and quite limited analytical resources, you can't make a career out of every difficult decision. When setting priorities, designers of affirmative action have to be careful, but not compulsive. They should be concerned about criticism and litigation, but not obsessive about research or constipated by caution. Life must go on; the goal is justice, not perfection.

## *Litigation Problems Ahead*

The moral judgments inherent in affirmative action will sometimes come under the crude scrutiny of the law, where related norms will be applied, using bizarre procedures that have their own reason and logic but that are not at all calculated to promote consensus, community, or enlightenment.

As I write this, a task force led by the Department of Justice is hard at work (when not furloughed by the budget impasse) reviewing an exhaustive inventory of federal programs that are, arguably, subject to the *Adarand* requirements of compelling justification and narrow tailoring. In anticipation of litigation, a few things seem disturbingly clear, based on work done earlier during the White House review.

Establishing the factual predicate for a "compelling governmental interest" is challenging, inasmuch as many federal affirmative action programs were neither enacted nor previously evaluated with an eye to empirical issues such as just how much discrimination there is today, what the evidence is of continuing effects of previous discrimination, what the evidence is that the absence of diversity has significant consequences justifying race-conscious measures, and so on. So the first challenge is to assemble the program data, Census Bureau statistics, and other relevant information. This is no minor undertaking. In several circumstances the raw data simply don't exist, while in others it is considered suspect by the very people responsible for collecting it. In many more situations, we don't understand the way the world works well enough to create reliable social science models that lend themselves to empirical testing. Take the question of estimating how many minority entrepreneurs there would be in a given industrial sector *but for* the various obstacles created by discrimination in lending, bid solicitations, subcontracting, and so forth. Econometric attempts to answer the question have evolved since the 1989 *Croson* decision from abysmal to crude, and it will be a steep uphill climb to get much better. If you think personal wealth has something to do with becoming a successful entrepreneur, then you have the problem of very little census data to make useful comparisons. And if you further want to control, in each industrial subsector, for education, age, various sorts of professional experience (which ones?) . . . The mind boggles. The social science is useful, and legal doctrine has made it necessary. But legal doctrine hasn't told us what to do when respectable scientists tell us: We don't know enough to answer the question you are asking us. This is not to say either that there are no data or that more can't be developed. My point is that this is a substantial undertaking, as those involved in the Department of Justice effort fully appreciate. Getting near the truth will require that judges and legislators be patient.

Assuming you have useful empirical work, there is also a fundamental, still unanswered legal question of whether the newly assembled data can be used in litigation to support the constitutionality of a law enacted years ago. Opponents of affirmative action might argue that the information must have been before Congress at the time the law was passed, and that post hoc analysis by well-meaning agencies is not acceptable. Assuming the courts nevertheless allow this post hoc fact-gathering to be presented as evidence, as is likely, judges will still have to allow the other side a chance to present contrary evidence. Battles of experts are not new to the courts, whether the issue is DNA identification or antitrust liability. And the ensuing battle of experts will enrich several consultants, including economists and, I hope, law professors. (The 1989 *Croson* decision, which first applied the standard of "strict scrutiny" at the state and local levels, spawned a cottage industry of "disparity studies," as jurisdictions scrambled to build cases that patterns of discrimination and lingering effects justified their affirmative action efforts in contracting.)

But the problem is that even in the most charitable characterization, adversarial court proceedings are designed to illuminate disagreements about what is or is not factually true, while they are less good at resolving tensions among competing values. And especially when the issues concern race, factual and methodological disagreements are often the manifestation of disagreements about underlying values.

All of that with regard to the justification. As for "narrow tailoring," the same problems of missing, post hoc, and disputed data apply. When it comes to considering alternative measures such as race-neutral mechanisms, the problematic position of an agency defendant in court is even more evident. Courts are traditionally somewhat deferential to agencies on matters within the agencies' institutional expertise. With a stretch, elaborate studies by the Department of Justice, the Department of Defense, the Census Bureau, the Bureau of Labor Statistics, and so forth will likely carry more weight with a judge than competing analyses that come from the anti-affirmative-action think tank *du jour*. A court might *prefer* that the facts had been presented to and adopted by the Congress that enacted the law, because that would represent democratic acquiescence in the derivative inferences (like the inference that yes, discrimination *is* a serious problem and the proposed program *will* help). On the other hand, when it comes to making more value-intensive judgments about this race-conscious measure versus another not-quite-so-targeted hypothetical race-neutral alternative, a court might balk at showing bureaucrats the same deference. The more explicitly normative the judgment—like: How effective must the class-based alternative be?—the more likely a court is to fret about needing a democratically accountable legislature to consider the matter.

This problem isn't insurmountable, particularly because it is not too hard to smoosh together elements of normative judgment and empirical science, hoping that courts will give the agencies a deferential blessing on the entire package. What I mean to emphasize is the potential ambivalence of judges as they consider "narrow tailoring" or lack of it, reflecting the dichotomy between the social science elements that are traditionally the province of technical experts (however much they may disagree) and the normative, value-intensive elements that are traditionally the province of our elected representatives. I will return to this theme in my final chapter.

Another practical concern is the harsh truth that litigation is in many respects a lottery. Are the courts the right forum to struggle with these questions about the acceptability of affirmative action? (I'm not suggesting we keep these disputes out of court; it's in the nature of things for courts to handle disputes when other mechanisms have failed to do so. Courts are *almost always* far less than the ideal forum.) The lottery starts with not knowing which controversies will get to court in the first place. There are disputes about affirmative action all the time—from peeves to grievances to outrage. If we want to find the most significant, or complicated, or interesting, or instructive of these disputes, relying on the random chance of someone getting ticked off enough to litigate, and of an agency having the stomach to defend its program, is not the selection mechanism to use.

The lottery continues with the question of where the cases end up. Judges vary in their attitudes on just about everything really important, and the further away from settled legal principles we get, the more variation we can expect among them in how they handle these disputes. Moreover, the appeals process is a slow and inefficient way to impose coherence on a decentralized national judicial system. There is also the resource lottery: Which plaintiffs have the money to mount an effective case, and which defendants can do the same? The government of the United States of America can put together a good empirical defense of a small business program, but can Utica or Lafayette or Chattanooga do the same if that city's name pops up in the litigation lottery?

By far the deepest problem is that the adversarial mechanisms of litigation have limited usefulness in helping us form and express consensus on race. The history of civil rights litigation since *Brown v. Board of Education* demonstrates that. I do not gainsay the potential for courts to work a transformation of society: only a handful of politicians have had careers of more enduring significance than cases like *Brown* or *Roe v. Wade*. But perhaps what we can—or should—expect from courts is only the routine of interstitial, humdrum decision making and of incremental elaboration of broadly accepted norms, punctuated by those rare acts of high drama and historic moment. We cannot expect courts to frame or sustain a coherent national conversation. For that, we must look to other civic institutions, and to ourselves.

## *Whom Should We Target for Affirmative Action?*

The problems of justification and tailoring lead naturally to the question of which groups should be included in affirmative action. In this book, I have focused on African Americans, but let me offer a few thoughts on the larger question.

First, it is not logically or morally necessary to have agreed definitively on the demographic scope of an affirmative action program in order to conclude that group A and group B should be included in it, but not groups E and F. That's because if we accept that context matters, then it makes no sense to insist that every hard question must be answered before we can proceed on some particular elements of the program.

Second, with respect to narrow remedial justifications for a program, we must focus on the seriousness of the group-based discrimination or risk of discrimination As a general matter, I have no doubt that the case remains strong for African Americans, Hispanics, and Asians. Even the comparative "success" of Japanese Americans and many immigrants from the Indian subcontinent has not immunized from discrimination these subgroups, much less the larger diverse community of Asian and Pacific Islanders. One must decide whether the nature and extent of the discrimination, as revealed by social science, warrants any particular kind of affirmative action. But these groups cannot be flatly excluded.

Third, I think the same analysis should be applied to recent black immigrants from the Caribbean and Africa. The poisonous and destructive influence of racism in America is such that we should predict that these immigrants will face discrimination roughly comparable to that faced by African Americans. It may be that these newcomers have endowments that make it easier for them to overcome it (e.g., middle-class Jamaicans); it may be that their resources are even more meager than those in the black underclass (e.g., many Haitians). What seems clear is that because so much prejudice still tracks pigment rather than immigration status, these new arrivals should not be flatly excluded from the reach of affirmative action. Further research, perhaps using the "tester" or audit methods discussed in Chapter 1, would shed needed light on the issue.

Fourth, there are clear embarrassments of excess in some policy measures adopted in the past. The classic is the Richmond, Virginia, ordinance struck down in the Supreme Court's 1989 *Croson* decision, which included Aleuts in the city's contracting preference program. That would presumably have made sense for Anchorage, but certainly not for Richmond. So, is the embarrassment in the sloppiness of the design—the apparent disregard for the moral cost of extensive race-based decision making—or in the inclusion of this rather rare (in Virginia) ethnic group at all? I insist that the problem is the former, because we know that discrimination and disadvantage *are* a shameful problem facing the Aleut and other Native American communities. But any reasonable tailoring in Richmond would leave Aleuts out. Mend it, don't end it.

Having included whatever are the appropriate groups, one still has to resolve the issue of whether the justification for a particular race-conscious measure is weighty enough. I do not mean to suggest that the moral claim each of these groups has on America, its institutions, or bystanders equals the claim held by African Americans. That is a complex inquiry beyond my present ambition, but here are just three of the questions to consider:

- Does experience suggest that members of the group are able to overcome any disadvantages related to group status in a reasonable period of time, or that the group in the aggregate is able to make meaningful strides toward morally equal opportunity, without the use of preferences? This question is intended to lead us toward such distinctions as that between Mexican Americans and Swedish Americans; there simply is no reason to expect that new arrivals from Sweden will have trouble, within a generation or so, gaining their full measure of the American Dream.

- How strongly does group membership correlate with socio economic disadvantage? As I argued in Chapter 4, any degree of socioeconomic inequality takes on a different moral cast if it is linked to immutable characteristics that we believe as a normative matter should have no bearing on welfare.

- To what extent have these newcomers voluntarily assumed the burdens of "otherness" in America? In Chapter 5 we considered the distinction between narrow remediation to address discrimination and broader remediation to create "morally equal" opportunity. Voluntary immigrants should not suffer discrimination, but not every disadvantage is discrimination, and not every group-linked disadvantage amounts to morally *un*equal opportunity. The voluntariness of their plight is an argument that society should be less willing than otherwise to shift to bystanders the costs of addressing some disadvantage. (This voluntariness point seems pushed to an ugly extreme in the xenophobic, draconian social welfare cuts proposed for *legal* immigrants. "Magnet" theories of immigration don't justify it.) This is not a "do nothing" prescription, because the inequality and exclusion are morally and instrumentally unattractive for America in any case. It does suggest, however, that in this hairsplitting business of priorities and vision, and bearing in mind the general force of the equally American belief in "personal responsibility," the voluntarily disadvantaged have a lesser claim on our solicitude if the remedy in question is the morally costly one of race-conscious decision making. All wrongs are not equally compelling.

The essential point is this: yes, affirmative action can be cumbersome, and vulnerable to sneers that every group under the sun has legislative allies to help it climb on board some imagined preference bandwagon. But these concerns matter little when compared with the deeper value commitments at stake. We are trying to decide the content of our vision of American opportunity and of an inclusive society. We are whom we include.

### Public v. Private Initiatives

To many of us, it matters whether a race-based preference program is adopted by a government or by a private agency. But closer analysis suggests that, while different values are implicated for each, it is not clear which is more (or less) objectionable. A privately imposed preference program can be defended on the grounds that private actors are entitled to autonomy, to be free of government interference to do as they think right. (This is, perhaps, what the drafters of the 1996 California ballot proposition against affirmative action have in mind when they propose to outlaw only *governmental* preferences.) On the other hand, one might argue that private preferences may allow for invidious reverse discrimination, meaning an abusive preference, and therefore that an effective antidiscrimination regime is needed to regulate and police such private preferences.

A government-imposed preference might be thought more acceptable on the theory that, if the justification for a preference embodies important principles and aspirations, then government should lead; that regulating abuses is not enough. Moreover, the aspiration of inclusion (in Vision III) has most weight as regards public institutions where it is seen to be democratic and to promote civic community. On the other hand, given that preferences have a moral cost, some will argue that the moral injury is more grievous if inflicted by one's own government—by the power of the state. This latter view is currently the law, because the constitutional scrutiny of government affirmative action is tougher than, say, Title VII scrutiny of private employer efforts. This approach honors private autonomy, but also signals some moral ambivalence, making racial preferences wrong for one actor but acceptable for another—wrong when people act collectively through government, but acceptable when they act personally.

This is unsatisfying. Surely if the state stands idly by while my neighbor injures me, I have strong grounds for complaint. The private-public distinction does not and cannot definitively resolve the issue of our responsibilities to one another. What works, in my view, is to engage in the moral conversation about what those responsibilities are; then, having decided, ask what enforcement mechanisms are appropriate in light of a variety of considerations—practicality, ethics, custom. It may be that we decide to leave enforcement to social norms and informal community standards of civility, or to religious or other community institutions. Or we may decide that the state should be involved in a regulatory capacity. In race as in smoking, obscenity, abortion and elsewhere: we should not make the typical lawyer's error of confusing the question of what is *right* with the decision about the role of government.

# 8

# POLICY CHOICES—LOOKING AT HARD EXAMPLES

*L*et's get down to hard cases. Some of the programs and situations I discuss here were among those we debated with President Clinton and Vice President Gore during the White House review of affirmative action. The range of contexts in which affirmative action policy must be considered is vast, and the details make it easy to lose sight of the forest. I've sorted my examples under four broad headings: measures intended primarily to make the government do a better job as a government; education, including college admissions and targeted professional fellowships; employment (including the problem of lay-offs) and the federal government's requirements for certain contractors (Executive Order 11246); and the desegregation of capitalism, including government efforts to promote entrepreneurship, such as contracting set-asides.

### *Affirmative Action and Making Governments Work*

*Presidential Appointments.* An early, dramatic signal of the tone President Clinton would take on matters of race and diversity was his statement during the 1992 transition period that he wanted a cabinet that "looks like America." At times during those hectic weeks, implementation of this well-advertised emphasis on diversity flirted with political peril as it appeared that various posts (particularly that of Attorney General) seemed to have been "set aside" to achieve the diversity goal. The President was reported to have grumbled about "bean counters" among the interest groups who were intent on holding him to his word on diversity and who had little sympathy for the new administration's eagerness to get personnel in place quickly. In the end, the gender and racial diversity of Clinton's cabinet was impressive, with five women appointed—at Justice, Health and Human Services, Energy, the Environmental Protection Agency, and the United Nations; five African Americans—at Agriculture, Commerce, Energy, Veterans Affairs, and the Drug Czar's office; and two Hispanic Americans—at Transportation and Housing and Urban Development. (Eight white males took over at State, Defense, Treasury, Interior, Labor, Education, the U.S. Trade Representative's Office, and the Office of Management and Budget. Clinton later bestowed cabinet status on the heads of the Small Business Administration, the Central Intelligence Agency, and the Federal Emergency Management Agency, and they, too, were white males.)

As I suggested earlier, the argument for special attention to the demographics of the cabinet makes little sense if framed in remedial terms: the motivation is not to correct a past history of government discrimination or a history of discrimination suffered by the individuals one appoints—Ron Brown, Mike Espy, Hazel O'Leary, etc. There is, perhaps, a "thin" argument for some remedial or compensatory purpose in bringing to national policy making members of certain groups that were excluded in the past. But surely the most compelling argument, drawn from Vision III, is that the cabinet will serve the President and the nation better if its members represent a reasonable diversity of American perspectives, experiences, and aspirations. Whether the issue is when to balance the budget, how to restructure the health-care sector, or the uses of military power in the post-Cold War era, the notion of a decision hatched by a homogeneous group of pooh-bahs is unsettling, to say the least.

President Clinton, Attorney General Reno, and their close aides have similarly insisted that appointments to the federal judiciary look more "like America" than in the past. The numbers demonstrate considerable success. And as President Clinton is fond of saying, this diversity has been achieved while simultaneously winning a higher proportion of "gold stars" from the American Bar Association's screening committee than any previous administration. Again, the argument is the same: judges apply a combination of legal "science" and value-laden "judgment" to the resolution of disputes that wind up in court because other mechanisms in society couldn't settle them. If we want judges who think and feel "like America," then they probably need to *look* like America too, in the sense of being representative.

What about judges or cabinet members who look like America but don't, in fact, think like America—who are outside the mainstream views of those they are supposed informally to represent? What about Clarence Thomas? Here I cannot pull my punches. When this conservative African American was nominated to the Supreme Court by President George Bush, I both wrote and testified in strong opposition, based on his judicial merits or lack thereof, not on any of the allegations concerning pornography, sexual misconduct, or character. I also wrote about the bizarre use of pseudo-covert affirmative action by President Bush, who proclaimed that Thomas was "the best qualified" candidate for the appointment—surely one of the most inept pieces of White House disinformation in the modern era. (It doesn't qualify as a "big lie" because the assertion was so implausible and silly on its face.) Was Clarence Thomas qualified? Perhaps—only barely. And what kind of diversity did his nomination promise for the Supreme Court? There was the strange experience of watching white male Republicans talk about how Clarence Thomas would be such a fine representative for blacks on the Court, making arguments so offensive to many blacks that a conspiracy theorist might have thought them a veiled effort to kill retiring Associate Justice Thurgood Marshall by inflicting a mortal despair.

History demonstrates, however, that African Americans are nothing if not too forgiving, too hopeful, and too faithful in the possibility of the white man's redemption. So something like that dynamic occurred with many blacks, who argued that perhaps the Clarence Thomas on the Supreme Court would be wiser and more progressive than the Clarence

Thomas who curried favor with Reaganauts and far-right think tanks. The evidence thus far is quite to the contrary. Clarence Thomas has been true to his past record. He is on the conservative right fringe of a conservative Supreme Court. On legal concerns about racial matters, he has been a reliable voice for something akin to Vision I—a color blindness that ignores racial realism or even pragmatism. Only he and Justice Scalia seem intent on arguing repeatedly that meaningful affirmative action is flatly wrong and illegal. This was predictable from his earlier record, as I and other scholars argued. Now Justice Thomas has a life appointment on the highest court in the land, and of course there will be no other African American on that court until he is gone.

One dilemma of diversity, therefore, is that the rationale for special efforts to include underrepresented groups in the centers of governmental power is that representativeness makes the government work better, but the decision maker has a problem of determining who is "representative," because the African-American community is not monolithic. If the forum and numbers are small, the problem is particularly tough. Clarence Thomas's views certainly represent those of a segment of the black community—let's generously say it is about 15 percent. In both proportions and absolute numbers, however, it is clear that he represents the views of more white Americans than minority Americans. President Bush's use of affirmative action, even covertly, to work such a perversely unrepresentative result is a cynicism of the most despicable sort. While appearing to advance the interests of black America, he actually dealt a crippling blow—not simply by appointing an archconservative, but by using that appointment to lock out any chance for a more authentic—viz., representative—black voice on the high court.

Who decides on authenticity or representativeness? The ideal solution would be to have the underrepresented group itself have a commanding voice in the decision. That certainly makes sense in the context of affirmative action in public service. But the reality is very different. Presidents pick judges and cabinet officers; the powerful have the power. The checks on a decision maker's discretion are primarily from the politics of the situation and from his or her values. But these, in turn, can be influenced by a clearer understanding of just what we seek to accomplish by using affirmative action in these contexts. One great lesson of the Clarence Thomas appointment is that we saw proponents and opponents alike fail to speak the truth about race, diversity, affirmative action, and the role of the Supreme Court. That failure deprived the nation of a chance to address some of the racial neuroses in our national character. A psychiatrist would bemoan the loss of a therapeutic opportunity. As for me, I'm just sick to tears when I read Justice Thomas's opinions.

For all the great success the Clinton administration has had in achieving racial diversity in the cabinet, the subcabinet, and the judiciary, the situation has been lame when it comes to the President's own White House staff. Lame, but interesting. As of spring 1996, there are three extremely able African Americans at the highest rank—Assistant to the President—all on the "political" side of the White House operation. Alexis Herman runs the Office of Public Liaison, which is responsible for working with key constituencies and associations to explain and rally support for the administration's agenda, and to carry feedback to administration policy makers and political strategists. Bob Nash is in charge of Presidential Personnel, the office which oversees the selection of senior and mid-level political appointees throughout the executive branch, including nominations requiring Senate confirmation. Maggie Williams is chief of staff to the First Lady. But while these officials are centrally involved in managing the political agenda and prospects of the White House, they are not centrally involved in formulating or implementing public policy.

The major policy organs in the White House complex are the National Economic Council, the Domestic Policy Council, the National Security Council, and—by far the largest—the Office of Management and Budget (OMB). There are also the more specialized missions of the Office of Science and Technology Policy, the Council on Environmental Policy, the Office of National Drug Control Policy, and the National Performance Review—I omit a few other cats and dogs. All told, as of early 1996, these offices have roughly 750 staff, of whom 520 are at OMB. Sixty or so senior policy officers are comparable in rank to subcabinet officers or above; they are all noncareer staff appointed by the President or his immediate advisors and removable at will. This is basically the set of people who have White House Mess "privileges" and use of White House cars for official travel. *Not one* is an African American (since my departure). *None* is a Hispanic American. *Only one* is Asian American. There are no White House policy units headed by a member of a minority, although women head the National Economic Council, the Domestic Policy Council, OMB, the National Performance Review, and the Council on Environmental Policy. In the powerful OMB, there is but one minority (that lone Asian American, Nancy-Ann Min) among fourteen top appointees working for the director.

What might account for the dramatically different record of minority inclusion on the White House policy staffs in comparison with other presidential appointees? First, it is a political reality that cabinet, subcabinet, judicial, and, to some extent, ambassadorial appointments are more visible (than White House staff jobs) because they require confirmation by the Senate. The confirmed positions have very public functions, though sometimes in a limited community of interest. Second, the bean counters to whom President-elect Clinton referred have made a habit over the years of counting only these kinds of beans, and not others, and they tend to hold the decision maker accountable only for that which they are measuring and monitoring. Third, without the glare of public scrutiny, even a well-intentioned decision maker falls back on easy habit. The inner circle of men and women responsible for recruiting and staffing the various White House offices naturally onough rely on the usual sorts of personnel mechanisms: connections, contacts, friends, cronies, old associates, candidates with powerful sponsors, candidates who "feel" familiar and comfortable, etc. As I have discussed, we know that these habits produce exclusion in private-sector hiring, and the same is true in the public sector. The diversity effort in the very visible cabinet, subcabinet, and judicial selection process is protracted and painful; it is sometimes hard to do affirmative action the right way. But habits are by definition easy, breaking them often hard.

Last, there's a difference between policy and politics. The importance of inclusion may, to the powers that be, seem more self-evident on the political side of the White House because, after all, a Democratic administration needs to attend to the politics of minority communities with some care. When it comes to setting policy, however, a different, mysterious calculus comes into play. This is an unattractive picture. As a committed policy wonk, I am saddened to see that when a tight circle is drawn around the President to make the most important policy choices for the nation, minorities are generally on the outside or, perhaps, the back bench. There has been progress in twenty years, but not enough. When combined with the impressive record beyond the President's own staff, the lesson is that even for those most committed to inclusion, it requires unstinting and perhaps exhausting effort. Sadly, interest-group pressure politics, including better bean counting, seems for now the only reliably effective tonic.*

*The Armed Forces.* Many observers, notably President Clinton, consider the U.S. armed forces, notably the Army, a good example of successful affirmative action. Indeed, after substantial progress since the Vietnam era, today's military leaders seem fully committed to what they insist on calling "equal opportunity," and it is clear that this commitment includes what most people would term affirmative action. The Pentagon, however, is allergic to inessential political controversy and over the comings and goings of Presidents and political fashions, "affirmative action" has certainly meant controversy.

Let's look at the numbers. In 1949, only 0.9 percent of all officers were African American; today, it is 7.5 percent and growing. In 1975, after the end of the Vietnam War, only 5 percent of active-duty officers across all services were minorities, and today that proportion is 13 percent despite a decrease in force size. There have been fairly steady increases at senior levels over the past two decades, except that the proportion of African-American generals and flag officers increased until about 1982 and has been more or less steady since then. This overall positive picture is clouded by lagging numbers in the Navy and Marine Corps, by the problems in integrating the technical specialties and certain technical career tracks, and by the career obstacles women have faced due to restrictions on job categories available to them.

---

* Near press time, the President announced his intention to nominate Franklyn D. Raines, a black, to succeed Alice Rivlin as OMB director. It is rumored that Raines first declined an offer to succeed Ron Brown at Commerce and requested OMB instead. He will be a phenomenal success.

Beyond the numbers, we were reminded by a double murder in December 1995 that bigoted intolerance has not been eradicated from the armed forces. Nor should we expect otherwise, since the services cannot be immune from the diseases of America at large.

What is the justification for these military affirmative action efforts? With de jure discrimination against minorities a distant memory, remedial justification is not the point. Moreover, Pentagon officials insist categorically that they are not pursuing diversity because it serves some broad social welfare purpose. Just as industry has an instinctive reaction against any form of government regulation no matter how sensible, Pentagon officials resist every effort to link its national security mission with other social or economic objectives, believing that in the long run such linkages only serve to make their budgets and legitimacy vulnerable by diluting their high purpose and distracting them from it. So the key concepts and principles are these:

- The current Pentagon leadership considers complete bottom-to-top racial integration and tolerance a military necessity, required in order to have a cohesive and therefore effective fighting force. They cannot fulfill their national security mission unless they meet the challenges of diversity: racial conflict in the ranks was a grave and even mortal concern during the Vietnam era, and that lesson is studied and understood. As a civilian Pentagon official told me during the White House review, "Doing affirmative action the right way is deadly serious for us. People's lives depend on it."
- Doing it "the right way" means ensuring that people are qualified for their jobs. In a sprawling personnel system covering millions of people, there are well-established performance criteria. The boards that select for promotion do not abandon these when pursuing affirmative action goals, but it is also true that the promotion criteria are inherently flexible.
- The Department of Defense works actively to integrate the equal opportunity goals in its management systems. For example, intensive training efforts are required of virtually all

ranks, and an individual's performance with respect to equal opportunity matters is a formal element in the personnel appraisals used by promotion boards.

- The armed forces have made substantial efforts and investments in outreach programs and in retaining minority career officers, as well as in training to "level up" individuals' skills.
- Finally, despite the formality of the system, there are variations. We see gross differences between, say, the successes of the Army and the lagging progress in the Marine Corps. The White House review found that different officials expressed slightly different perceptions of how the system operates. This is certainly to be expected in any giant, hierarchical bureaucracy, but it underscores the difficulty of managing this agenda in a clear, consistent way.

Let me elaborate on a few of these points. The services have concentrated recently on the "pipeline" problem in the officer ranks. For example, the Navy and Marine Corps in late 1994 and early 1995 finally set explicit goals to increase minority representation in their officer corps. The old benchmarks had been loosely informed by college graduation rates, but the new approach seeks to ensure that the group of officers commissioned in the year 2000 will reflect the racial composition of the overall population: 12 percent African American, 12 percent Hispanic, and 5 percent Asian American. There are also year-by-year goals.

The key to such goals is that they are not numerical straitjackets but simply help the organization to mobilize needed resources and strategies. For example, all the services have outreach and recruiting activities in ROTC, the service academies, and other channels. These include obvious race-conscious recruitment tactics—the high schools and colleges you pick to visit, the enlisted personnel you recruit for Officer Candidate School, and so forth. The Army has operated a very successful "preparatory school" for students nominated to West Point whose academic readiness is not all it could be; the enrollees are disproportionately but not exclusively minority. (At this writing, funding for this effort is in jeopardy in Congress.)

On the specific issue of promotions, there has been a great deal of confusion and misinformation. Let me quote the description, approved by senior Pentagon officials, in the White House report:

All of the services emphasize racial and gender diversity in their promotion procedures. The Army, for example:

- instructs officer promotion boards to "be alert to the possibility of past personal or institutional discrimination—either intentional or inadvertent";
- sets as a goal that *promotion rates for each minority and gender group at least equal promotion rates for the overall eligible population*; if, for example, a selection board has a general guideline that 44 percent of eligible lieutenant colonels be promoted to colonel, the flexible goal is that promotions of minorities and women be at that same rate:
- establishes a *"second look" process* under which the files for candidates from underrepresented groups who are not selected upon initial consideration are reconsidered with an eye toward identifying any past discrimination; and
- instructs members of a promotion board carefully so that the process does not force promotion boards to use quotas. Indeed , , , *the minority and women promotion rates often diverge considerably from the goal.*

Revealingly, when interviewed, some Pentagon officials argued that this creates a "color-blind" promotion system, while others insisted that it permits race to be considered as a flexible factor that does not compromise the merit system and does enhance national security. In my view, the latter position accurately describes the practice. If the system were color-blind, there would be no need for the elaborate instructions to promotion boards.

There are several implications here. First, the goals have been critically important to the success, which is not surprising to anyone familiar with the challenges of managing complex organizations. The risk of conflict between goals and merit is addressed through management vigilance, motivated by a clear sense of the relationship between diversity and the national security mission. Moreover, there is an ample array of measures—from targeted recruitment to personnel appraisals to analytical studies of organizational performance—designed to help make those goals attainable.

Second, the armed forces are in some respects unique. They have a hierarchical, *disciplined system* in which dissenters from the equal opportunity mission either are "converted" or, probably, exit. It is a *controlled system*, in that managers have tremendous discretion to assign, train, retrain, and promote as they see fit. And it is a *closed system*, with no "lateral hires," so competition for promotions is among a closed group identifiable far in advance. The up-or-out promotion system means that underperformers tend to leave. This control of the pipeline is in significant contrast with, for example, a university faculty trying to hire new physics professors.

Third, there are nevertheless some transferable lessons. The thoroughness of the implementation, over a wide range of management and mission-related issues, is critical. In contrast, most other organizations take the equal opportunity mission and stick it in a little box in a marginalized bureaucratic Siberia. The top-down priority given to equal opportunity and affirmative action is important both symbolically and practically. Doing it the right way requires resources, rewards, sanctions, and tenaciousness, which the organization won't supply continuously unless the leadership sends a continuous message of support. Among the elements most sensitive to this top-down commitment, and to resources, is the investment in building a first-rate group of individuals from which to choose; for the Pentagon's closed system, the dividends earned from this investment are easier to enjoy than they might be for, say, a corporation that trains junior managers and then loses them to the competition. All of the foregoing must be combined with an emphasis on (authentic, whole) merit, a certain degree of patience, and serious efforts to measure results.

The armed forces did not—*could not*—create senior-grade minority officers overnight, because the pipeline just doesn't function that way. There are similar constraints in many other organizations. While tackling these energetically and creatively, organizations must recognize that a commitment to equal opportunity and affirmative action cannot be made for only one or two seasons; it is, instead, a task that must be marked in generations.

### Affirmative Action in Education and Training

I have already said a good deal about affirmative action in education, about education as America's opportunity engine, about the importance of the diversity rationale to the quality of educational institutions, and about the issue of merit. Three additional points concerning admissions to selective colleges and universities should be made here. There are obvious implications for other selective or "elite" contexts, from newsrooms to boardrooms.

*Admissions and Faculty Hiring.* The crux of the matter, it seems to me, is whether a college will go beyond recruitment of promising minority applicants to adopt a selection system that uses race as a flexible "plus factor." (Quotas are illegal, and *Bakke* ruled out inflexible set-asides for public institutions under the Fourteenth Amendment; *civil rights statutes apply the same prohibitions to any private school that accepts federal funds, which virtually all do* under student loan programs or otherwise.) In making this decision, an institution implicitly reveals its measure of the benefits and costs associated with inclusion. My sense is that much of the variance we see in the racial makeup of otherwise comparable schools is due to differences in the weight those institutions attach to diversity. Even within Harvard University, for example, there are considerable differences across faculties and departments. Faculty hiring at the Kennedy School of Government is abysmal with respect to racial, ethnic, and gender diversity, while the Law School seems better with respect to African American men and (less so) white women; both should be embarrassed as regards Latinos and Asians.

We should expect that internal forces at many colleges and

universities bias their judgment about the importance of inclusion. Conservatives warn about "political correctness," and claim that preference mavens exercise an iron grip. But, apart from a few high-profile examples like the University of California at Berkeley, the numbers make this claim laughable: college-going rates for African Americans and Hispanics are volatile; minority faculty members remain a rare and endangered species in most of academia; and most selective universities consider that campus diversity is precarious. The far more important internal dynamic concerns the challenge to entrenched hiring conventions—conventions often correlated only imperfectly with a rigorously justified conception of merit. A fundamental conservatism of these institutions leads people who are already inside to believe that the mechanisms that selected and promoted *them* are, of course, the best ones for determining merit and desert; to challenge those mechanisms is to challenge the desert of those who have already won in that game.

Yet it is still true that educational institutions are exemplary in showing how the benefits of inclusion spill over to society as a whole. When educational policy makers focus exclusively on what's in it for *them*, they "underinvest" in inclusion from the perspective of society as a whole. Enlightened institutions try to avoid this by using a more capacious notion of self-interest. Whether it's pretentious or legitimate, elite universities always claim a concern for educating "leaders" and creating "knowledge"; state universities usually claim a special mission of community service; professional schools—law, medicine, teachers colleges—may recognize their responsibility to shape a specific sector of the society, and to do so in a way reflecting broad social needs.

Finally, there is a special difficulty, not unlike the one I mentioned in discussing the armed forces, concerning the long and chancy preparatory road that matriculants and faculty must travel. Selective universities have little influence over the quality of the people who apply to study or teach. Even if a college were to tutor high-school students, say, it is unlikely to benefit much from the effort. But there are at least three obvious responses to this observation. First, a college can make tightly targeted investments—selecting people and settings that maximize its own chances of gain. It could have a summer "enrichment program" for selected students from local "feeder schools," or a super-early admissions process for promising students who have completed some such program. It could invest in the faculty pipeline with targeted postdoctoral programs or innovative mentoring strategies. Second, it could make investments collaboratively; a consortium could both have a greater effect and together benefit more. Third, leaders in higher education, who have been virtually silent in the great public debates over social policy about the opportunity agenda, could speak out. The pipeline feeding students and faculty into colleges depends on government policies in K–12 education and social welfare. If those systems fail, higher education suffers. The policy debates need more than the muted participation from an occasional do-good college president or editorials in trade newsletters that only educators see and only administrators read.

Colleges most often cite diversity as the justification for their affirmative action efforts, rather than confess a need to remedy past discrimination on their part. The question, in the post-*Adarand* world, is whether will suffice as a matter of constitutional law for university officials merely to cite Justice Powell's opinion in *Bakke* and quote statements from social philosophers and university leaders, dead and living. A skeptical federal judge might well demand more concrete factual evidence that diversity has identifiable and even measurable benefits to the enterprise. (The same can be said in other contexts, such as law enforcement. Will defendant police departments be required to present facts demonstrating that a more inclusive patrol force does a better job?) The literature is not reassuring on this point; again, it is because the importance of inclusion has become such an article of faith that its proponents seem not to have taken the trouble to document what they so strongly believe, all but unanimous. (Put aside the confused debates over same-sex education at Wellesley or The Citadel, or the nearly same-race education at many historically black colleges and universities. The question is whether, when an institution voluntarily chooses inclusion because it values diversity of a certain kind, the choice is morally and legally supportable. The question whether Wellesley, Morehouse, or The Citadel ought to be *compelled* to change its admissions policies is related but separate, involving the difficult boundary between permissible exclusion and impermissible discrimination, rather than the boundary between permissible, affirmative inclusion and impermissible discrimination.

*Financial Assistance.* The two immediate policy issues are: is it appropriate to have racially targeted financial assistance; and is it good to design government programs to increase the numbers of underrepresented groups in certain professions—research science or medicine, for example.

Consider the facts surrounding recent litigation involving the University of Maryland's flagship College Park campus (UMCP). Maryland was fairly late in undertaking serious efforts to dismantle its Jim Crow system in higher education, with de jure and de facto violations of law continuing for decades after *Brown v. Board of Education.* Indeed, federal civil rights enforcement authorities at the Department of Education worked for years with University of Maryland officials to negotiate a mutually acceptable plan for ending the vestiges of the dual system of segregated colleges. The plan had many elements, including measures intended to help attract and retain black students at UMCP, one of which was an academic scholarship program, named after Benjamin Banneker, to run in parallel with the university's color-blind, honorific Francis Scott Key Scholars program. The somewhat lower scoring threshold for the Banneker Scholarships meant that black students could win a Banneker grant when white students with comparable scores could not win a Key grant. A disappointed white applicant sued.

The university argued, with support from the Departments of Justice and Education, that the lingering present effects of Maryland's confessed history of discrimination provided the necessary predicate of compelling justification for a *remedial* program; they argued further that the Banneker program was narrowly tailored, inasmuch as such a scheme was needed in order to attract to the competitive flagship campus a meaningful number of black students likely to succeed academically. The U.S. Court of Appeals for the Fourth Circuit, however, essentially concluded that the facts did not establish clearly enough that the racially disparate enrollment patterns in the state's multicampus college system were traceable to the prior discrimination. Nor

# INCLUSION AND EXCLUSION IN HIGHER EDUCATION ADMISSIONS

| | PERMISSIBLE | IMPERMISSIBLE DISCRIMINATION |
|---|---|---|
| **INCLUSION** | • Proponents of affirmative action programs want to be here<br><br>• Historically black colleges and universities [HBCUs] want to be here; they don't *formally* exclude anyone | • Rigid preferences—such as certain set-asides—are impermissible; what else is, or should be?<br><br>• Opponents of "plus factor" admissions either insist on color blindness or deny diversity's important benefits |
| **EXCLUSION** | • Women's colleges want to be here—arguing they justifiably exclude men<br><br>• Men-only military academies want to be here<br><br>• "Black-only" male secondary schools want to be here, by analogy with women's colleges; but is race different? | • Flatly exclusionary practices are rigid and problematical; which circumstances provide adequate justification?<br><br>• Opponents argue that male academies discriminate; can the alleged benefits withstand constitutional scrutiny? |

*Dilemmas:*

• The current Supreme Court majority refuses to distinguish between suspect categorizations burdening versus benefiting a historically disadvantaged group (women, blacks, etc.). So is it impossible to distinguish between Wellesley and Virginia Military Institute?

• Does the fact that HBCUs admit a few non-African Americans convert those programs from ones of exclusion to ones of inclusion? Federal policy makers in both branches and both political parties think so.

• Is the inclusion/exclusion distinction any more defensible than the beneficent/invidious distinction currently rejected by the Supreme Court?

was it convinced that other, less racially exclusive measures would be ineffective.

Although the defendants' theory of the case was based on the remedial justification, Maryland having conceded prior discrimination, the diversity consideration was also at work. The result of the litigation (which we should not overemphasize in its particulars, because it is only the analysis of a single, three-judge panel in a single federal circuit court) makes clear that courts have to struggle to find the line between remedial and diversity purposes, and struggle still more to decide what evidence is needed to meet the burdens of proof for each. In my view, the Maryland case was unfortunate because the evidence of lingering effects was a hodgepodge, with little drama, and there was no persuasive trial evidence that the university had made a hard-nosed effort to consider race-neutral or, at least, less race-conscious means. As I have argued all along, it seems reasonable that when we make legal and moral judgments about the acceptability of affirmative action we implicitly link the strength of the different prongs of the analysis. Let me be clear: The appellate court's decision discarding the trial court's positive findings of fact was a bad one. It raised the evidentiary hurdle to unreasonable heights, but the conceptual framework within which it reasoned poses the right questions.

I recall a conversation in the late spring of 1995 with Donna Shalala, Secretary of Health and Human Services, who expressed strong support for the Banneker grants and mentioned a similar program she had instituted when she was chancellor of the University of Wisconsin. I asked whether Wisconsin had explored alternative race-neutral measures before choosing a minorities-only scholarship program. She was somewhat dismissive of my question, which only underscored to me the danger that proponents of affirmative action are sometimes so clear in their own minds about the benefits of remediation and inclusion that they do not attend to the moral (and sometimes political) costs of using such preferences. Of course, a month later, in *Adarand*, the Supreme Court took what seemed to me a useful prudential principle and, unfortunately, made it a constitutional necessity.

*Federal Grant Programs.* The need to consider less restrictive alternatives also arises in government programs designed to correct the underrepresentation of minorities and women in certain professions. At the federal level, these are concentrated in the Departments of Education and Health and Human Services and in the National Science Foundation. There are many similar state, private, and charitable efforts, including fellowships and scholarships established by foundations.

As in the Banneker case, there is reason to believe that a purely remedial justification for such measures has only limited force. The formal exclusion of minorities from the various professions has ended, and the lingering effects of the old discrimination are by and large dissipated, certainly when compared to other factors that produce underrepresentation. For example, too few African Americans aspire to be planetary scientists, and that is to some extent because they have no role models, a consequence in part of discrimination in the not too distant past (if not the present) by the relevant institutions. It seems likely, however, that the much stronger explanation is the pervasive disadvantage suffered today by African Americans, and its effects on both preparation for and aspiration to hard science. So the more plausible rationale for these programs rests with the broader remedial objective I have termed "morally equal opportunity" and the value of inclusion to institutions and to the nation.

Here are some federal examples from the White House review. They are all small in dollar terms—the proliferation of programs is not correlated with the magnitude of taxpayer investment. (The enthusiastic congressional *authorizers* operate without the budget constraints faced by congressional *appropriators* and agency officials.)

- *Program to Encourage Minority Students to Become Teachers.* The Department of Education gives grants to university and college schools of education to improve recruitment and training opportunities for minority individuals; increase the number of minority K–12 teachers; and identify and encourage minority students in grades 7–12 to prepare for teaching careers. The programs prepare and place minority students as teachers in both urban and rural K–12 schools with at least 50 percent minority enrollment.

- *Faculty Development Fellowship Program.* DoEd awards grants for support of postgraduate faculty who are members of targeted groups. The recipient institutions must have a "demonstrated record of enhancing the access to [graduate education for] individuals from underrepresented groups."
- *Institute for International Public Policy.* This program addresses the chronic underrepresentation of minorities in international service, including both the State Department Foreign Service and private international voluntary organizations. Funded by DoEd, it provides a single grant to a consortium of higher education institutions which operate the Institute.
- *National Science Foundation.* A variety of NSF programs address the underrepresentation of minorities and women in mathematics, science, and engineering; some grants go directly to individuals, and others go to institutions for local administration. An example is the Graduate Fellowships for Women in Engineering and Computer and Information Science Program.
- *HBCUs and HSIs.* Several federal programs assist the 103 historically black colleges and universities (HBCUs) in various ways—from financial aid to students, to improved physical plant, to scientific equipment. HBCUs have nonracial admissions policies, but remain vital to African Americans, educating, for example, a disproportionate share of African Americans entering higher education and the graduate professions. They are especially important and successful in serving very-low-income students. Similarly, there are efforts to support Hispanic-serving institutions (HSIs), principally through a DoEd program that helps institutions whose enrollment is at least 25 percent Hispanic (of which half must be both low-income and first-generation college students, and another quarter must be one or the other).
- *NIH Programs.* The NIH, a division of the Department of Health and Human Services, has several programs supporting underrepresented minorities in research and education. Some focus on minorities because of a statute, while others do so

based on regulations the NIH adopted using its discretionary power to set funding priorities. For example, the National Center for Research Resources has a Minority Initiative that gives grants to high schools to identify, encourage, and train members of "ethnic or racial group[s]" who are "underrepresented in biomedical or behavioral research." And the NIH Minority Predoctoral Fellowship Program supports Ph.D. and M.D./Ph.D. candidates through grants made to universities.

These are only samples. For example, HHS administers more than forty programs dealing with the education of health professionals, most of them are designed to assist "disadvantaged populations" and are race-and gender-neutral on their face; but those and other programs use flexible selection criteria, and details in program administration show some use of race and ethnic "plus factors."

What can we make of all this? First, the opportunity-results grid I described in Chapter 7 suggests that because education is more closely related to "opportunity," affirmative action measures in education should be more acceptable there than they are elsewhere. And in the legislative process, creation of these programs has been relatively noncontroversial—so far. Second, the premise for these programs seems always to emphasize our national interest in avoiding the serious threat of human-resource crisis in the years ahead: in field after field, experts project that there will be too few willing and able people prepared to do the hard work in the next century. In the sciences and in research generally, forecasters unambiguously predict disaster if we continue to rely so heavily on white males, who are sharply declining as a proportion of the workforce. We *must* add substantial numbers of women and minorities to the pipeline.

Third, most of these programs are too small to have been the focus for detailed evaluations—or any evaluation at all, for that matter—as we discovered during the White House review. While administrators were generally passionate in defense of them, that passion hardly amounts to the kind of evidence a court would require under equal protection strict scrutiny. The Department of Justice has been helping federal agencies to develop a more rigorous presentation of the human-resource argument, which would support the "compelling interest" prong of the constitutional test, and to explore race-neutral alternatives as required by "narrow tailoring." Results of that work are expected by late 1996. Fourth, it is important to bear in mind that these programs are only small elements of a much larger, richer government effort. In the Department of Education, for example, funds targeted on minorities amount to only 40 cents out of every $1,000 spent on student aid. This cannot be counted a significant practical diminution in opportunity to nonminorities and, outside the absolutist color-blind framework, that fact seems morally significant.

But one aspect of these programs goes beyond the national interest in staffing critical professions. Research scientists, academics, teachers, and health professionals occupy important social and economic stations in the United States, and to the extent that most of them continue to be white (and largely male), there is something wrong with the picture. The rigid logic of constitutional doctrines may make it difficult to weigh this in the balance, but somehow there must be scope to ensure that tomorrow's picture is better than today's. If race-neutral measures can do the job, fine. But if they can't, isn't more needed?

## *Affirmative Action and Employment*

It is affirmative action in employment that seems to generate the most political heat across the nation. Interestingly, though, in Washington there has not been a great deal of ruckus because the federal government's policy role as regards private employment is rather limited. Title VII of the Civil Rights Act, outlawing employment discrimination, applies if affirmative action is abused and rises to the level of "reverse discrimination"; otherwise, courts have consistently interpreted the statute to permit it, and Congress has implicitly endorsed that interpretation. President Clinton has made clear that he would veto any efforts to amend Title VII and curb affirmative action, and all but a fringe of congressional critics of "preferences" shy away from such provocative and legislatively pointless proposals.

One much debated area is whether quotas result from the implementation of the requirement, in Executive Order 11246, that certain companies with federal contracts adopt goals and timetables. The answer in the executive order context presumably informs our view about the risks of quotas in countless voluntary affirmative action settings where numerical goals are used. A settled but still argued issue concerns so-called race-norming. I begin, however, with the question of whether Title VII permits employers to use race (or gender) as a factor in deciding whom to lay off when downsizing.

*Layoffs, Promotions, and Hiring.* Imagine yourself in the following situation. As a member of a local school board, you must decide which of two teachers to lay off when budget pressures and declining high school enrollment make downsizing necessary. The superintendent reports that Ms. White and Ms. Black were hired at the very same time, have equally excellent records, the same educational credentials, and so forth. The *only* difference seems to be race. For some years, the school board and administrators have worked diligently to increase the number of minority teachers, in hopes of achieving some reasonable correspondence with the demographics of the school population while keeping an eye on the pool of qualified job applicants. Victory is not quite in sight, and the possibility of layoffs over the next several years makes board members worry that the diversity gains will be wiped out.

Here's the question. Should either the law or our values *require* the board to decide between Ms. White and Ms. Black by flipping a coin, or in some contexts might the board be permitted to take its diversity goals, and hence the race of the two teachers, into account?

I could be accused of concocting a law professor's typically strained hypothetical question were it not that these facts are modeled closely after a case in Piscataway, New Jersey. The Bush administration's Department of Justice sided with the white teacher, who was laid off, but the Clinton administration reversed that position to support the school board's argument that neither Title VII nor the Fourteenth Amendment absolutely precludes taking race into account in such a circumstance, provided the facts are compelling. The layoff problem might be considered this way:

*Vision I.* There's no predicate of identifiable discriminatory acts and victims; Ms. Black is not the beneficiary of a remedial order based on discrimination against her. The color-blind principle requires that the school board flip a coin. There's nothing to debate.

*Vision II.* Does some broad conception of remediation or morally equal opportunity provide an adequate justification? It is doubtful, inasmuch as the purpose of hiring teachers under an affirmative action scheme is only very indirectly related to the purpose of providing opportunities *to those very teachers* or to remedying the morally unequal opportunities of a disadvantaged group by hiring those individuals—these are indirect and quite secondary considerations.

*Vision III.* Is the school district's interest in diversity, furthering its mission, weighty enough to justify the concentrated cost imposed on Ms. White by dismissing her? The answer would depend on many particulars about the demographics of the school and its faculty and, ideally, about the education dynamic at stake.

The second and third assessments here are quite debatable, and they would shift if one changed the hypothetical employer from a school board to, say, an Alabama steel mill, the Boston Public Library, the First National Bank of East St. Louis, the Oakland police department, or Microsoft. Context matters.

During the White House review, our discussions of this problem focused on two competing formulations: (1) if race is a permissible factor in hiring and promotion, then it should be a permissible factor in layoffs; (2) layoffs are different—you can and should draw a bright line when it comes to someone losing a job they already have. The difference between these two is substantially a difference over the extent to which the costs associated with race-conscious decisions are accorded weight and specifically whether concentrating the cost on an identified person increases the cost's moral significance.

A middle ground—by now the reader can anticipate the method—stresses context and balancing. In the layoff example, the cost is concentrated on Ms. White. In a promotion, the cost is lessened and diffused, and in a hiring situation, the cost is further decreased and diffused. Within Visions II and III, as one moves from layoff to promotion to hiring, the moral cost of race-conscious decision making is of decreasing concern at any level of remedial or diversity benefit.

Interestingly, as best we could determine, it is not uncommon in the private sector for nonunionized employers to take diversity into consideration in making layoff decisions. (Unionized firms usually have seniority provisions in their contracts that constrain the structure of layoff plans; the Piscataway case is unusual because the two employees were identical in all characteristics relevant under the contract.) The only thing clear from this pattern, if true, is that a flat rule prohibiting consideration of race is inconsistent with common good judgment. To the extent that layoffs *are* different from promotion and hiring—and I do believe the concentrated injury is morally significant—the difference is not usually considered absolute.

For companies committed to equal employment opportunity and diversity, to have their progress wiped out by forced layoffs is a bitter pill indeed. Having worked to create an organizational culture valuing diversity, such a bureaucratic imperative may seem weighty, as against the barely noticed injury to a few identifiable bystanders. If this organizational dynamic of indifference to employees is at work, it is not agreeable. What we want is a judgment about the desirability of affirmative action based on a considered review of the justifications, implications, and need for "tailoring."

*The Executive Order Program and Quotas.* As we have seen, President Johnson issued Executive Order 11246 prohibiting employment discrimination in firms with federal contracts and requiring them to implement affirmative action to ensure equal employment opportunity. After a few years of experience, it was clear to Department of Labor officials and civil rights activists that the affirmative action obligation was ineffective, which is why the Nixon administration in 1970 issued regulations requiring firms to develop written affirmative action plans with goals and timetables. Attorney General John Mitchell made it clear that the required flexible goals were quite different from quotas.

EO 11246 applies to federal contractors and subcontractors with contracts worth more than $10,000 per year. This includes roughly 200,000 firms, divided almost evenly between construction and nonconstruction, employing some 26 million people, performing contracts worth roughly $160 billion. (These are 1993 figures, but the numbers are fairly stable from year to year.) The obligations for nonconstruction and construction firms differ, since they have very different payroll and personnel practices. *Nonconstruction* firms with more than fifty employees or contracts above $50,000 must have a written affirmative action plan kept on file for possible compliance review. To develop a plan (almost always with a consultant), the employer conducts a workforce analysis and a labor-market analysis to determine whether women or minority group members are "underutilized" in any job category. The employer then establishes goals to address any underutilization, and must make a "good-faith effort" to achieve those goals. The regulations do not require specific goals but have a "safe harbor" presumption that goals within 20 percent of proportionality would be accepted. *Construction* firms don't have to maintain written affirmative action plans but must make "good-faith efforts" to meet the demographic goals set forth by the Department of Labor based on region-specific census and workforce data for minorities, and based on a nationwide goal of 6.9 percent for women (established in 1978 and based on labor-force analyses at the time). Goal-setting in the affirmative action plans is based on estimates of the number of qualified individuals in the labor market. The regulations explicitly prohibit quotas and preferential hiring or promotion under the guise of affirmative action numerical goals. As for penalties, the Labor Department may order a contract to be terminated or suspended for a violation of EO 11246, and it may also bar a firm from future federal contracting. These administrative actions are very rare, and are taken only after attempts at conciliation, followed by formal hearings and appeals.

The White House review described the process as follows:

[A] contractor's failure to attain its goals is not, in and of itself, a violation of the Executive Order; failure to make good faith efforts is. [The Department of Labor's Office of Federal Contract Compliance Programs] undertakes compliance reviews for certain contractors flagged by a computer program as having below average participation rates for minorities or women. OFCCP also conducts reviews of contractors selected randomly and identified through complaints. (Roughly 80 percent of reviews are "triggered by" [the] computer-based selection system.) In FY 1994, OFCCP conducted more than

4,000 reviews, roughly 3.26 percent of its supply-and-service contractor universe, and 1.55 percent of its construction contractors. If a firm is found to violate affirmative action requirements (or antidiscrimination requirements) OFCCP attempts to conciliate with the contractor; in a very small percentage of cases, no agreement is reached and the case is referred for formal administrative enforcement.

The report went on to survey the social science research evaluating the effects of the executive order program. Generally it found only modest effects on employment levels as compared with firms in the economy at large. We then described and explored the standard criticisms of the program. Our conclusion:

> The available evidence, from court and administrative litigation, refutes the charge, based on anecdote, that equal employment opportunity goals have led to widespread quotas through sloppy implementation or otherwise. Quotas are illegal under current law, and can be used only as remedies in extremely limited court-supervised settings involving recalcitrant defendants found to have engaged in illegal discrimination. [Equal Employment Opportunity Commission] and court records simply do not bear out the claim that white males or any other group have suffered widespread "reverse discrimination."
>
> Undeniably, however, there is anecdotal evidence of certain managers taking impermissible shortcuts—hiring and promoting "by the numbers" rather than by using affirmative action in a flexible way to broaden the pool and then ensure that the effort to be inclusive does not compromise legitimate merit principles. . . . These anecdotes, if true, may in fact be stories about illegal discrimination, and are grounds for more attention to enforcement and education. Nevertheless, the balance of the evidence, based on complaints and litigation, indicates the problem is not widespread. The notorious paperwork burdens appear to be greatly exaggerated but are being reduced anyway as a part of the overall regulatory "reinvention" effort spearheaded by Vice President Gore.

The true debate about this program, in my view, is at a deeper level. First, assume there is some abuse, with flexible goals being implemented in a way that results in de facto quotas—for the sake of argument let's say 5 percent of the time (a very high guess). Whether one views that 5 percent as morally acceptable or as an outrage requiring an end to affirmative action goals, or as something in between, depends on your values—on the weight you accord alternative kinds of risk. There is always some risk of quota-type abuses when flexible goals are coupled with management carrots and sticks along a spectrum of forcefulness; but without goals, experience tells us we risk having no genuine improvement in opportunity. (That's one reason why the Nixon administration acted; that's why corporations use measurable goals to define key management objectives.) Second, there is a still more subtle point about human nature and discretion. The value-intensive choices discussed in this book are tough ones, and Edley's Maxim states that there are more tough jobs than there are good people to fill them. Are the careful, subtle judgments required to make an affirmative action program both morally fair and instrumentally effective *too hard?* Too hard for us reasonably to expect that tens of thousands of decision-makers in corporations and colleges and governments will be up to them? Affirmative action needs lots of discretion. Can we trust all those organizations and people with that kind of discretion, given the moral costs of error?

A moment's reflection will demonstrate that these two problems—the trade-off in risks and the worry about delegating subtle judgments—are really different ways of presenting the same imponderable: we have a pretty poor understanding of human character, when it comes right down to it, and we have a poor understanding of the extent to which we can mitigate—by regulation, training, or enforcement—the damage done when character fails.

Much of this also applies to the voluntary use of numerical goals in a variety of private and public settings. Instead of detailed OFCCP regulations, employers often operate with human-resource manuals, and personnel professionals in large companies go through training programs of varied quality. Admissions officers at colleges are more likely to be trained informally on the subtleties of goals and preferences—perhaps from local lore. As we saw in Chapter 1, there certainly is no evidence of rampant quotas—i.e., reverse discrimination—but our mechanisms for inventorying *any* kind of discrimination are imperfect. It is important to monitor these efforts with care, guarding against abuses.

*Race-Norming.* Race-norming is the widely criticized practice of taking tests of various sorts and adjusting the raw scores for different subgroups—blacks or whites, for example—so that the averages and distributions of the "normed" scores are the same across the subgroups. Suppose you have a test for selecting civil servants in which, you observe, whites perform better than blacks on average. If you hire the new civil servants on the basis of the raw scores, you will hire proportionally fewer blacks than in the applicant pool. If, on the other hand, you "norm" the raw scores (in this case by raising the black scores) so both groups have the same distribution, then your hiring on the basis of the highest scores will give you a workforce with proportional representation. Just about everyone, myself included, agrees that this is wrong, it being a rigid way of getting proportional representation that smacks of quotas and that appears to insult the merit principle. But I want to note a caveat.

Much of the criticism depends on the test's being a good test, truly measuring factors that are relevant to the job at hand. If the test is lousy, it should be scrapped and replaced with a better one. But if no better test is available or can be devised with current scientific understanding about the job at issue and the psychology of testing, what then? (This happens quite often.) Suppose the test isn't good, in terms of its job-relatedness, but not exactly terrible either and the best we can do for now. Shouldn't you supplement the test with other considerations so that you can make decent hiring decisions? (In college admissions, for example, an application includes letters, essays, reports on extracurricular activities as well as test scores, and then a committee does something mysterious in a conference room.) If, in Vision II or Vision III, we are concerned to correct manifest racial imbalances for either remedial or diversity purposes, and this not-so-good test is producing a poor list of job candidates, then *must we be slavishly loyal to the raw scores from the not-so-good test?* The sensible answer is no, but it doesn't follow that we should use race-norming. Race-norming in this situation is offensive not because of the insult to the merit principle, since the test wasn't a good predictor of merit anyway, but because it would be inflexible and would ignore the moral cost of pursuing proportional representation. Instead, the selection system should be redesigned to put less emphasis on the test *and* to consider race more flexibly, together with using other ways that a "careful tailoring" analysis would recommend (outreach, training, etc.): this would be a good-faith affirmative action effort. And it would have the added benefit of reinforcing the merit principle by forcing the organization to revamp its selection process.

This is easier to write than to do. The problem is that Americans on all sides of the race problem have spent generations *doing* what was easy, and the resulting slow progress tests *everyone's* patience.

### Desegregating Capitalism

A recent *Business Week* article headlined "The Top Managers of 1995: What did it take for a manager to succeed in the past year?" listed twenty-five people, not one of whom was a black or Hispanic. What is noteworthy is that this is so unsurprising. When you survey the leadership ranks of corporate America, when you measure the wealth of whites versus blacks, when you turn to corporate executives for civic leadership on the opportunity agenda—in short, when you look at the largest shareholders in the American Dream—you certainly have the impression that there's one Dream for some of us and another for the rest. America's original sin meant that minorities were excluded from the IPO, the "initial public offering," that let most of our forebears in on the ground floor of economic growth and prosperity. Now, still, there are areas in which illegal discrimination operates to deny would-be entrepreneurs equal opportunity, and this is difficult to remedy with ordinary antidiscrimination enforcement regimes. Discrimination in lending, subcontracting, hiring—you name it. Even more significant are the informal barriers created by networks, connections, cronyism, referrals, *relationships*. You tend do business with the people you know, the people you trust, and the people to whom those folks introduce

you. That natural process, superimposed on our socially and economically segregated society, perpetuates the opportunity divide and the
two-track character of the American Dream.

Narrowing the opportunity gap includes accumulating and creating
wealth by participating in the mainstream economy as owners and
managers of substantial companies. Except in some heroic trickle-
down theories, however, this is not closing the gap faced by the great
masses of black folks who are poor, striving, or even middle-class. So
the black capitalism agenda can be dismissed as mere affirmative action for black millionaires, an effort to see that minorities have a proportionate share of imported luxury cars and private jets. Indeed, I've
been at too many meetings in the past two decades when black entrepreneurs talked pretty much like that.

But deeper issues are at stake. First, the Dream is a lie if it's not for
us all. There's something to be said for being true to the ideal, for root-
ing out the corrupting forces that led to the corporate reality revealed so
unsurprisingly in *Business Week.* Second, powerful capitalists are powerful Americans. They shape our communities, our culture, our politics. They influence, directly and powerfully, the fate of their workers
and their workers' families. They make important decisions and are
held accountable by the invisible hand of the market (if at all), not by
votes and democracy. We can lose sight of their power because corporate leaders are usually invisible to the public at large—that, too, is
part of our culture. Name twenty of the hundred most powerful political
leaders in America? If you are reading this book (and you are), you can
do that easily. Now try to name twenty of the hundred most powerful
*business* leaders. Much harder, at least for most of us, but they are there
nonetheless. Isn't there something wrong if the people on the list of
twenty, or one hundred, or five thousand are overwhelmingly white and
male? Is it good for America? Is it fair? Does it tell us something positive about who we are? If not, then what is to be done?

If the opportunity engine works, then nondiscrimination, quality
education, self-reliance, and so forth will eventually create a black
entrepreneurial class. Yet—unsurprisingly, again—it would be
damned hard to find many African Americans who believe this prescription will cure the problem within a couple of decades. An econ-

omist acquaintance told me years ago that if one extrapolates, optimistically, the black-white wealth accumulation trends of America from 1945 to 1985, we can expect equality no sooner than a century from now. It is chilling that this is so believable. As challenging as the opportunity agenda is, we should appreciate the even greater difficulty of reaching and navigating in the most powerful currents of the mainstream economy.

This chapter is about hard policy choices. On this topic, the most basic choice is whether the remedial, broadly remedial, and inclusionary justifications for race-conscious action are sufficiently weighty. One could agree in principle that the problems discussed above are legitimate concerns, but nevertheless feel that challenges in education and employment are far more pressing and also more deserving of public and private response. The rationale might be that education has more the quality of an "investment" in "opportunity," while programs promoting entrepreneurship are more like "rewards" and "results." The employment arena is in between. Alternatively, one might accept that desegregating capitalism is a worthy goal, but then argue pragmatically that we don't know how to do it very well, it's politically perilous, and it diverts attention from more important elements of the racial-justice agenda. For me, the jury is still out on these contracting programs. My White House experience persuaded me that several changes should be made—as a matter of moral judgment and sound policy, not necessarily because the Supreme Court would require every last one of them. (Interested readers can find the full analysis, and recommendations, in Chapter 7 of the report itself. Will the political and bureaucratic forces swirling around these efforts permit such reforms? If those who believe the cause is critical cannot agree to work for some incremental changes that will substantially improve fairness and reduce the political fallout on other affirmative action measures, then the programs do not deserve to survive: Mend it, else end it.

# 9

# A DIVIDE OVER DIFFERENCE: NATIONALISM AND BEYOND

**W**ithin many of us, seemingly inconsistent perceptions and aspirations live a confused coexistence. We see in America the possibilities of racial conflict, but also of healing. We often work toward and within identity politics that express our narrow interests and group membership, but we also dream of greater community. I do not believe we can dissolve these tensions—by reason, by passion, or by experience. The challenge, instead, is to understand them and make a constructive peace among them. If racial policy making is a roiling, treacherous stretch of countercurrents and white water, then our safe passage will come not by calming the waters—likely an impossibility—but by discovering how to navigate the currents.

## *Difference as a Value in Racial Politics*

*Nationalism v. Universalism.* One way to view race relations is through a prism that separates *nationalist* and *universalist* perspectives on *difference*. Difference is both good and bad, of course. And one can think about difference both descriptively and aspirationally—i.e., about the significance you ascribe to difference in people's lives today or about the significance you hope (or, pessimistically, fear) that difference will have in some preferred future.

In the nationalist conception of race relations, the distinctive social or other elements that make one racial group different from another are valued as an important source of strength, to be developed and exploited positively (rather than exploited as the basis for victimization). Black nationalists, proud in their blackness, want unity in order to defend against white racism and discrimination, and to mobilize political and economic power to promote affirmative policy agendas. White nationalists want unity in order to preserve a hierarchy that benefits them, to defend against any minority's usurpation of it, and to promote an affirmative agenda of cultural hegemony. (I've struggled to find a more sympathetic expression for white nationalism, but cannot. Nationalism as an ideology of a dominant group seems to me inescapably oppressive in its implications; it is antithetical to tolerance.)

The universalist conception is that the things that unite us as Americans are more substantial than those that divide us into racial groups. The positive sense of this is the familiar one about universal brotherhood; the negative is intolerant assimilationism or cultural hegemony. That is, one can preach universality with an integrationist's optimism that racial tolerance and pluralism can manage with differences because powerful, transcendent values and bonds ensure domestic tranquillity; and one can also preach universality with a xenophobe's pessimism that demands the subordination of differences because the bonds of community are intrinsically too fragile.

Whatever your views about biologically determined group identity and affinity, it is impossible to deny the long-standing and nearly universal experience of socially created racial groupings. Race *matters*. But everything turns on the matter of degree, and on perceptions of the trends. Conservative and liberal optimists alike believe that the social significance of race and discrimination is declining; pessimists see race relations as deteriorating. The objective truth of the situation seems of only limited importance: *perceptions* of the reality certainly color one's interpretation of experience and evidence, shaping one's attitudes and reactions. If I believe discrimination is disappearing, I

| ALTERNATIVE CONCEPTIONS OF RACIAL DIFFERENCE | | | |
|---|---|---|---|
| | | POSITIVE, OPTIMISTIC | NEGATIVE, PESSIMISTIC |
| **UNIVERSALIST** | *descriptive* | diversity makes for richness and competitive strength | differences fuel distrust, even animosity, and undermine community |
| | *aspirational or predictive* | differences fade in significance, communities are inclusive; ties uniting Americans are stronger than differences dividing them; networks, norms, and trust overcome animosities | the melting pot becomes the food processor: assimilation, as pressure for conformity demands that groups abandon identity politics; cultural homogeneity |
| **NATIONALIST** | *descriptive* | group identities balance the majority's political and cultural dominance | identity politics leads to balkanization; leaders encourage the zero-sum politics of resentment |
| | *aspirational or predictive* | group cohesiveness provides a base for cultural, economic, and political strength within a broader community of tolerant pluralism | breakdown of national community; intergroup barriers offer surest form of safety; sharp interset-group politics make coercive assimilation the only alternative to the escalating conflict |

will dismiss the studies that demonstrate otherwise as flawed and the episodes as aberrational, clinging to my optimistic conviction. A pessimist will do the opposite.

*Responsible versus Pathological Nationalism.* The responsible version of black nationalism was well displayed by the throng below the podium at the Million Man March on Washington in the fall of 1995. It focuses on the positive good of community unity and, in the American tradition, fosters a sense of shared interest in collective political and social action. It is both defensive and assertive without being hateful. What is the responsible version of white nationalism? It is, I believe, the promotion of a defensive attitude on status quo white-majority economic and cultural status and hierarchy—in short, a conservative agenda. I mean more than simply conserving the good and suppressing the bad—few would disagree with that—for it all depends on the definition of what is good and what is perverse. One element in policy conservatism tolerates the widening of socioeconomic inequalities, and another is the historically maintained, but counterfactual insistence that markets and charity produce social justice.

In contrast, the sociopathic version of white nationalism is found not only in the preachments of racial supremacists but also in the irrepressible cottage industry of their more respectable intellectual consorts—from William Shockley to *The Bell Curve* to Dinesh D'Souza. The sociopathic version of black nationalism is found in the anti-Semitic, white-devil preachments and disinformation of Minister Louis Farrakhan, the cult of violence implied by bandoliered Black Panthers nearly thirty years ago, and the bizarre critiques made by a few blacks against police crackdowns on teen gangs and by those who consider drug thugs to be community heroes.

But there is a mild form of white nationalism as well, expressed by conventional political conservatives who vigorously defend the traditional distribution of political and socioeconomic power, which today in America operates to the advantage of whites. Few policy conservatives of this stripe are racial supremacists of the old school, though there are certainly closet exceptions. Instead, I think, they are adherents of the credo "What's mine is mine, what's yours is negotiable." And they allege that this will expand long-run opportunity for everyone. The mild form of black nationalism is expressed in conventional pleas for political solidarity, community coherence, and racial self-respect among blacks. The great African-American novelist Ralph Ellison wrote of the invisibility of blacks in mid-century America. Jesse Jackson has voiced a hopeful, assertive, nationalistic prescription for the cure: "*I* am *somebody!*" And being somebody did not, in his formulation, require hating anyone. Just loving ourselves.

*Strong v. Weak Universalism.* To add another element to the picture, we should note the strong and weak forms of universalism as well. Here the distinction is between assimilation and tolerance. To favor assimilation is to believe that racial or social groups must shed their distinctive differences because they undermine the imperative of universal community. Social and other significances of the differences must be made small and, over time, all but vanishing. For example, the fact that the distinction between Presbyterians and Methodists seems to make little difference in American society except on Sunday morning is a measure of great progress having been made, grinding away the significance of difference. A radical universalist agenda would, I suppose, have us keep grinding the edges until ecumenical consolidation had everyone worshipping at identical services. Few Americans would accept this, however, because in our liberal tradition it is hard to imagine such a development without unacceptable coercion. Instead, we usually embrace a weaker form of universalism emphasizing *tolerance.*

As relates to racial differences, antidiscrimination and even de-segregation remedies are a form of tolerance. More aggressive forms of integration—which some white and black critics alike view (from a nationalist perspective) as disruptive social engineering shade toward assimilationism. We should note that assimilation can be viewed as violently coercive or not, depending on the nationalist perspective of the viewer as well as on the methods. The African-American community has been divided from time immemorial between integrationists and nationalists, and this disagreement continues in full force: *Should we struggle to build a bridge and cross over to join* them? *What of our selves will we lose, and is it realistic to believe that they will truly accept us even then?* A strong nationalist believes that to assimilate is to risk forsaking our fulfillment as a people; a weak nationalist believes that to assimilate brings nearer the possibility of fulfilling our potential as individuals. Both are right.

*Inescapable Ambivalence and Duality.* The final complexity is this: here we are, living both as Americans and as members of a subgroup—racial, ethnic, gender, sexual orientation, religious, whatever is the focus of the moment. There is every reason to expect that we will hold different tendencies toward nationalistic solidarity or toward universalist community, depending on the context. Put differently, *intragroup*

## STRONG AND WEAK NATIONALISM AND UNIVERSALISM

*What are the implications of an ambivalence about group identity and the wider appeal of community?*

|  | STRONG UNIVERSALISM | WEAK UNIVERSALISM |
|---|---|---|
| **PATHOLOGICAL NATIONALISM** | *Minimum alienation*<br><br>*White:* Engagement in coercive assimilationism<br><br>*Black:* Advocacy of separate but equal status | *Minimum tolerance*<br><br>*White:* Hierarchy, hegemony, oppression<br><br>*Black:* Separatism and revolutionary politics |
| **STRONG NATIONALISM** | *White:* Coercive assimilationism<br><br>*Black:* Assertive group identity within coalition politics and liberal policies | *Both:* Interest-group competition and rivalries; insular communities; conservative white vis-à-vis radical black politics |
| **WEAK NATIONALISM** | *Maximum tolerance:*<br><br>*Both:* Steady erosion of group differences; identity and growth of one-community consciousness | *Maximum alienation:*<br><br>*Both:* Death of civic life; moribund community displaced by market-consciousness |

affinities and cohesions vary, and so do *intergroup* dynamics. The first concerns the integration of self, while the second concerns the integration with other selves. This distinction creates instability or uncertainty in our politics. It also explains such common sentiments as those felt by African Americans who (like me) simultaneously feel a strong attachment to *group* aspirations and a strong commitment to the values and ideals of American society as a whole. To some extent these nationalist and universalist impulses are in tension, as when I must decide whether to participate in the Million Man March or a race-based independent political campaign. That tension is often expressed and debated in the languages of aspiration and of reality: *You may want a world in which mainstream politics gives blacks an effective avenue to seek redress for wrongs and disadvantages, but the hard reality is that America's two political parties won't provide that and we must go elsewhere, brother.* Or that can be flipped: *You may want a world in which protest politics can effectively secure racial justice, but the hard reality is that in America the only way to get anything done is in mainstream politics.* So, even though we may think that our ambivalence about nationalism and universalism is a confusion about hopes versus realities, it is more complicated than that: an additional cause of the ambivalence is our complex identity as members both of subgroups and of the national group, which results in at least some inevitable tension of divided loyalties.

How, then, should we understand American racial politics—our disagreements within and between the races over issues such as integration and affirmative action and ethnic solidarity and social welfare programs and aid to Africa and even, perhaps, the O. J. Simpson verdict? Simplifying the disagreements to crude left-right, black-white dynamics misses the subtleties. This kind of reductionism fails to describe the jumble of values and imperatives that thoughtful people hold in their minds and hearts. I think it's as impossible to resolve the contending values as it is to separate the yin from the yang in Confucian cosmology, or the smell from the taste of your favorite gumbo. The very tensions I have described express our human condition, individually and collectively. And that condition is in its nature not static but, rather, a dynamic flux, as we experience the changes in how those tensions are played out moment to moment within us and within society.

The better question is: Can our society master that dynamic, or is it the master of society? We are certainly unlikely to master it if we do not first work to understand it.

Because the underlying factor in the tension between nationalism and universalism is one's stance toward *difference*, we should ask what it is that makes intergroup differences salient. When and why do differences matter?

In October 1995, Americans watched in wonder as our Canadian neighbors seemed on the verge of ripping their national state asunder for reasons we couldn't quite understand. Francophone Quebec had long made secessionist complaints, alternating with demands for constitutional reforms under which Quebec would be accorded a still more special status within Canada's federal structure in recognition of its "unique traditions, culture, and status." Before the fateful referendum on October 31, the American media conducted endless person-on-the-street interviews about the secessionist sentiment, but these were singularly unilluminating because every speaker seemed impressively inarticulate about precisely what was at stake, apart from the language factor. There was loose talk about "oppression," but also fairly compelling expert opinion about the grave risks of serious economic dislocation for an independent Quebec. In any case, it is difficult for most (parochial) Americans to understand the depth of alienation the secessionists claim to feel since their plight seems not too serious in comparison with the condition of racial minorities in the United States. Yet the almost 50 percent vote suggests more than a mere "claim." (I recall traveling to Montreal as a youngster and being taunted, in French, with racial epithets hurled at me by white boys on a passing bus. It's difficult to think of white francophone Canadians as my fellow victims.)

Meanwhile, Bosnia, and Rwanda, and Chechnya, and a dozen other places from Mexico to Northern Ireland to . . . (one fears) South-Central Los Angeles and Brooklyn and points in between. Religious strife is rarely the proximate cause of death in the United States today, but that is not true in many places in the world. That and other stories entitled us Americans to be proud of our tolerance ideal, however imperfect the implementation. But comparing the reality here with the reality of societies in extremis is too easy. An African American should take no more solace from the fact that she is more fortunate than an oppressed member of a minority in Bosnia than an American blue-collar worker faced with a layoff does from the fact that her unemployment benefits are munificent in comparison with a Bangladeshi's wages. It is fairer and certainly right, instead, to compare American practice with America's ideals, and American life with America's dreams.

In discussions of affirmative action and of race relations generally, skeptics often ask whether race really matters as much as class, whether differences of race are by definition more important than differences of, say, occupation or sexual orientation or political affiliation. (Wise guys irritatingly ask about hair color and height, expressing their impatience with the whole subject by trivializing it.) The question arises in many contexts. What groups, if any, ought to be beneficiaries of some form of affirmative action? Is divisiveness about race the most important obstacle to creating civic cohesion and community? Given America's ability to manage other intergroup differences, must we be pessimistic about the future of race relations?

In the spring of 1988, I was working as national issues director in the Dukakis presidential campaign, and I accompanied Dukakis to a living-room discussion outside Racine, Wisconsin, with a group of dairy farmers. In preparation for the Wisconsin primaries, I had studied the economics and politics of the dairy programs and understood the difference between Class I and Class II milk, and so forth. Dukakis had reviewed the briefing materials. To me, the striking thing about the session was how sophisticated these dairy farmers—small businessmen, really—were about everything from the regulatory complexity of the programs to the different economics faced by dairy farmers in Texas, Florida, Vermont, and Wisconsin, from the Senate politics of the issue to the consumer politics of it. In that room, the most important thing to those farmers seemed to be their shared identity as Wisconsin dairy farmers—not religion, race, or party affiliation, not age, veteran status, or region per se. In other settings, those men and women would have come across with a more complicated and multidimensional civic character. But for the moment, they were simply *dairy farmers,* not foreign policy pundits, right-to-lifers, gun owners, or Lutherans.

The questions are these: How often, or in how many contexts, does being black, or a dairy farmer, or a Lutheran, or a woman provide the structure for your life in that moment? Which of the many groups we belong to matter in an undeniable way? And are there choices you can make in how you live your life that *give you some measure of control* over how often a situation thrusts a particular group identity upon you?

And relatedly: You are a member of a certain group; *can you exit?* Can you leave and join another one, or none at all? I believe a strong case can be made that, in America, race *is* a different distinction than the other ones in our political, social, and economic life. (The only serious question is the uninteresting one of whether race is uniquely different in kind or merely *very* different in degree.) The puzzle for me is that so many whites—on both the ideological left and the right— do not see the truth of this proposition, no matter how many facts scream it at them.

I can understand this denial only as the consequence of two things. First, many whites have so little contact with blacks that indeed for them race has little or no social significance. Just as there is no social significance to homosexuals they've never encountered, or to Native Americans. Not on the radar screen, period. Less pejoratively, that's like our American difficulty in understanding the social significance of being a French-speaking Canadian. We just don't get it, and the explanations of how meaningful their distinctive culture is don't res- onate with us. Second, some whites are in a state of serious, deep denial, because they cling to the aspiration of an American universal- ity. Facts about deep difference bother them, or at least threaten to undermine the determination to achieve universality. So they discount the significance of those facts.

On the other hand, even as many whites may have a tendency toward universalism which deafens them to some strains of difference, so too may there be a tendency among blacks to exaggerate or manu- facture their differences in aid of nationalism. Insouciant universalism is the luxury of those who are dominant; a Potemkin Village solidarity-in-difference is the contrivance of those who are not. Let me elaborate. A colleague has suggested to me that at certain places and occasions differences are manufactured or exaggerated, seemingly beyond reason. Might racial differences in America be one such case? (He points to the deep divide between Armenians and Azeris in the Caucasus, but I don't know enough to have a view on their dispute.) Undoubtedly, "actual" differences, cultural or otherwise, are sometimes exaggerated in order to imbue them with social or political significance, and then they take on a reality of their own, become critical in the construction of nationalism. All that a leadership cadre needs is *enough* of a difference to calculate the possibilities of making a political or economic gain by heightening it: by consciousness-raising, in the familiar phrase of the 1960s. I don't see that it is possible to say there is a moral right or wrong to this process of seizing, magnifying, and mobilizing differences. Particularly in the United States, that seems to be a major motive force in much of our pluralist politics—the genius of our system if you like it, our curse if you don't, but ours nonetheless.

Heightening differences in the service of nationalism is one phenomenon. Another is proxy compensation, or virtual representation. Critics of affirmative action often argue that by emphasizing group differences and injustices, a few advantaged blacks—intellectuals, academics, businesspersons, journalists—can "win" affirmative action benefits for themselves, but in doing so accomplish almost nothing of benefit for the very people whose suffering supposedly provides the moral justification for the affirmative action in the first place. In a slightly different form, the charge is also made as part of a larger attack on civil rights and antipoverty leaders, who, critics claim, are interested not in service for those they purport to represent but in professional self-preservation. Most of these criticisms should be summarily dismissed for what they are: ad hominem and politically motivated efforts to discredit people who have unpopular or irritating agendas; the rest of it simply recapitulates the disagreement over remedial and nonremedial moral justifications for affirmative action, and over arguably too-inclusive remedies.

The very practice of affirmative action creates winners and nonwinners in the African-American community. This is the inevitable consequence of its lotterylike quality, which requires that you be at the right place, at the right time, with the right stuff. It's not just that the remedy is selective rather than universal; even creating formal and universal equality of opportunity creates separation or difference because individuals vary in how well they can take advantage of those new opportunities. So even traditional nondiscrimination creates separation and distance, as when a decline in residential discrimination enabled the traditional group of successful "strivers" to move out of racial ghettos. The question is whether separating the more mobile strivers and affirmative action beneficiaries from the masses indicates progress or ethical bankruptcy in the struggle for social transformation. I turn now to that issue.

### *Affirmative Action and Theories of Social Transformation*

The common criticism of affirmative action that it has benefited only a few blacks, principally so-called elite ones, seems sweeping and inaccurate. It is admittedly difficult to separate out the effects of antidiscrimination measures and other affirmative action measures in, say, blue-collar employment. Yet it is fair to say that among the most dramatic consequences of affirmative action has been the desegregation of many (far from all) elite centers of social, economic, and political power. Increasing numbers of African, Hispanic, and Asian Americans—and of women—are found in corporate boardrooms, prestigious university faculties, and media editorial offices, holding high political appointments, and so forth. In what sense is this a meaningful kind of progress, given the continuing misery of the underclass?

There are several elements embedded in this issue—including the wisdom of investing scarce political capital in this particular strategy. But the two key concerns are these: From *the left*: Isn't the effect of affirmative action to give select individuals a stake in preserving the fundamental elements of "the system," when they might otherwise become an effective, militant leadership cadre pressing for more radical changes in capitalism and in American politics? Call this the "Band-

Aid" critique. And from *the right*: Aren't the elite blacks who benefit most dramatically from affirmative action somehow not truly deserving, their gains ill-gotten by trading on white guilt about or empathy for the underclass? Call this the "racial spoils" critique.

The "Band-Aid" critique has an element of truth, and no doubt identifies one reason for the lack of leadership in the national African-American community. The "racial spoils" critique also has an element of truth, but it is substantially blunted by several considerations. First, it is not accurate to say, for example, that a middle-class black being considered for a corporate promotion has faced no race-based disadvantages. Certainly the disadvantages are less than those faced by less fortunate blacks, and certainly class-based disadvantages faced by less fortunate individuals of *any* ethnicity are considerable. But in the United States today, *any* black man or woman is likely to face continuing, serious disadvantages because of race, relative to white peers. (Then there's a separate argument about whether those disadvantages are serious enough to warrant a given form of affirmative action, but that's a different discussion.) Second, as we have seen, there are important reasons other than remediation to engage in affirmative action in a given setting. As I've argued, a particular institution and the nation may both have a strong interest in inclusiveness in order to help that institution be more successful on its own terms and for the general benefits to society. Third, the individual benefited by affirmative action may be able to do something for other blacks as a result of his or her new position. We have black entrepreneurs employing African-American workers, black teachers serving inner-city students, and black government officials working to shift public priorities when previously the government paid scant attention to the black underclass.

Oddly, what the two critiques share is a skepticism about the conception of social transformation which we might term "trickle-up incrementalism," in contrast to structural upheaval. The contrast is descriptively important because it determines whether, for example, you see the incremental gains from affirmative action as meaningful, hopeful, and a harbinger of greater progress to come, or as limited, trivial, or even counterproductive. And the contrast is important prescriptively, because it tells us whether those who would be change agents ought to focus on more sweeping and necessarily confrontational strategies.

So one can consider the isolated, sometimes solitary beneficiaries of affirmative action as the vanguard elements of a slowly rising mass. More will follow. It just takes time. It takes a while for people to rise past the obstacles. Twenty-five years of stop-and-go, here-and-there affirmative action and advances in civil rights may not be enough to judge the potential of the trickle-up strategy. On the other hand, one can see the few who have "made it" as destined to be isolated exceptions, believing that only some deeper, more thorough upheaval can transform society enough to help those stuck below the barriers created by race and class. The trickle-up strategy may work but will take too many generations and cost too much misery and wasted human potential.

Where the left and right differ is in their prescriptions for the kind of transformative change required. The conventional left thinks of class struggle and the end of capitalism as we know it. The new conservatives think of a militant orthodoxy of values and culture—stressing personal responsibility, self-help, individualism, the overthrow of state-sponsored welfare dependency, and the virtual extirpation of public altruism. (I have an opinion about this.)

I cannot choose between trickle-up reformism and radical transformation as strategies for racial justice or, for that matter, any other kind of justice. Much depends upon what time frame you believe is relevant and how patient you are, and our brand of democratic capitalism seems flexible enough to reinvent itself when social and political forces require. As the New Deal reformers saw it, for example, the creation of big government—what we now variously call the administrative state or the welfare state—was a shrewd maneuver to protect capitalism from the Depression-fed global wildfires of totalitarianism, fascism, and illiberal collectivism. A brilliant example, you might say, of the evolutionary imperative that one must adapt or die. The dramatic civil rights gains of 1954–68 are perhaps comparable. (And the burst of environmental protectionism may also fit this pattern: it was needed in order to save the planet from capitalism and hence save capitalism from itself.)

But consider these interesting implications of the two schools of thought:

- Trickle-up theory will work only if one optimistically believes that the changes required of the system are within its evolutionary grasp, that the impediments to change that will bring greater justice to the underclass can all be overcome in time. But for a racial pessimist, who considers the distance between the races to be so great and the very core of our politics so poisoned as to make good solutions unattainable, this trickle-up theory is a share and a deception.
- For a left-leaning racial pessimist, the prescription for class-based transformative upheaval is just as unappealing as trickle-up strategies are, because the poison of racial division undermines the class solidarity needed for successful struggle. A left-leaning racial optimist would simply have to be satisfied that a preferable alternative to democratic capitalism really exists. (I myself have not seen it.)
- The right-leaning prescription for salvation, a conservative values-oriented revolution, makes sense if you accept the basic conservative analysis of the situation: that race is not the problem, social pathology is. As a host of conservatives have put it, if you eliminated discrimination and racism tonight, not one person in the black underclass would be better off tomorrow. (And therefore we shouldn't bother to try?) So this conservative presentation for social transformation, like the leftist prescription based on class struggle, is premised on a judgment that race matters, *but not much*.

If this presentation of the various implications is correct, the choice is easy: none of them has much going for it a priori. So the way to choose is to be pragmatic. What seems achievable today, next month, this decade? Some people have a revolutionary vision—what Louis

Farrakhan and Pat Buchanan have in common deserves its own book—but most of us know no better than to march, and sometimes run, by putting one foot in front of the other, again and again.

Why am I suspicious of the radicals on the left, even when I share so many of their values? For one, they assert a need for deep structural upheaval but only vaguely define it. Not only is the institutional detail lacking, even the aspiration is uncertain. How much of the order of things must change? Capitalist relations and institutions? Religious orderings of social life? Gender roles? Family structure? And we are to replace these with what? How?

To my mind, the question whether the pillars of capitalism or other major institutions must be brought down should be answered consequentially. If the goal is emancipation of all peoples, how is that most likely to be brought about? To me, thinking as a "race man," this is not in the first instance an ideological inquiry (though an answer requires interpretation, prediction, and hence subjectivity reflecting inchoate ideological presumptions) but, rather, a matter of policy analysis, social empiricism, and trial and error. Plenty of error.

We don't have a good alternative to appropriately reformed democratic capitalism, and we don't have proof that a sweeping transformation is required to achieve racial justice. (We should apply Occam's razor to keep our revolutionary ambitions modest.) And there's certainly no reason to believe that sweeping change would be more achievable than conventional reform. Thus it seems entirely true that the prospects for American racial justice are bound up in the prospects for American democratic capitalism. I fleetingly had other views in my youth, but now I think: Mend it, don't end it.

## The Racial Gap in Perceptions—from Taxis to Criminal Justice

On the day of the Million Man March, October 16, 1995, President Clinton gave a widely praised speech, the central theme of which was a plea for honest conversation, for truth-telling, across the racial divide. He said, for example, that blacks must understand that "it is not racist" for a cab driver to pass by a young black man trying to hail him, given that he has a plausible fear of inner-city crime. A few weeks later, the following item appeared in *The Washington Post*:

*Cabbies in Lincoln's City Told to Rebuff Black Men*. Springfield, Ill.—A few blocks from the tomb of the Great Emancipator, a notice posted at Lincoln Yellow Cab Co.'s headquarters made it clear that getting a taxi can be a question of race.

"Effective immediately Do not pick up any black males unless you feel it is safe," the note read. "If you do not feel safe with the way they look Do not pick them up! There has been too many robberies lately, and they have all been by BLACK MALES."

The sign, posted on a bulletin board visible to customers, came down yesterday shortly after a reporter asked about it. Company manager Earl Reno said his lawyer advised him to take the sign down and "put up a sign that says do not pick up any suspicious-looking persons."

The issue of cab drivers being unwilling to pick up minorities has arisen before, most often in big cities. Last fall, former New York mayor David N. Dinkins (D) said a cabbie snubbed him by driving no more than 20 yards farther to pick up a white fare.

The issue of discrimination has special resonance in Springfield, in part because Abraham Lincoln spent most of his adult life here, but also because of the city's history since his death.

In 1987, a federal court ruling brought an end to a system of commission government that opponents claimed was designed to dilute black voting power. The system itself was instituted after a 1908 race riot that prompted the founding of the NAACP.

Black leaders sharply criticized the latest episode.

"That's like saying all black people are robbers," said David Livingston, state president of the NAACP. "You can't judge a person by just looking at them. That's discriminatory and stereotyping."

"You always have hopes that attitudes are changing," said Frank McNeil, a black city alderman who was a leader in overturning the commission government. He said he will ask city officials to seek evidence for potential punitive action against the taxi company.

Legal experts said a policy against picking up blacks also probably violates state and federal civil rights laws.

Reno denied that the note reflects an effort to discriminate, saying

the company does a large business with blacks and that he was trying
to alert his drivers "for their safety."

What is really at stake in this conflict? Most people seem to believe
that a cab driver should be free to decline to serve someone the cabbie
fears, perhaps with the additional proviso that the fear must be *reasonable*. So the question comes down to what is reasonable. Some conservative civil rights critics argue that race-related generalizations
based on experience or statistics are rational and therefore legitimate.
According to this logic, the Yellow Cab manager was acting reasonably
and permissibly. The counterargument must be one of the following:

- The generalization is not statistically valid—the numbers
  don't add up.
- Although it is statistically valid, the difference correlated with
  race is too small to be an *ethically acceptable* basis for making race-based decisions about individual people.
- The statistical difference may be substantial enough, but we
  nevertheless want a rule that "trumps" the statistical inference—a rule *prohibiting* people from doing what might otherwise be considered rational. In essence, we decide that
  compelling social-justice concerns about race mean that pure
  rationality is not, given the broader concerns, reasonable.

There's not much to say about the first argument, except to note
that when prejudice may skew subjective judgments and the interpretation of data, there is a special danger that the numbers will be cooked
or the analysis botched. Extra grains of salt are needed whenever
claims are made that racial discrimination is not discrimination at all
in a certain instance because the statistics make some stereotype sci-
entifically plausible. But it's not really a response to say, "You can't
generalize," because, of course, we generalize all the time about lots
of things. But when are the generalizations analytically and ethically
appropriate? The Yellow Cab manager isn't claiming that *all* black
males are criminals, which would be nuts. He is claiming that criminals
are disproportionately black. This is accurate; participants in the Mil-

lion Man March would agree with him. He is also claiming that this disproportionate criminality means a special risk for drivers who pick up black men. But what does the arithmetic tell you? It may be that the odds of getting mugged by a white fare are one in a thousand, and three times greater with a black fare. Is the Yellow Cab manager estimating the risk from a black fare at three in ten when the real statistic is three in a thousand? Anyway, what odds give a rational or ethical justification for generalizing and deciding about that dude on the corner?

The second and third arguments concern the context. In the taxicab setting, we have two competing interests: the driver is concerned with personal safety and his personal freedom to make decisions about how he works; the interest of the would-be customer can be stated trivially as an interest in getting a convenient cab ride, or, more legally, as an interest in fair treatment at the hands of someone who is, by regulatory law, supposed to provide nondiscriminatory treatment to all who request service, or, with still more moral gravitas, as the fundamental interest in being treated equally and with dignity.

I find that most of the disagreement people have over the problem of the taxicab—once you get past the statistical issue—concerns the interests at stake and how weighty they are. For people who have been victims of discrimination, the issues couldn't be weightier: stigma, dignity, the right to be judged as an individual. It's the *merit* principle, if you will, which in other situations conservatives protect with boundless passion. Given the fairly low level of risk for the driver, this account of the interests at stake would lead you to push for regulations prohibiting practices based on stereotypes and ready generalizations.

But for many other people, the discrimination issue may not be so weighty, the injury to the would-be passenger may be considered minor, and there would be a general disinclination to regulate the cabbie's decision making intrusively. After all, attitudes about risk vary widely: in everyday life we all take risks that far exceed those which we expect government agencies to eliminate through health, safety, and environmental regulations. Who is to say what increased risk to a cabbie is "low"? We are hardly consistent and rational in these matters.

Going still further, we realize, though, that the heart of the disagreement is not over the worth of the cabbie's freedom or life but over the value of the black man's dignitary interest. If I believe you have insulted me, if I feel denigrated, it is nonsensical for you simply to assert that I shouldn't feel that way and leave it at that. Your actions have an effect on me, and my subjective reaction counts for something in measuring the extent of the harm. On the other hand, if my hurt feelings and diminished self-esteem are *unreasonable* responses to the events, then it certainly doesn't warrant any kind of attention from public policy or the authority of the state. But then again, who decides what is unreasonable? Based on what expectations and experiences?

At one extreme, some may say that there is no dignitary interest involved. Although I may feel insulted and denigrated, the argument goes, that is an unreasonable and insubstantial subjective concern if you did not *intend* to denigrate me, or at least if a reasonably objective outsider would not view it as denigration. Lawyers will recognize this familiar move in tort law—for example, in negligence suits—where the subjective expectations and injuries of the plaintiff-victim are not the measure of the matter. Instead, tort law looks to the more *objective*, or outsider's, assessment of the defendant's reasonableness.

Unfortunately, defining the full measure of discrimination and racial conflict in a given instance by reference to some neutral objectivity will not work, I believe. The impulse to escape the subjectivity of the plaintiff-victim makes sense, but in tort the supposition is that objectivity is reliably found in the norms of disinterested third parties—the putative "reasonable person" role in which jurors and judges are cast. In the race context, however, when the outsiders are predominantly members of the white majority, who may be assumed to have a "white idea" about the social structure of race relations in our divided society, there is nothing objective about the outsider's viewpoint. To use it would be to substitute the subjectivity of the cabbie for the subjectivity of the would-be passenger, the subjectivity of the white for that of the black, that of the perpetrator for that of the victim.

The move to focus on "reasonableness" rather than subjectivity is a normative one, even if we cloak it in scientific trappings by calling it a search for objectivity. Whether the imposition of such a norm is on balance good or bad is a subject of some debate among legal theorists. But in the context of race, this move to replace one set of subjective or normative perspectives with another has the great and real danger of recapitulating and reinforcing racial hierarchy. It's as if, in tort, we let the doctors and hospitals decide what the standard of "reasonable care" should be when we adjudicate whether a patient's injuries were the result of negligence. The law makes doctors' opinions very important, but in practical effect it permits juries to impose on the medical profession a duty of care that is more protective of patients than the medical establishment might legislate for itself.

In the race context, is there an obvious basis for choosing between the perspectives of victim and perpetrator? The victim's view may be skewed by the psychology of victimization—the sense of ever present oppression. The perpetrator's view may be skewed by the psychology of the hegemon—the desire to retain power and control.

Let's get back to what President Clinton said. When he seemed to assert that it is obviously not racist to do the kind of thing that the Springfield Yellow Cab Company in fact did a few days later, he was dead wrong about its being *obviously* not racist. The only obvious thing is that it's a hard problem. You can only enjoy the luxury of believing it is an easy problem if you excuse yourself from the civic responsibility to understand the perspective of folks on the other side. It may be that the process by which the President's speech was developed in the White House failed on exactly the criteria of civic inclusion and conversation which he established for the nation as a whole: to reach out to understand.

That same month, October 1995, public reactions to the O. J. Simpson verdict reminded us of the great gulf in perceptions between most blacks and most whites in the United States. Polls immediately following Simpson's acquittal indicated that blacks agreed with the verdict by more than two to one, and whites rejected it by the same margin. The contrast in emotional response was comparably sharp, with so many blacks elated and so many whites enraged. The gulf presents several scientific and social puzzles:

- What is the truth as regards the actual fairness of the American criminal justice system, in Los Angeles or elsewhere?
- What has given rise to such sharp, group-correlated differences in perception?
- What are the social and political implications of such differences?
- What will happen if we allow the differences to persist or worsen?
- If we believe it is important to narrow the differences, how can we?

The first issue, truth, is almost too difficult to discuss. It may be unknowable: although objective facts can be found to some degree of certainty, the evaluation of whether the given facts, the evidence, establish "fairness" is a matter of judgment and, in this context, of politics.

Shortly after I returned from the Clinton administration to my teaching at Harvard, a student asked me to supervise a paper on something having to do with race. (Yes, they are often that unfocused.) My questioning revealed that she had an interest in becoming a criminal prosecutor, so I suggested that she write on some aspect of race in the criminal justice system. Our conversation came on the heels of a new study indicating that almost one-third of all black men aged twenty to twenty-nine are in jail, on probation, or otherwise under the supervision of the criminal justice system. I suggested she try to develop a conceptual framework for assessing what kind of evidence would constitute "unfair" or discriminatory disparate treatment of blacks by the system. I put this hypothetical situation to her:

*You are a young prosecutor in the Brooklyn District Attorney's office. Because you have demonstrated so much promise, the boss offers you your choice of communities to work in. As between two equally crime-plagued communities, one white and one black, which would you choose to serve? Would it matter whether their crime rates were different?*

The student, an African American, said she would choose the black community. I said, "Right. Because you care more about combating crime in your own community." She nodded. But then I pointed out that, on the basis of her anti-crime reaction of solicitude for the security of the black community, she could not jump to the conclusion that an observed statistical disparity in incarcerations or arrests would—in her own terms and from a "black perspective"—be unfair, unjust, or undesirable. The problem is more complicated than that. And so is the truth.

Moreover, one is tempted to say that the truth is of less practical significance than what people *believe* the truth to be. The connection between the two is imperfect, shaped by subjective and social influences. As I have said, for example, your reaction to new evidence about discrimination against minorities or police abuses will depend upon how the new evidence compares with what you think you already know. Statisticians put this in terms of Bayes's Theorem, which describes mathematically how a tentative prediction based on limited information should be updated to reflect added information provided by new data. Imagine flipping a coin. You naturally begin with the assumption that it is "fair"—equal chances of heads or tails. If over a series of tosses you see a great many more tails than heads, you begin to get suspicious. There is a scientific way to compute the changing probability—a prediction, really—that the coin is balanced and fair. But science aside, research has shown that people doing the experiment will likely shift their views in different ways.

Similarly with our expectations about the fairness of a police force or a criminal justice system, or, perhaps, a nation. A common phenomenon is that we are, *irrationally*, more accepting of new evidence that reinforces what we already believe, and more doubtful of new evidence that is challenging or threatening. It takes sustained exposure to the new information to teach us new attitudes. Prejudices die hard, especially when occasional experiences seem to validate them. ("You see? I told you so.")

Racial preconceptions and prejudices are not incurable. But the disease is highly resistant, and sometimes the patient refuses treatment. One thing, at least, is clear: truth is no miracle treatment.

The answer to the second puzzle—about the causes of sharply different worldviews—is at once obvious and complex. Blacks and whites see the world differently because they live in different worlds. There is more to this than the familiar facts about ghettos and well-to-do suburbs, or continuing patterns of residential and social segregation. The gulf in perceptions exists *despite* how much we actually share, and this is an indirect measure of the power of what holds us apart. For example, most middle-class folks get their ideas about the criminal justice system from the mass media, especially television. But for poor people, contact with crime and all that goes with it is far more common. The disproportionate number of blacks in poor and high-crime neighborhoods means that they have a disproportionate exposure to the criminal justice system. For them, the mass-media picture is far from being the only basis on which they form opinions.

And there is more. Beginning with the civil disturbances in Watts, Los Angeles, and other cities across the country in the mid-1960s, police departments came to recognize that they faced what I term a "trust deficit," separating them from the minority communities they are sworn to serve. The black nationalists of that day derided the police as an army of occupation and as "pigs." Many departments reported difficulty getting civilian cooperation in investigations, a phenomenon which became a movie and television cliché. The Kerner Commission Report documented the alienation between police forces and their citizenry. Dozens of jurisdictions faced lawsuits challenging the long-standing practices of exclusion in the police rank and file and then in the officer ranks. All of these are symptoms of the trust deficit. Civilian review boards, community relations initiatives, and now "community policing" are among the measures that cities have tried, with varying success, to remedy it. But these new measures, however fine their intentions, come in the wake of bitter experiences. And old habits— be they habits of misconduct in a police department or habits of distrust in a scarred community—die hard, and draw occasional rejuvenation from fresh wrongs, from hatred, and from destructive forms of nationalism, black or white.

In sum, the gulf in perceptions is evidence not only that we live in different worlds but also that we have different histories and, therefore, different expectations about what the world will be. Since we are conditioned to expect what we have experienced, it is all the more difficult to change our expectations. Most important, there is no reason to believe that healing words alone will much matter, whether spoken by a minister at a march or by a president on a podium.

The implications of this gulf are chilling. The trust deficit which our criminal justice system has in the African-American community is currently only the most glaring trust deficit. Other public and private institutions are in a deficit situation as well—the media, the political process, big corporations, social welfare bureaucracies, public schools, the very machinery of economic opportunity and upward mobility in the United States. . . . In each area, there is some perception gulf between the races. Take the alienation and corked-up frustration so apparent among blacks in anticipation of the Simpson verdict and multiply that by so many other areas. The innumerable speeches and articles after Simpson's acquittal were well-justified hand-wringing about our divided society, but reflected an appreciation of only one piece of this problem. Their concern was not proportionate to the full range of the dangers we face.

Again, the dynamic bears analysis. Just as accumulated historical experience makes it harder to pull communities together because of the inertia of distrust, so too the extensive distrust generated over varied settings multiplies the impediments to community-building. That is, the trust deficit burdens us in many contexts; the whole of the burden is greater than the sum of its parts.

No measures sufficient unto the task are in sight. The immediate forecast is for more drift and polarization, with increasingly militant black and white nationalisms. One might expect that American society has what macroeconomists used to refer to as automatic stabilizers. Just as the national economy after the Depression was thought to have mechanisms for self-correction that would prevent deep recession or hyperinflation, so too we perhaps have automatic social stabilizers that will prevent a downward death spiral in race relations and tolerance, some combination of political forces and social sense that will rescue us from our worst selves.

I see little support in the news of the day for this cheery possibility.

The news media are filled with ever less tolerant voices, black and white, on the left and right. Yes, some responsible and calming voices are heard on the pundit circuit, and President Clinton has spoken constructively. But the genie of subtle racial intolerance is out of the bottle and not easily recaptured. We see the consequences in ballot initiatives and legislative proposals attacking affirmative action, campaign ads subtly inviting solidarity along racial lines, and political leaders and factions whose self-interest impels them along a path of divisiveness.

Moreover, we face more than a few exceptionally difficult policy and political problems at present—heated election campaigns, desperate budget battles in Washington and in statehouses coast to coast, uncertainty in foreign affairs, an alienated electorate. This is not a time when a President or other politicians are likely to push such matters aside in order to lead a cool, constructive national conversation on an issue as tough as they come. If automatic social stabilizers will indeed prevent us from careening into the abyss (a few commentators have gingerly raised again the specter of race riots), it seems clear that those mechanisms will not prevent many pains and perils short of that.

We ought to be able to figure out how to narrow the trust deficit. The trust-building efforts made by various police departments, for example, could be examined to see if there are general lessons about the determinants of success. Beyond the criminal justice system, though, things get more complicated. History offers lessons, and I suspect we do study too little and emulate only rarely the successful strategies of yesteryear for bridging racial divides. In part, this is because virtually everything written about the civil rights struggle has been composed in a historiographical mind-set of either celebration or revisionism. We need something quite different, perhaps the methodology of an anthropologist, an ethnographer, or even a carpenter carefully disassembling a miraculous piece of cherished cabinetry in order to learn how to replicate it with new materials at hand. *Who got together with whom? How were the coalition pieces assembled, and from where? How did they communicate? How did they work through their disagreements? What broke? Who quit? Who joined? Is now like then?* And are we like them?

• • •

I mentioned earlier the growing awareness and criticism of the sharp disparity in sentences given to defendants convicted for possession and distribution of crystalline crack cocaine and those given for the same crimes involving powdered cocaine. Crack has been the drug of choice in many inner-city areas, and when people feared an "epidemic" of its use, and came to appreciate how powerful the dependency was that crack users so quickly developed, a crackdown began, with an emphasis on tough sentences. After a while, the federal judges imposing the sentences mandated by the official guidelines began to see that the disparities were unconscionable, while jails and prisons filled. The United States Sentencing Commission recommended a reduction in the crack sentences, but Congress passed a bill blocking that; after some internal White House debate, President Clinton signed the bill, saying that this was a drug and law enforcement issue, not a civil rights issue. Well, that's obviously wrong. It is all of those, plus politics.

Jesse Jackson said, "Crack is code for black." And the otherwise quite thoughtful Representative Mel Watt (Democrat of North Carolina) said that it was unfair to send a poor black kid, who could only afford crack rather than the more expensive powdered cocaine, to five years in prison while the rich white kid in the suburbs caught with powder got a suspended sentence and stayed home.

There is something disconcerting about solicitude for people caught in the criminal justice system based on their income or class or race. (In this respect, the President's response seems correct.) A common old-style liberal argument in the 1960s was that moral blameworthiness was diminished when the defendant's social environment and various deprivations had created special incentives for his criminal behavior, or a kind of normative subculture more tolerant of lawbreaking. Conservatives pointed out that this kind of environmental determinism was unfair to victims and their communities, and tended to ratify and promote a distinct set of social norms that were dangerously inconsistent with those of society at large. At its core, environmental determinism *was* a perversion of the traditional understanding of free will and of principles of personal responsibility. It took the moral excuse from blameworthiness provided for centuries in the insanity defense and expanded it beyond all recognition. The correct response to the environmental deprivations, conservatives argued, is to alleviate them with an array of private and public measures, not to treat criminal sentences as a social welfare intervention analogous to income maintenance or charity.

Given the massive trust deficit, however, the liberals have another argument: that the criminal justice system has lost its aura of justice and seems to be just another feature of the harsh, oppressive environment in which so very many things seem wrong and *un*just. More is at stake than the efficacy of the system in the immediate circumstances of this defendant and that victim. There must be a way, over time, to attend to the matter of legitimacy and trust. Otherwise, there is every reason to expect that the racial divide will worsen. In short, we may see a tension between justice in the moment and justice in the large. We must construct and operate the criminal justice system in a way that reduces that tension, and sharply disparate sentences contributing to incarceration, or court supervision of one-third of black males in their twenties only worsens it. Undeniably crack is a scourge of enormous proportions. What many people are arguing is that this response by the criminal justice system is tantamount to a scourge of another sort. The cure is itself debilitating. *Isn't there another way?* Political leaders have failed to offer one, content instead to watch the battle of the scourges fought out in someone else's community.

I am not sanguine about the ability of politics to resolve this problem, despite the theoretical instruction that politics is a useful process for mediating our most contentious value conflicts. I suspect—although I have never discussed this with my former White House colleagues— that from the President's perspective the question of crack sentencing seemed quite simple because the politics were so compelling: whatever the substantive merits of reducing the disparities in sentencing, it would have been impossible from a *communications* standpoint to explain to the American people that it was anything but a soft-on-crime retreat in the war on drugs. One of President Clinton's singular political achievements was to eliminate the national GOP's almost thirty-year edge in opinion polls as the party that is tough on crime. I suppose it was thought that nothing should be done to destroy that achievement. Sad to say, I can't disagree, given the political stakes. But there should be an affirmative, complementary strategy.

As we can see, the political dynamic on issues of criminal justice is so colored by color, and the perceptions of truth and fairness so filtered through and refracted by race-based differences in experience, that one simply cannot expect politics-as-usual to mediate our differences. Politics seems merely to recapitulate our problems.

Nor am I sanguine about the ability of law to resolve this problem of what is fair and what is just, despite law's imperial claims to jurisdiction over such matters. Some weeks after my conversation with the law student about whether she would choose to work as a prosecutor in a black or a white community, the Supreme Court agreed to review a case from California that was very much on this point. A federal district court had decided to permit defendants to use "discovery"— the court-supervised process for subpoenaing documents and sworn testimony from your opponent in preparation for trial—against federal prosecutors. The defendants in the particular case had made a preliminary showing suggesting that drug prosecutions in the San Francisco Bay area were racially targeted, and argued that such targeting, if proven, would violate the Fourteenth Amendment's equal-protection clause. (The Court's decision will come sometime in 1996.) Given the imponderables and the general solicitude courts have for prosecutorial discretion, it seems unlikely that a conservative Supreme Court will make the effort to establish some norm of fairness and chisel it in the concrete of constitutional doctrine. I'd expect it to stress the mountainlike height of the hurdle defendants must surmount in order to make a preliminary showing of wrongful conduct compelling enough to warrant rummaging around in the prosecutor's files or subjecting prosecutorial discretion to judicial review. But, in the larger scheme of things, the question concerns not these *legal* technicalities about racial justice in the allocation of enforcement resources, but the *ethical* judgment about fairness.

## *Leadership*

The Million Man March was an impressive demonstration of racial solidarity and purpose, but it also provided an inadvertent but deeply painful showing of the inadequate leadership in national African-American community. A few days before the march, I participated in a symposium with Cornel West at the famous Schomburg Center in Harlem, a library and research center that is hallowed ground on the cultural and intellectual map of black America. Chatting before the event, Cornel described his unsuccessful efforts to persuade a group of leading black women that they should not protest against the march; one could "separate the message from the messenger," he told them. Acknowledging Minister Louis Farrakhan's apparent flirtations (at least) with racism, sexism, and homophobia, Cornel insisted that the noble purpose of the march he had helped to organize—the affirmation of values shared and solidarity enjoyed among black men—was simply too important to derail by protesting because Farrakhan's had been the first and loudest voice calling for a march. The difficulty was, Cornel agreed, that no leader but Farrakhan and no organization but the Nation of Islam had the imagination and organizational resources to make the event happen. To say this is to make a powerful and painful indictment of African-American leaders, and of those who would be leaders.

Or is it?

The argument that the message and messenger could be separated underestimated the determination and skill of Minister Farrakhan and his communications machine, I believe. He had never had such an opportunity for getting attention and being granted legitimacy; no one should have harbored any illusions that he and his closest followers would graciously accept being one-among-equals, or that he would demur from his acolytes' assertions that the marchers were there to support *him*. Indeed, even as West and others were trying their hand at campaign-style political "spin control," Nation of Islam representatives and the march's director of operations, the Reverend Benjamin Chavis, issued press statements scoffing at their attempts and saying pointedly that the success of the march would be a testament to Farrakhan's leadership, that he would be *the* keynote speaker.

Some leaders and commentators also misunderstood the dynamic of the media. In the days preceding the march, they argued that one could turn the major news media away from Farrakhan by stressing instead the message of healing and the values of community. This was naive in the extreme. News reporters and producers always search for the "edge" in a story, and Farrakhan is nothing *but* edges—with his talk about black versus Jew, black versus white, men versus women, straights versus gays, poor versus rich, believers versus infidels. This was—and is—too good a story to drop or even mute for the sake of some peace-and-love rhapsody recycled from the 1960s.

Three days after the march, I hailed a cab at 2nd and C Street SE, a couple of blocks from the Capitol, headed for National Airport and a flight back to Boston. The cab driver was a forty-something black woman with her head wrapped in a colorful galé, which reminded me of my first wife during our college days, and she was using her cellular phone to leave a voice-mail message about quitting time; she signed off as "Newt Gingrich." Sensing a kindred spirit, I opened up for a chat. In addition to being witty and attractive, she proved to be extremely intelligent and articulate. A traffic plug on the Southeast Expressway gave her time to present a fully developed argument that African Americans are, on balance, worse off because of integration, in her view. Problems ranging from family structure to crime to schools have exploded, as achievers take advantage of new opportunities created by integration to abandon blacks who, increasingly, live in concentrated poverty. More troubling than this plausible bit of folk science was her willingness to tolerate Farrakhan's messages of hate, especially his anti-Semitism. She acknowledged the ugliness of such sentiments, but suggested that it *may* be that externally directed anger is necessary to create more internal community and unity of purpose. After all, she reasoned, the strategy of integration-plus-assimilation has failed miserably.

This woman driving a cab, like so many people interviewed in the media about the Million Man March, was caught in a quickening black nationalism, with both its positive and its negative possibilities, reflecting the truths of both nationalist and universalist perspectives on the American condition.

On the positive side, almost every social and political challenge facing black communities seems all but impossible without strong leaders and positive values that bind people together in a web of shared respect, commitment, and aspiration. The nationalist thesis is that these ties—or at least many of them—must be internal to the racial group rather than universal and assimilationist. Here again is the difference about difference—between those who think of group identity as a threat to an American ideal and those who think that denying racial difference means either the threat of violent assimilationism or a tactic to enforce marginalization. The nationalist thesis is that the black community *must* come together with an external agenda and its own leaders. The universalist thesis is that group-centered agendas, instrumentally valuable in the moment, are ultimately offensive and self-defeating. Bosnia.

There has never been a period in African-American history when the leadership in the black community was not divided between these strategies. Perhaps the negative aspects of nationalism are on the rise when despair is on the rise, in which case the growing sympathy for this brand of grass-roots leader is unsurprising. There is too little progress to offer as proof of a contrary strategic wisdom.

Where will that struggle go now? In the last few years of the tenure of the Reverend Benjamin Hooks as executive director of the NAACP, that organization's fractious board of directors meddled more and more in operations. When Hooks was finally ousted and replaced with the Reverend Ben Chavis, the Association's problems went into remission, but only briefly. Chavis tried to align the NAACP with young community leaders and more nationalistic sentiments, and proposed steps for a reconciliation and perhaps alliance with the Nation of Islam. Financial scandals and collapse provided the occasion for Chavis's departure, but the result of it all was an unprecedented moral (and fiscal) wound to the nation's oldest civil rights organization. Among the highlights of 1995, therefore, must be counted the decision by

Congressman Kweisi Mfume (Democrat of Maryland) to resign his office and take the helm of the NAACP. Mfume is an outsize talent who had been the subject of more than idle whispers about someday heading the Democratic Party in the House of Representatives. An exceptionally effective politician, legislator, public speaker, and negotiator, he immediately created grand possibilities for a renaissance in the NAACP.

At the same time, the National Urban League has a new leader in Hugh Price, a former foundation executive and member of *The New York Times*'s editorial board. Price is a policy intellectual of the first rank who well understands the processes of social change and the dos and don'ts of crafting agendas for change, of building coalitions to press those agendas. Price does not immediately register as a grass-roots-kinda-guy, but he has already proven himself an able ambassador to corporate and opinion elites from African Americans and communities in need.

That this kind of leader has appeared in two important organizations is cause for long, deep celebration. But to understand the magnitude of their task, we should consider the conditions relating to the dangerous decline in the effectiveness of black leaders over the past two decades. First, the situation is in some respects intransigently difficult. The simple, powerful injustices of the Jim Crow laws in the South, supported by law enforcement officers who were proud to be racist, like "Bull" Connor, and commonly condoned overt bigotry, are rare enough now so that most of the country believes that racism in America is unusual, unimportant, or both. Rallying the troops in these circumstances isn't easy. Second, many able blacks who in earlier times might have stayed in their communities have, instead, used the opportunities opened up by the civil rights movement and moved into the semi-integrated mainstream world. Third, we have not understood, as some corporations and the military do, that leadership is too important to be left to chance. Future leaders must be found and trained. We must reverse the tradition of doing almost nothing to prepare people who will battle effectively for better neighborhood schools, greater voter turnout, or wider employment opportunities. This is more than a generational problem. We surely have that, but we must also think differently about the nature of leadership. Occasionally in African-American history we've been blessed by the miraculous arising of a prophet. But God helps dem who help themselves, and we have to do more than await miracles.

Fourth, black communities, like white communities, have experienced a decline in civic engagement in many forms. In his work on "building social capital," my Harvard colleague Robert Putnam has pointed out the steep decline in the United States and many other industrialized democracies in the levels and quality of the *networks, norms, and trust* that create strong civic communities and sustain both democracy and economic vitality. Analyzing numerous indicators—voter participation rates, church attendance, membership in voluntary organizations, opinion surveys, and much more—Putnam observed declines in all racial and social groups. But in the United States, the levels of civic engagement are lowest, and dramatically so, among African Americans. Poor leadership may be both an effect *and* a cause of declining community.

Fifth, too few minority leaders have bridged the worlds of mainstream politics and identity politics, the worlds of church supper and legislative back room, the worlds of the media and the policy conclave.

Sixth, and finally, too many African-American leaders fail to grasp—as Martin Luther King, Jr., did—that their task is not simply to lead blacks but to lead blacks and whites—taking seriously the need to show all Americans where we should be going, encouraging them in that direction. Of course we need many kinds of leaders for many different purposes and in many different settings. But we have had too few who spoke *from* the souls of black folk while speaking *to* the souls of us all.

We all know that there is far more difficult work to do than there are good people to do it. The leadership of the African-American community measures up well enough against other leaders. (I say this more with concern for the United States than with pride in my black leaders.) But the peril is all the more acute for people who must depend for their survival on the quality of their leadership. As usual, the African-American community has to be *better* in order to be equal.

• • •

Well, this chapter was a dose of gloom and doom. Its central question concerned community—understanding and mediating the differences that define community. Within each of us, and in the polity as a whole, are inevitable tensions of identity and community. These can be understood but not dissolved.

What oppresses me is a sense that a poisonous dynamic has developed concerning these differences. There can be no end to the values battle over race policy, no healing of the racial diseases, until that poison is eradicated. We must build bridges between communities and, indeed, create *better* communities. How?

# 10

# VALUES AND COMMUNITY

### *The Rights Rhetoric Trap*

**W**hy can't we reach consensus on affirmative action? The question is a bit daunting, as we have a crisis in persuasion to which almost everyone responds by increasing the volume or complexity of their arguments, yet few people change their minds. In this book, I've tried to suggest ways of thinking about race relations that will help us move to a different plane and get us unstuck. For all the attention I have given thus far to the legal and moral choices, *the harder question is how we persuade each other to make one choice rather than another.* Our familiar rights talk does not move people any longer, at least not on its own.

At a very simple level, it is easy to explain our robust disagreements over affirmative action: perhaps there is broad consensus on the aspirational ideal, *but disagreement over means.* We agree that racial difference ought not mean disadvantage. After all, this is the essence of racial justice, and affirmative action is simply one means of attaining it. Disagreement over means can be regarded as a technical detail about which reasonable people, like-minded as to goals ex hypothesi, can reach an accommodation if only they would communicate effectively about their differing instrumental calculations.

There are three important errors in this rosy formulation. The first is that, as we have seen, the supposed empirical dispute about affirmative action is attributable partly to the differing vantage points: black and white observers see things differently. The second error is to claim that the dispute over the instrumental correctness of affirmative action can be resolved because it is an argument about objective "facts," not subjective "values." Facts and values are not neatly separable, and a dispute about values lurks within the empirical dispute, indeed sometimes dominates it. The crux is not the varying estimates of how long it will take, say, for race-blind hiring to produce equitable minority representation in a workforce; the disagreement has more to do with how urgently one wants to make progress, and one's willingness to pay particular kinds and levels of costs for it. There is also the related matter of risk aversion: people differ on what risks they will accept in order to make progress. Many disputes about remedies, such as thumb-on-the-scale ("plus factor") affirmative action, are disputes about risk aversion and, therefore, about different underlying values and commitments.

Third, and most important, racial justice is only one of several ideals that describe the kind of community we want. As we have seen, defining the appropriate forms of and limits to affirmative action requires subjective, controversial choices, and the several sometimes inconsistent goals require subjective, conflicting accommodations. This is, at root, a choice among alternative moral visions.

So the conflict over affirmative action is not an empirical dispute about instrumental means to achieve a well-understood, accepted end. Indeed, a helpful distinction between means and ends is impossible in this value-laden field. The conflict is inescapably *moral*—lifting what would otherwise be a dispute between the willful political preferences of this or that legislator or judge, and expressing it in terms of legal and moral principles and rights. An elevated plane, and admittedly one with little sunlight and much fog.

Arguing about rights on this plane hardly resolves the matter, since claims concerning rights are notoriously controversial and anything but objective, particularly in the race context. So an argument that appeals to "rights" undermines most of the desired objective basis for agreement. A knock-'em-dead, objectively compelling, rights-based argument to end all argument has not been found because it cannot exist. It is the mythic holy grail of civil rights advocacy. Nevertheless, we continue searching. While it may be futile, it's a living. A noble one.

Political and legal advocates in our culture have become adept at stating positions and demands using the rhetoric of rights. The effort to distinguish rights from "privileges" has been wisely abandoned in constitutional jurisprudence, but continues in political discourse. Indeed, increasingly since the 1960s, advocates seem to express an interest group's stake in a controversy in terms of "rights": farmers have a right to price supports; present or prospective homeowners have a right to the deduction for mortgage interest payments on their federal tax returns; commercial and recreational interests have rights to exploit fish, wildlife, and other natural resources. That we have this accelerating use of such rhetoric and the simultaneous devaluation of rights currency reflects the essential dilemma within rights-based theories. Most rights are, by nature, alienating to someone, because they allow a barrier to be built around the individual or group that holds them, ostensibly to protect against hostile acts by the state or others. My colleague Roberto Unger puts it this way:

> [O]ur dominant conception of right imagines the right as a zone of discretion of the rightholder, a zone whose boundaries are more or less rigidly fixed at the time of the initial definition of the right. The right is a loaded gun that the rightholder may shoot at will in his corner of town. Outside that corner the other licensed gunmen may shoot him down. But the give-and-take of communal life and its characteristic concern for the actual effect of any decision upon the other person are incompatible with this view of right and therefore, if this is the only possible view, with any regime of rights.

Unger is a leading intellectual of the left, but another of my colleagues, Charles Fried, is a leading intellectual on the right who has written to much the same effect by going so far as to define the ordinarily communal notion of "equality" in the rather alienated terms of self-protection.

For better or worse, these "rights" make for barriers separating people or groups within a community, which thereby give that community a certain character—in some respects an impoverished one. A right protects the minority from being forced into a majoritarian democratic consensus by placing the group outside the reach of that consensus, and perhaps outside the community's processes of consensus formation or reform. In other words, to the extent that a right trumps a community's democratic processes, those processes and the sense of community they would create are impaired. We usually consider this desirable in the end—that's what the Bill of Rights is about—but it has its costs. Relatedly, by asserting the right to stand apart from the majority view and not be drawn into a consensus, the holder of a countermajoritarian right is boycotting the continuing, dialectical process of community formation and self-definition of which democratic processes are a part. So, while the familiar, positive idea of rights is that they provide an escape valve when democratic processes go awry, it is also true that rights distort structures of inclusion, participation, and accountability. *Members of a community are the same in that each enjoys certain rights, but any individual asserting a right sets himself apart and becomes different by insisting on exemption from the collective purpose or judgment.*

We can thus be properly skeptical about the power of rights-based analyses, inherently alienating, to dissolve the value-laden conflict over affirmative action. But what other modes of analysis do we have? The common-law framework for liability, which stresses individual fault and causation, is closely related to, if not derived from, rights-based theories: it generally presumes that everyone has a "right" not to be a "victim" of private or state action unless one has been at "fault."

Conservative intellectuals like to press this tendency of the common law to an extreme, believing that in order to protect liberty we must impose liability only in cases in which the defendant intended the act, because only the voluntariness implicit in intention gives us the moral justification for invading the personal sphere. Liability must proceed from moral choice, and moral choice requires intention, not merely volition. This very conservative approach tries to avoid the slippery slope of subjectivity, negotiation and politics implicit in liability rules that are based on "reasonableness," causation, or foreseeability, but does so by forcing a destructively alienating emphasis on the individual vis-à-vis the community. And anyway, their approach doesn't escape subjectivity when it comes time to define or characterize the intentional "act" required for liability. What is the required scope of the intention? And what constitutes evidence and proof of intent, if not some version of "reasonableness"? No solution to these issues of definition avoids subjectivity.

It does us no good to define racial justice using common-law notions of individual fault and liability because both the conservative and conventional versions of those notions have the same difficulties as rights rhetoric. We would still have *subjectivity*, because fault depends on assessments of reasonableness, on the debatable content of a given duty, and on how short a causal chain we demand between an act and its injurious consequences. And we would still have *anti-community alienation*, because the common-law approach requires proof of personal fault and causation, and thereby simultaneously protects the defendant from state-enforced loss-shifting and gives him a barrier against responsibility for the problem of the needy plaintiff-citizen, even if sharing responsibility is demanded by the politics of the community. Obligations are defined with an eye to personal autonomy, rather than community aspirations.

There is another connection between the rights framework and the fault-causation framework, but this time it concerns the victim. To the extent that rights are conceived as protective devices for individuals against others and against the community (as the community might act through the state), it has been argued that rights belong to individuals, that "groups do not have rights," as race-based measures seem to presume. This individualist conception of rights divides and alienates members of the minority group one from another. An alternative, group-based conception of rights would instead emphasize the shared social experience of the group. In the affirmative action context, one might focus on the group's social condition and opportunities, rather than searching for evidence that each would-be beneficiary of affirmative action had somehow been a victim of identified acts. Consider the claim that justice and morality require that a black worker recently hired in a program to reverse decades of black exclusion should be protected from layoffs, to the detriment of more senior white workers. The claim has at least some force if and when it evokes a certain aspiration for society. In that aspiration, lingering effects of past discrimination are finally eliminated, and sooner rather than later. But this moral vision is not fruitfully expressed in terms of rights because of our inability to order those competing black and white claims convincingly—that is, *persuasively*. The reciprocal checkmating of rights claims is inescapable and, hence, a draw. But neither side will abandon the game.

### Who Are the Victims?

We need an ontology of victims. Public policy decisions almost always benefit some people and hurt others. When a new highway is built over there instead of over here, a few people get financial compensation for condemnation of their property, as required by the Constitution's Fifth Amendment, but people injured or burdened by the traffic, the noise, or the fact that another neighborhood gets the commercial benefits, just have to bear the loss. There are many structurally similar situations. Have your taxes been raised to finance a government program that you oppose or that doesn't help you except in the most remote sense (a new attack submarine, welfare benefits, a levee in Nebraska)? Consider the fairness when you pay insurance premiums but never have occasion to file a claim. All of these demonstrate the inevitable loss-shifting and overhead that come along with living in a community and engaging in collective activity.

The central, familiar criticism of affirmative action is that it creates a new class of victims, victimized because they happen to be white. This is a politically clever attack because Americans usually love victims, and our legal system tries to favor them with relief. Courts, however, consistently reject such sweeping logic. Chief Justice Warren Burger, who was never accused of extremism in these matters, wrote that "a 'sharing of the burden' by innocent parties" is permissible if the remedy is carefully tailored. That view is sensible because virtually every form of collective action entails some elements of sacrifice from many. Usually the sacrifice is by the less politically powerful, but sometimes a principle or law forces the majority to sacrifice in aid of the minority. I suppose that, in such situations, the continuing frustrations of the majority will make any such policy of sacrifice perpetually unstable. And that's where we are on affirmative action.

In the contexts of public policy choices burdening certain individuals or groups, the moral content of the category "victim" is quite different from the criminal model that comes so readily to mind. And it is different from the tort context, dominated as tort is by the concepts of fault and duty. So the question is, in what respects are the social and economic burdens associated with racial policies morally equivalent to the burdens associated with other public policies? *Must* we think of racial justice as being so different?

We can imagine several ways of analyzing the assignment of social burdens. The first is that of *culpable causation*; this emphasizes that the state should let a loss lie where it falls unless a specific defendant is at fault in the sense of having caused the injury. With affirmative action, the white bystander will argue that he is not at fault, hasn't done anything. If background and/or past events far beyond his control disadvantaged the black, the state should let the consequential losses lie unless the black finds a culpable, discriminating defendant to bear the costs of any remedy. But why should this be so? Is the faultless white a victim of black aspirations, or has he simply found himself on the expensive side of a redistribution, in which both the disadvantaged black and the innocent white are caught up in a problem bigger than all of us? The two perspectives of these hypothetical white and black individuals mirror the contrasting values we discussed: color blindness versus morally equal opportunity and effective antidiscrimination. Each vision is coherent. *But to be persuasive you have to stand outside both.*

A second approach to assigning social burdens might be labeled *collective correction*; it emphasizes collective responsibility for certain dangers and injuries because we are all in this together and the costs of corrective action should be distributed among all of us rather than heaped on the unlucky (innocent). It accepts responsibility for healing the injury. There is also the possibility of taking responsibility for the injury itself, accepting the blame, but the two are distinguishable. Accepting responsibility for healing need not entail accepting blame and the moral judgment associated with it; however, conversely, accepting collective blame would definitely mean assuming the moral obligation to help. This is the argument for reparations. In some respects the collective-correction approach is consistent with either Vision II or Vision III, because the predicate for remedies is not limited to some narrow notion of bigotry or racial animus. In other respects, collective correction is not consistent with those frameworks because it gives no principled attention or moral weight to the burdens imposed on bystanders by race-conscious measures, no recognition to the widely shared intuition that race *is* different from other policy subjects. It is almost the antithesis of the color-blind vision, which holds that the moral cost of race-based decisions has the greatest possible weight. Indeed, we'd have to consider pure collective correction a distinct Vision IV, in which the means of achieving racial justice are subject only to the same moral limitations we apply to public policies concerning highway construction or farm subsidies.

A third approach is *interest accommodation*, a pragmatic advance on the first two. Rather than the winner-take-all vision of moral calculation, rights-based litigation, or raw majority power, the interest accommodation vision emphasizes the search for common ground, compromise, and community. Perhaps the majority and minority can each give a little, rather than insisting that one has all the entitlement marbles and the other must bear all the costs. For example, in a situation where layoffs of last-hired workers may obliterate the gains from affirmative action, some commentators have suggested job-sharing or wage-reduction schemes; a touchstone in the legal analysis of race-based college scholarships is, under "narrow tailoring," whether such scholarships are a small portion of total scholarship spending. This is a familiar tactic in pluralist politics, in which the moral calculus balances the contending values. It is not a moral determinism in which absolutes or definitive hierarchies of values define a nifty analytical

# VISIONS OF RACE, LIABILITY AND REDISTRIBUTION

| | VALUES: THE MORAL PERMISSIBILITY OF RACE-CONSCIOUS DECISION MAKING | LIABILITY: THE PREDICATE FOR IMPOSING REDISTRIBUTIVE BURDENS | RACE AS A FACTOR IN DESIGNING POLICY |
|---|---|---|---|
| VISION I | *Chapter 3*: the moral cost of race-based thinking is always too high to pay, except perhaps for narrow remediation | *Culpable Causation*: the required predicate for imposing a redistributive burden on defendants or bystanders | race cannot be a basis for redistributive government policies; notion of "remedy" is very narrow |
| VISION II | *Chapter 4*: there is a moral cost to race-based decisions, but it may be justified for remediation, including the remediation of lingering effects needed for morally equal opportunity | *Interest Accommodation*: the implicit model for weighing justifications and tailoring race-based measures when redistributing opportunity; moral weight of interests depends on many factors; bystanders have a voice, but not a veto | race can be used only with predicate of justification, plus tailoring of the measure |
| VISION III | *Chapter 5*: there is a moral cost to race-based decision; but justification not only as in Vision II, but also for diversity | *Interest Accommodation*: as above, but with recognition of additional nonremedial interests | same as above; in both Visions II and III, the tailoring shows that benefits must be *balanced* with costs |
| VISION IV | *Chapter 10*: there is *no particular moral cost* to considering race, provided the motive is beneficent—that the decision does not burden a historically disadvantaged group (the Supreme Court rejects this view) | *Collective Correction*: suggests that the legitimacy of using race is based on a communal vision intended to correct the consequences of the past and/or reconstruct the present distribution of opportunity; reparations | race is no different from income, geography, or any other basis for rationally allocating the redistributive consequences; fault or blameworthiness is immaterial; neither careful justification nor narrow tailoring is required (this is not the law) |

purity. Instead, its results seem contingent, indeterminate, and subjective. Moreover, in important respects it is unconventional—indeed, troubling—when looked at legally because it lacks the conventional trappings of "objectivity" as the Rule of Law seems to demand. Interest accommodation is attractive because it appeals to our pragmatism and rejects moral absolutism. That honesty has its advantages, but also its costs. One cost is legitimacy if, for example, the parties to the dispute have it in their minds that "rights" are at stake—and that is precisely the mind-set with which many of us approach civil rights issues, reinforced by the rights rhetoric of legal and political discourse. Accommodation does not square with the objective demand that justice be done. Yet, in truth, the search for objectivity (as in culpable causation) offers only illusory certainty, and it quite evidently doesn't offer a means to achieve consensus. The search for common ground through interest accommodation has the very great value and virtue of pointing in the direction of healing and building *community*.

If we approach affirmative action and remedies for racial injustice with an emphasis on collective arguments as distinct from familiar patterns in private law, new possibilities might, in fact, arise. Before the *Stotts v. Memphis Fire Department* decision by the Supreme Court in 1984, federal court of appeals in the First and Sixth Circuits had ruled that seniority rules of last-hired, first-fired could be modified at the expense of white workers in a situation of threatened layoffs in order to preserve some of the recent minority employment gains brought about by court-approved affirmative action plans. In those opinions, there were suggestions that white workers had benefited from the employers' earlier discrimination and, therefore, must bear the social costs of the struggle to end racial injustice. These suggestions were made timidly, but it was noteworthy that they were made at all, even though eventually rejected by the Supreme Court in *Stotts*.

The attractiveness of those ideas comes, to me, in the way they treat antidiscrimination as a matter of understanding and structuring *social categories*, rather than private rights, and therefore a matter more appropriate for collectivist modes of analysis. Most people—apart from a few academics—do not regard the theoretical conceptions that govern property, contract, and tort as matters of social category and culture, matters contingent on social organization or policy, but simply as legal attributes or claims tied to the individuals. But when a court looks at antidiscrimination as something different from private law, it can—or we can—think about remedies in a different way.

If, that is, we can shed a few inhibitions. Among those is our sense of what kinds of argument and reasoning are appropriate for political, as opposed to judicial, institutions. The rhetoric of causation, rights, and duties is deemed judgelike; the rhetoric of pluralist accommodation, deemed inconsistent with objectivity and the Rule of Law, is the province of the political branches. Ultimately, giving resolution of disputes and formulation of rules to courts and legislatures, respectively, is at root less about the nature of the problems or the *feasibility* of resolving them with judges or legislators than it is about the kind of analysis we suppose to be needed and appropriate. Yet, if you see that the various modes of analysis (politics, Rule of Law fairness, and instrumental efficiency) are inextricably linked and impossible to describe in isolated purity, then you see that assigning each to an institutional pigeonhole is wrongheaded. Part of our problem, indeed, is that we think about racial justice in terms of what a *court* might do, but we have courts, in their decisions, applying principles and processes rooted in common law and Rule of Law traditions, traditions which lock in the stalemate we must escape. When courts review policy choices made by legislators and politicians, whose eclecticism draws from varied conceptions of fairness, desert, and reason, the conflict is between modes of reasoning, not just between institutions.

The upshot is that we shouldn't expect to escape stalemated rights rhetoric and find common ground on racial justice by relying on the way lawyers think and legal institutions operate. In the realm of what each of us should believe is fair or just or desirable, we need not be bound by the abstractions of institutional role and competence, or by centuries-old notions of fault and liability. Instead, we should focus on the debate and choice about values that has been the focus of this book.

## *Persuasion and Conversion: Escaping the Stalemate*

My first proposition was that we should put aside the wishful thought that our disagreements over affirmative action are based on mere differences in empirical judgments about the instrumental need for racial preferences. My second is that we should put aside the naive view that a proper understanding of "rights" as now defined in legal doctrine (or plausibly accommodated by it) will solve the problem. These two renunciations are not easy, politically or intellectually, because they require that we rethink many familiar ideas—such as the pretense that we agree on definitions of racial justice, or that we must rely on fault-based liability—and come up with an alternative way of reasoning and persuading. To what extent do our ways of discussing affirmative action recapitulate the problematic, unresolvable divisions inherent in these concepts I would have us put aside?

There are three axes of rhetorical battle, or general forms of argument—arguments (not all true, of course) that find their way into both legal analysis and political discourse:

- Proponents of affirmative action are concerned with results and substance; opponents with opportunity and procedure.
- Proponents stress the public or state role and the social importance of group identity and group rights; opponents stress autonomous, private spheres of action and individual identity and individual rights.
- Proponents emphasize welfare and reparations; opponents emphasize fault and injury. This is a variation on the preceding argument.

Is it any wonder that consensus eludes us, when the underlying dispute is drawn along these lines, when contenders understand the problem as one of choice between equally incoherent, unsatisfactory alternatives for stating their beliefs? We must understand the disagreement in different terms. To explore why this is so, let's consider each of these three ways of framing the debate.

*Opportunity v. Results; Procedure v. Substance.* This disagreement looks like one between those who want to make sure that the footrace is "fair" and those who pay attention to the winners and losers. One group seems to have an eye on the process rather than the outcome: they just want to make sure that the contest is not fixed and that the neutral criterion of "fleetness" controls the result. Recall again President Lyndon Johnson's explanation: "You do not take a person who had been hobbled by chains, liberate him, bring him up to the starting gate of a race and then say, 'You are free to compete with all the others,' and still justly believe you have been completely fair." But you can put aside this difficult—I would say impossible—search for unbiased process and neutral rules, and examine instead the distribution of winners and losers, making a judgment about whether the picture reflects the kind of fairness you want in your community. There are three basic choices, necessarily subjective: either you think the observed distribution is fair or you think it isn't; or you don't really care, so long as the race was won by the fleetest. Having accepted the unavoidable problem of subjective choice, however, you may decide it's the wrong game. (Why a footrace? Why fleetness? Why measured in this way?)

Let me elaborate. It is now fairly common for law teachers to demonstrate to students that they should be especially wary of doctrinal arguments based on supposedly neat distinctions between substance and procedure. In most circumstances, something that seemed procedural can be recast as substantive, and vice versa. At the very least, any problem that at first glance appears to be quite largely the one can, on close inspection, be seen to contain important elements of the other. Thus, the seemingly "procedural" notion of assuring people equal opportunity has "substantive" content of enormous significance: opportunities available to different individuals or groups must be compared, and a value-laden decision must be made as to when these are equal. This entails deciding which differences among opportunities and among individuals to ignore and which to count. So grounding the debate over racial policy on the opportunity-results distinction has the same conceptual and practical problems as the procedure-substance distinction: both are problematic whenever things get interesting.

A better a way of thinking about this is to consider whether the measures taken to affirm "equal" opportunity ought to acknowledge the genuine disadvantages still worked by the lingering poisons of racial caste. As I argued in Chapter 4, *morally equal* opportunity must take into account the need to redress at least certain of the race-linked disadvantages in the socioeconomic endowments we bring to the game. (One may or may not need overtly race-conscious measures to do so.) There is the related conflict over the very definition of "discrimination"—whether it should focus exclusively on disparate treatment (which superficially sounds like opportunity) or should also encompass disparate impact (which superficially sounds like results). Someone properly skeptical about a strict opportunity-results or procedure-substance dichotomy would put it this way: *If an employer or policy maker has a malign indifference to the observed inequalities generated by a seemingly neutral hiring rule—i.e., doesn't care about the disparate impact—then his substantive choice to ignore those effects, and continue the practice that is feeding that inequality, is itself a culpable choice about the content of opportunity.* Put this way, substance loops back into procedure, and results loop back into opportunity. To many supporters of affirmative action, this conceptual "move" seems obvious and compelling. To many opponents, it is sophistry. They want to insist that *no*, there is a distinction. I think they are wrong.

And it doesn't help to talk about intent. People who say that "discrimination" should be limited to disparate treatment want to do so because then they can hold perpetrators accountable for their intentional acts. But those who want to include disparate impact would say that perpetrators also "intend" the reasonably foreseeable consequences of those intentional acts. After I show you the results, you can't continue with your past practices and deny that you intend those results; if you want moral immunity, you will have to base your defense on some notion other than absence of intent. My point is, intent doesn't work as a defense precisely because procedure and substance, opportunity and results, are difficult to keep separate.

*Private v. Public; Individual v. Group.* Well, if the familiar opportunity-results distinction is an unhelpful (yet common) way to organize the affirmative action debate, how about the equally familiar public-private distinction? One school of affirmative action opponents believes that a sphere of private autonomy must be preserved and protected against encroachments by the state; that private interests and values should be subordinated to public will only under extraordinary circumstances; and that inasmuch as many racial policies represent a form of intrusive social regulation, they can be justified only on a very narrow basis corresponding, perhaps, to judgments about criminality. This is the inescapable import of the libertarian argument, and such views are extreme. On the other hand, proponents of affirmative action and related policies are prepared to displace the primacy of individual autonomy with emphases on the importance of group identity and government coercion. Then there are nuances about when and how.

To distinguish public and private in this way is intellectually coherent only in the extreme form of libertarianism, if then. This is because once we admit the possibility of any kind of collective action to obtain social welfare goals, we cannot but blur the line between individual and community spheres. Suppose the state acts to advance or protect the interests of person X, but does so at the expense of person Y. Then Y may perceive the action as an incursion on his or her autonomy, but X's perspective is different. Whose is correct? Neither. The public-private distinction is of little use in answering the question; the issue is one of power and fairness, and it cannot be satisfactorily addressed with absolute rules such as radical individual autonomy. We gave that up long ago when we came into the cave together to escape saber-toothed tigers and the cold. To most people this kind of radical libertarianism just seems weird. It doesn't describe the world we live in. The opposite extreme view, that the public sphere absorbs the private, is just as untenable: we have not surrendered everything to the state.

If we must choose to side with either X or Y, and we sensibly refuse to embrace extreme views about what the citizen's life should be, then we must argue about the messy, bloody dispute at hand. It isn't all black and white. The context is almost everything. Elements of the civil rights dispute express the tension between public and private spheres familiar throughout America's history, but the unresolvable nature of that tension in turn explains why casting the dispute in these terms makes for stalemate. The public-private dichotomy, the counterpoint of individual and state, recurs in countless other areas of the law, and is, in every instance, in theory an undissolvable antinomy. But in practice we live with this conundrum; and we must, because it is who we are as a polity.

Extremists to one side, therefore, the typical opponents of aggressive affirmative action are concerned not with the possibility or appropriateness of government intervention in a general, theoretical way— they don't mind tort, bankruptcy proceedings, highway construction, or reasonable environmental protection—but with the moral and social case for intervention on behalf of racial minorities. The debate often sounds it, but the problem really is not individual versus state. At times, it's black versus white.

*Fault v. Welfare; Injury v. Reparations.* Here's yet a third way of stating—caricaturizing?—the debate. Opponents of affirmative action want to base legal and social policy on notions of individual rights and wrongs (fault, injury), while proponents are willing to press claims based on supposed group interests (welfare, reparations). Thus, in one view, the African American benefits from a preference given to minorities by virtue of being black rather than by virtue of some individualized victimization; meanwhile, the white bystander to an affirmative action program feels penalized without the familiar demonstrations of personal fault and proximate causation required in much of our legal order. In the other view, discrimination and morally unequal opportunity are today's greater problem, not individual acts of racial bigotry, so that effective remedial measures can sometimes fairly impose burdens on those who are comparatively advantaged by the status quo and the history that produced it. I have argued earlier that alternative moral visions frame the choice between these views. The words "fault," "injury," and "wrong" are woven into arguments on both sides of the debate—but their meanings differ, depending on the vision. The words sustain the debate, and will never resolve it.

But imagine instead *collective correction* of wrongs done to blacks—wrongs reflected in and implemented by the state, not just by specific old or dead people. This alternative conception of a fair and just remedy proceeds from a conviction that society has the collective responsibility to repair injuries inflicted by the collective, quite apart from pinning blame on particular people. In other words, society has a duty to provide a remedy. For these purposes, privity—a centuries-old legal concept meaning a connectedness substantial enough to trigger liability—flows from community.

A few decades ago, in a detailed analysis of reparations, Boris Bittker of Yale Law School suggested that the appropriate solution to these problems is a public fund to compensate victims. But our political society is democratically controlled not by the victims but by the perpetrators and by heirs and beneficiaries of perpetrators. The majority declines to establish such a public fund, yet recognizes, by statute, that legal causes of action exist for discrimination. No one is brought before the courts to bear remedial burdens except individual defendants and associated bystanders, such as white male workers. So now what? If you accept the framework of collective historical correction, you argue that these defendants and their associates have a social-contract obligation to bear some of the costs. In the alternative fault-and-causation framework, with individual rights pitted against the claims of community, no such obligation can be found. As I suggested earlier, a middle ground can be found in *interest accommodation* and in the emphasis on the community's common ground.

So your choice in matters of racial policy is made not solely in terms of the "rights" of the individual. It involves considering a person's responsibilities as a community member. The disagreements are both empirical and value-based: Are the lingering effects of America's history of condoned racism significant enough today to deserve political and legal attention? Does the white "victim" of affirmative action programs possess a precious autonomy that should immunize him from the demands of community, in this case demands stemming from the community's aspiration to right racial wrongs? Such questions demand moral choices, not logic-chopping about injury, fault, or causation. And I say that as a person who does logic-chopping for a living.


The axes of policy debate parallel the conceptual conundrums: the rhetorical counterposition of opportunity and results, process and substance, is the unworkable contrast between instrumental means and

| DISCOURSE STALEMATE AND VALUES CHOICES | | |
|---|---|---|
| | *Here's how we tend to argue about race:* "THIS" versus "THAT" | |
| **RIGHTS RHETORIC** | rights of the "bystanders" right to be left alone right against reverse bias | rights of "victims" rights of the needy/ disadvantaged right against bias |
| **AXES OF POLICY DEBATE** *unresolvable, manipulable dichotomies provide fuel and confusion* | opportunity fault/wrong/animus intent private | results redistribution/welfare effects public |
| **THEORETICAL RESONANCES** *some familiar themes from social theories?* | means self individual nationalism | ends other community universalism |
| **MORAL VISIONS** | color blindness the moral cost of race-based decision making | remediation, effective opportunity, inclusion the moral cost of race-linked, "endowed" disadvantage |

racial-justice ends; the tension between the regime of private autonomy or fault-based liability and the regime of communal aspiration or welfare equity parallels the stalemate of rights talk.

Of course, American society as a whole doesn't approach affirmative action and preferences within any single moral framework. There is no collective moral judgment, only a collection of private ones. Nor could it be otherwise, absent the sustained national conversation and political focus our culture requires to accomplish those rare upheavals in civic values.

What seems to happen *in practice* is a pragmatic process of rights accommodation, which graciously recognizes many interests—those of black victims, of whites enjoying the status quo, and of blacks and whites who hope someday to enjoy the status quo. Compromises are "fair" only in the semi-principled sense that comes from their being "political" and in that respect legitimate. Assuming a given decision maker is cautious and reasonable, the remedy will not be too offensive. In fact, the range of achievable remedies will change over time, because attitudes of the various groups evolve to reflect changing norms. Thus, school desegregation remedies, which in 1955 might have seemed far too intrusive to be politically supportable, were by 1975 entered into voluntarily. By 1985, the Justice Department was trying, with little success, to reopen and dismantle those remedies. But by 1995, the federal courts were increasingly signaling that desegregation remedies had run their course, and that both lingering and new diseases in our schools must find new prescriptions. The dominant sense of fairness changes every time, for better and for worse.

I am not arguing that rights are unimportant. Even in their bloodless positivist form, they are an undeniable component of justice and an indispensable tool of advocacy. As Ronald Dworkin has put it, justice requires rights, with equality foremost among them. But if I am correct that rights rhetoric is necessarily an unreliable strategy for persuasion in the affirmative action debate, what alternative or additional strategies are available?

### Creating Community

My point of departure is a loose analogy to the religious concept of conversion. When and how does a person decide to embrace a religious doctrine, or a cause like abortion?

In the early 1980s, not long after I began teaching at Harvard Law School, I was invited to join a handful of other colleagues at an informal dinner with Boston's new Cardinal, Bernard Cardinal Law. I'm not sure why I was invited, since I am neither Catholic nor particularly religious. (Affirmative action, I suppose.) Cardinal Law was reportedly a conservative on matters of church doctrine, but he had an impressive record of progressive activism in the cause of racial justice during years of great service in the Deep South. At the time, Boston was in the throes of one of its periodic bouts of racially motivated violence, with gangs and police brutality, with random acts of thuggery; the situation was quite ugly, and many feared a return to the violent chaos that characterized the worst years of the anti-busing hostility in South Boston and elsewhere in the city. I told the Cardinal that I was somewhat despairing of bridging the great gulf in Boston's racial attitudes and the terrible animosities, and asked whether he was optimistic. Would we really be able to come together?

"Yes, I am hopeful," he replied. No elaboration.

"Why, Your Eminence?" I asked. (I hoped that was the proper term of address.)

"Because," he said, "I believe in the possibility of redemption." Well, that was interesting. I suppose that the change in values, commitments, and perceptions that you need to turn a bigot into a brother is a sort of redemption. But that still left the Cardinal's answer incomplete.

So, playing law professor, I pressed further. "But why?"

"Because I have faith," he said. When I looked uncomfortable, he anticipated my next question and continued, "And I have faith because Christ has risen."

There was a genial finality to it. I could understand how, for a person of deep religious commitments, this was a complete analysis and a dispositive answer. But for the rest of us, it left something to be desired. I persisted: "But what reassurance can you give for those lacking your religious faith?"

He replied by voicing confidence in human nature (despite the immediate evidence, I thought to myself). What he may have meant was a collection of human qualities: our desire for stable, civil communities; our inquiring and flexible natures; and, developing from those two, our ability to adapt our conceptions of community and self over time in response to experiences and reflection.

Days later, still puzzling over his reply, it occurred to me that redemption is a product of a conversion, and the conversion is itself a product of a religious experience of some transformative sort. The question, therefore, is: *What secular experiences will have a transformative effect on people so that their racial thinking is redeemed*—so that their values and sense of community, connections, and possibilities are transformed to make possible a different structure of race relations?

Advocacy and debates in recent decades have been dominated by political-legal rights discourse, as we have seen, and they have not explored this plane of community experiences and transformation. But to move beyond the impasse, beyond the stalemate, and thereby to create possibilities for influencing the values we hold, I believe we need self-conscious efforts to construct transformative secular experiences. A decade ago, writing on this theme, I put it this way:

> The kind of conversion I have in mind cannot plausibly be accounted for in terms of the power of rational argument that tips the balance and makes someone understand the "Word of God." [For example:] It will not be some particularly well-crafted argument about rights that finally persuades the apartheid supporter in South Africa that his or her society is diseased. There may be political, economic, or military developments that coerce acceptance of a new moral order. However, whether those are sought out or thrust upon him, the actual conversion of the moral universe of that South African will come about through transformative experiences. Of course, those experiences may well include rational arguments, among them rights-based arguments. But the power will be from a collection of such experiences, because rights rhetoric alone will have difficulty doing anything more than legitimating what is already that person's moral reality.

We do a certain amount of explicit instruction in values when we raise our children, hoping to shape their character and perspective. But perhaps even more than that, we shape our children by consciously selecting and constructing *experiences* for them, believing that these will transform them in desired ways. We may steer them toward play with certain children, or away from others. We decide for or against television shows or warlike toys. We insist on music lessons or team sports or homework discipline, or none of the above. And we even "construct" experiences designed to counteract the untoward effects of experiences we dislike. What "good" teenager hasn't been "taught a lesson" by being "grounded" for a minor infraction of rules? So the notion of using constructed experiences to shape values is familiar to all of us. One of the original premises of school desegregation measures was, in fact, that shared experiences across racial lines would transform that generation of students and help to usher in tolerance and community. The results were mixed, not because the premise was wrong, but because the execution was problematic. Still, integration in the workplace and at all levels of education has generally been thought to hold out our greatest hope for instilling racial tolerance. I cannot fault that logic, but it needs elaboration.

We have learned that it is one thing to throw people from different worlds together in a classroom or an Army boot camp and yet another thing to make them feel a connection that produces a sense of community and mutual commitment. More is needed than proximity. The construction of that experience may be a complex undertaking, depending on the social distance between the people involved and on the context. There is more to this than sitting around a campfire holding hands and singing "Kumbaya."

If this notion of conversion and moral development generated through experiences is plausible, what are its implications for strategies of persuasion?

I recently spoke at a convocation of Episcopal clergy and lay leaders in the New England region. In the Q&A session, we explored my proposal to embark on a course of self-consciously constructed experiences in order to build community, and it became clear that some of them believe this is precisely what they are about when they operate a soup kitchen or deliver meals to elderly shut-ins. I demurred. In my view, such individual Christian acts are not the same as creating the connections and social capital that make for community. Serving someone on the other side of a table at a soup kitchen does not necessarily create the sort of personal connection and reciprocity of interests that is transformative in the needed way. It may be transformative in that someone unfamiliar with the plight of the needy will be enlightened by doing volunteer work, may be affected in profound ways. That is all to the good; charity is virtuous, and it is endangered. But a still deeper effect, I believe, arises from experiences of a still deeper sort, perhaps captured in the expression "Walk a mile in my shoes."

The ultimate goal is to shift the boundaries of the "other" and "community." The charitable impulse makes the boundaries permeable, at least, but does not shift them. The difficulty is that the charitable impulse is contingent. It ranks low among many competing claims upon us and, for most people, it is just about the first commitment they drop in a pinch. The disruptive, uncomfortable adjustments we need to make in order to achieve racial justice will amount to far more than a pinch.

In race relations, the boundary between you and the "other" that defines your community is etched on the national experience in patterns of segregated life and underscored by countless Technicolor differences in social, economic, cultural, and political affairs. Constructing the needed transformative experiences will be very hard. Short of a blueprint, some possibilities are suggested by "postliberal" efforts to emphasize communal values and goals, which acknowledge (and try to avoid) the alienated conception of rights and eschew the search for objectivity. An emphasis on people's connectedness, rather than their autonomous liberty, is consistent with my previous argument that conversion is most likely to come about as part of reimagining community membership and relations. Connectedness, therefore, must be the goal of the experiences we consciously construct to accomplish the transformative conversion. This is the integrationist ethic writ large and extended, but with no implication of self-denying assimilation. To extend Cardinal Law's thought, it is a strategy that both depends on and nurtures the human spirit in its qualities of curiosity, bonding, and caring.

What practices would be consistent with this, given our objective of achieving a consensus on affirmative action? To begin, there must be more shared experiences with the "other." For example, black and white members of Congress on opposite sides of the issue might spend time with each other's constituents—richly textured and intimate time, not stilted panel discussions. Black and white workers should work at understanding each other's experiences and perspectives rather than drawing battle lines and arguing about "rights." How can employers or unions instigate this? These shared experiences might promote understanding and thereby create the possibility for different answers to shared, and very real, problems. The same approach can be appropriate for people in almost any context: in newsrooms of major papers, among school administrators, with parents of pupils in integrated school systems, in a police precinct station. You can't feel a sense of community with someone you don't know. The point is not that exposure makes us see that our similarities are more significant than our differences—that may not even be true in particular circumstances—but that it gives us a better understanding of our differences, which encourages acceptance or accommodation of them.

To seem academically plausible, this strategy of constructing transformative experiences may require a fancy theory of psychodynamics. More concretely, however, this is a program of grass-roots politics, not a call for multiracial encounter groups. Politics usually flows from a sense of community, but it can also be a force in creating a community. The integrationist tenet, that racial injustice can wither away in an integrated society, is consistent with this theme. Rubbing shoulders in classrooms, workplaces, and social life adds the decisive experiential element that an argument simply about blacks' right to be equal cannot have. This, at least, is the integrationists' hope, and rights rhetoric codifies it but does not inspire it.

The history of the civil rights movement in the United States is itself suggestive. The moral transformation brought about during the two decades following *Brown* is one of the more remarkable accomplishments in American history. Racial discrimination went from being entrenched state policy (de jure or de facto) in most of the country to being the target of nearly universal moral condemnation. Was it the rhetoric that converted millions of Americans, or was it experience in combination with that rhetoric? The power of those television images was enormous—the growling dogs, the fire hoses, and "Bull" Connor on the one hand, the dignity of the black children and protesters, of Martin Luther King, Jr., on the other—and, too, President Kennedy and other white leaders focused on the policy issues about racial inequalities in everything from child mortality to retirement poverty. My contention is that these experiences and images had at least as much to do with the process of conversion as the rhetoric did. Experiences led people to reimagine the kind of community they wanted, and that community did not include ugly racism and innocent children condemned by accident of birth to dispiriting disadvantage.

I discovered support for this view in a conversation I had ten years ago with Donald Cunnigen, a doctoral candidate in Harvard's sociology department, who had conducted many interviews for his research on liberal white Southerners in 1954–80. Contrary to what he had previously imagined, his interviews showed that whites did not abandon their support for segregation or their sympathy with ideas of racial superiority as a result of being struck by lightning or being persuaded of the correctness of an argument concerning rights. Usually it was a gradual accretion of experiences, combined with reflection about general moral values (especially what they took to be "Christian values"), which finally changed them into relative progressives.

To state my thesis more precisely: The conversion may involve reimagining both what the membership of the community is and the terms of social relations within it; some tolerance of racial injustice and inequality continues so long as blacks and whites view each other as "others" and social relations between them are strictly stratified; law and litigation merely reflect socially transformative shifts in the vision of community adhered to by elites in the judiciary, the legislature, or the media (this was true during the upswing of the Warren Court and it is true in the downward slide of the Rehnquist Court); the legal experience in turn reinforces the transformative vision and projects it beyond the intellectual and social elites to society as a whole.

This is, of course, only one possibility. There is no fixed relation between the legitimating and transformative functions of law. It depends on the moment, the problem, the other social forces, and even the individuals on hand. Whatever one's view of the past importance of rights rhetoric in either motivating or merely codifying social transformation, as a theoretical and practical matter today the strategically "correct" function for rights rhetoric is up for grabs. It may well be a trap, keeping us from persuading each other to reach a new consensus.

Meanwhile, the value and purpose of the civil rights and anti-poverty movements have lost the attention of the American people, while other messages have come to the fore in mass organizing or political agendas: the environment, arms production, capital formation, tax reduction, "Christian" education, "basic" education, abortion. Crudely put, Madison Avenue skills are needed. Yet the civil rights movement has among its cadres far more people who understand the problems of proving discriminatory intent under the Fourteenth Amendment than it has people who understand how to organize a media campaign to focus attention on black unemployment, voter registration, or victimization by crime. Thankfully, there are no figures who are as visible, scarily legitimate, and morally compelling (repellent) as Lester Maddox with his ax handle, and White Citizens Councils. What images and experiences will generate the next stage of America's moral conversion to a better ideal of racial justice?

The victors in *Brown v. Board of Education* knew the Constitution did not require that change occur overnight. When the Supreme Court announced its ill-starred "with all deliberate speed" formula, it was implicitly attempting to reconcile the civil rights of blacks with an interest in the Court's legitimacy, if not an interest in the very stability of society. Now, over forty years later, opponents of effective affirmative action, those who would settle for aspirational equal opportunity, argue that white rights are at stake and must not be compromised. This is a straightforward issue, and the position you take on it depends on which you care about more: the moral and worldly urgency of African-American progress or the moral and other consequences of deviating from the newly embraced principle of a color-blind society. That principle is a convenient invention, and an oppressively ahistorical one. As constitutional principle, it is both two hundred years late and two generations early. Of course, some people made up their minds on this question a long while ago and refuse to revisit the hard issues. For them, I suppose, low gear is deliberate enough speed even some forty years after *Brown*.

Justice Harry Blackmun said it well in his opinion in the *Bakke* case: "In order to get beyond racism we must first take account of race

. . . (a)nd in order to treat some persons equally, we must treat them differently. We cannot—we dare not—let the Equal Protection Clause perpetuate racial supremacy." Indeed, rights rhetoric may be a trap.

## A National Conversation: The President and Personal Responsibility

Public figures from President Clinton to Newt Gingrich, and Lani Guinier to Patrick Buchanan, have called for a national conversation about race. While it is difficult to dissent from this call for civil dialogue, it is also evident that our expectations ought to be pretty low, unless innovative ground rules overcome several serious obstacles. I count at least six: the issues are too hard; the President is too busy; politics is about winning; journalists are corrupt; elites are isolated; rights rhetoric is a trap.

I have failed miserably if the reader is not by now persuaded that the issues of affirmative action and race relations are extraordinarily hard. Over the years, I have thought and thought about what makes certain public policy challenges so seemingly intractable, even when just about everyone agrees that action is needed. In the 1980s, when the savings-and-loan crisis and the Third World debt crisis loomed, the powers that be dithered at great cost and human suffering, and with destabilizing effects on fragile democracies around the world. Now there is a health-care crisis, with unsustainable growth in costs and insupportable gaps in access to care and insurance. There is the inner-city horror of lives lost to drugs and crime, and the socioeconomic cancer of third-rate public education, killing opportunity. (And there are crises to come—perhaps in the financial soundness of our mutual funds and insurance companies, or a catastrophic surge in HIV infections, or the poisoning of vital aquifers.) The full explanation for our inability to come to grips with these in an effective and timely manner differs from case to case, of course, but a few factors are at work repeatedly.

One factor is the extent to which solving a problem requires very complex and diffuse private actions (perhaps regulated), rather than focused government action alone; also, the more ambitious the needed public-sector activity, the harder it is to build a political consensus and design the policy mechanism. When it comes to race, we know that much depends on countless complex acts of merchants, employers, police officers, teachers, preachers, and children. We know that these acts cannot all be regulated effectively, even if it were desirable to do so. And we know that much depends on personal values and attitudes which are only indirectly and imperfectly affected by policy measures.

Another factor is the extent to which the costs and benefits of the problem and its solution fall on distinctly separated and alienated communities. Third World economies are a world away from most American voters; so are America's own isolated inner cities and rural communities suffering from desperate poverty and social disease. Still another factor—there are many—is the extent to which there is a strong consensus among serious people about the one or two best ways to "solve" the problem. You might think that this is the most important factor, but I don't believe it is. Sometimes, all the experts pretty much agree, but the policy-making system remains stuck in the mud. So a real sense of the answer is not sufficient and may not even be necessary. Occasionally, the system stumbles on an answer without expert consensus having known it in advance—like a second global war helping to end the Great Depression. In race matters, all we do is stumble along, and few serious people claim to know the truth. (Be suspicious if they do.)

In light of all of this, a national conversation must spend time on the nature of the problem and other preliminaries, since we aren't ready for a thoughtful debate about solutions. We remain at the muddling-through stage because we haven't talked enough to share a sense of the problems, let alone the answers. Seeing this, however, brings us face-to-face with the question of whether our leaders, the media, and the public have the patience and fortitude to wrestle with such tough problems. The difficulty starts at the top, because . . .

The President is too busy. And he's not alone in that. Most of the leaders with the political and moral authority to guide us through this quagmire are inevitably distracted—by Bosnia, health care, special prosecutors, the deficit, or natural disasters (not to mention political campaigns). "Conversation" implies something more than a one-shot exercise, more than episodic staged events and town-hall meetings. With one exception, I know of no circumstance short of crisis which can produce the sort of engagement we need, and the exception occurs when the political parties make an issue the focus of an election campaign. As to that . . .

Politics is about winning. Political leaders are occasionally courageous, but when they are it's worth preserving in books or on celluloid. So it is safer to assume that *political* leaders will make a *political* decision about whether to engage in a national conversation. When I began to work on the affirmative action issue for President Clinton, it seemed clear that the story one could tell about the political benefits of speaking out on this issue was a pretty implausible one. The political risks seemed much larger and more likely than any benefits. It boiled down to asking whether "doing the right thing" would show character and in that way score political points. That is not the kind of gamble politicians like to make, even if they have the mettle.

The campaign dynamic is similar. As I've said, I've watched at close hand the tactical decisions in two Democratic presidential campaigns—Carter-Mondale in 1976 and Dukakis-Bentsen in 1987–88. The competition among various interests and agendas is hard-fought, and countless variables come into play—poll numbers, the tactics of the competition, the needs of fund-raisers or party allies, and so on. Somewhere in the mix—either underlying the tactical choices or emerging like a hazy landscape on a pointillist canvas—one should discern who the candidate is, where he wants to go, and how he will lead. But in a typical campaign strategy meeting that vision is a bit hard to spot. (The candidate is never there to help, being sealed inside an aluminum tube at 40,000 feet, and too deprived of sleep and family time to trust with deeply serious decisions. When the candidate insists on making decisions anyway, disaster looms.)

It is not realistic to expect that candidates or campaign operatives will make resource allocation decisions on any basis other than efficient construction of a majority in the electoral college. If a campaign is to be courageous, it is likely to be so on some issue on which the candidate has no real choice, because it can't be ducked and the choices are too sharply defined to fuzz in campaign-speak. Race fits neither test, so a constructive national conversation seems unlikely in a campaign.

What are we to do? The old adage "Think globally, act locally"? And then there's Tip O'Neill's instruction: "All politics is local." We can hope for leadership, but community is *our* responsibility. Individuals and local groups will have to participate in this conversation and in the experiences designed to transform values. After all—to return to the religious metaphor—one doesn't generally experience conversion and redemption vicariously, televangelism notwithstanding.

Local action can take many forms. Here's a sample of what I have in mind:

*Education.* While there is much concern and gnashing of teeth about the dangerous inadequacies in much of public education, there is far too little grass-roots activism on the issue. Entirely apart from the need for community-building in aid of racial justice, America needs a potent, grass-roots school-reform movement. Improving local and state K–12 education is a cause that can unite people across lines of color, class, and political party. Coalitions focused on shared goals will encourage shared values and community. Focusing on education makes substantive sense too. Moreover, experience demonstrates that meaningful reform of K–12 education will come about if and only if there is strong state and local action, which is most likely only with sustained, intense, politicized community pressure. The best strategies for constructing transformative experiences depend on local contexts; education is not the ideal target of opportunity everywhere.

*Religious Institutions.* Churches and other institutions in the faith community are obvious candidates for leadership. Soup-kitchen altruism is a start, but next must come the networks and shared concerns that create community. Churches are among the most segregated institutions in society, yet they are committed to instruction in values. Conversion and redemption mean taking values from the pulpit and helping parishioners to put them into practice, which is never easy. One can imagine efforts to be more inclusive and diverse, whether through outreach for new parishioners or collaborative community works with other congregations, leading to bonds among parishioners.

*Community Works.* Projects like Habitat for Humanity (led by former President Jimmy Carter) seem, in their best form, to forge relationships rich in mutual understanding and emotional investment. The same approach should work in areas other than housing, which is Habitat's focus, but it probably helps if the projects create something visible and lasting and if the tasks bring everyone to a common level. Then there is a memorial, created with minimal hierarchy.

*Community Security.* Crime-watch and other neighborhood anti-crime initiatives create a sense of community. The impetus often comes from frustrated, fearful citizens. But there's no reason why more police departments and political leaders can't take the lead in pulling people together. (Of course, this only works if the community is somewhat integrated.)

*Community Defense.* Some problem may threaten a community— a construction project, an environmental hazard, or the closing of a military base—and ironically this creates a possibility for collective action and shared enterprise.

In contrast to these, the traditional leftist prescriptions for class struggle on behalf of a progressive economic agenda may simply fall flat when faced with racial divisions, as I have argued. Collective action based on shared economic interests has had only occasional success in the United States—one of the puzzles of our national political culture. Consider the long years of decline in organized labor and the inability of the national Democratic Party to develop any energy in the populace over the stagnation of working-class and middle-class incomes and the rising insecurity of the past two decades. Perhaps America's opportunity engine and its democratic capitalism dissipate class-based pressures before they threaten fundamental structures. But perhaps the puzzle also is due to our race neurosis and its poisonous consequences for coalitions and community.

## *The End of Affirmative Action?*

In conversations at the White House, we often spoke about what "Joe Sixpack's" views and responses might be on affirmative action and racial justice generally. Joe was always a blue-collar white male, of course (and probably living in a key electoral state). I won't deny that some folks mentioned him in order to suggest that it might be nice to think about how to communicate effectively to, or keep from alienating, a key voting bloc. But I noticed two striking things about the discussions. First was the tendency to put Joe's concerns and attitudes in the middle of the conference table, but only rarely to put alongside them the comparable concerns of an African-American Everyman (or Hispanic, Asian, or white woman). Joe Sixpack was the common, almost automatic analytical device. The closest analogous device for minorities was to think about how the Congressional Black Caucus might respond, or feminist leaders like Judy Lichtman and Marcia Greenberger. It generally fell to women and minorities in the discussion to "integrate" the Everyman by saying, "Look, it's not just about how Joe Sixpack feels, not just about *his* dreams and frustrations." The apparent capacity of most participants in the discussion to project themselves onto the barstool next to the white Everyman, chatting him up, was in marked contrast to their use of real-life minority and women political figures as representatives for the Otherman. Interesting.

Second, the attention to Joe Sixpack didn't, for the most part, *sound* like political calculation. It sounded like something else, especially when it came from Bill Clinton. But what other reason could there be to worry about Joe Sixpack? The President talked loosely about being President and leader of *all* Americans, not of some subset of factions or interests. In puzzling about this months later, I realize there's a fairly deep point in that impulse, difficult though it may be for cynics to grasp. Putting aside those who object to affirmative action just "on principle"—the bulk of this book concerns them—there is not just one Joe Sixpack but at least three. *Joe #1*, over there on the barstool, is angry about affirmative action. He's resentful and even seething because he is a bigot—a racist, or pretty close to it. *Joe #2*, sitting toward the back, in the booth, is upset about affirmative action because he believes *incorrectly* that he or someone he knows has had opportunities diminished somehow as a result of affirmative action. He thinks he has suffered, but he's wrong, though his resentment is real enough. *Joe #3*, just returning from the men's room, is upset about affirmative action because he believes—*and he's correct*—that he has suffered some diminution in his opportunities because of affirmative action. Perhaps he had to wait a little longer for a promotion, or his company has been getting less business from the local Air Force base than it used to, so he's getting less overtime.

Faced with these three characters, do we care about the views of all three? Do we care about their views equally? When I put this question to my seminar students, several immediately said that we shouldn't pay any attention to the racist *Joe #1*. One woman said we shouldn't pay attention to *Joe #2* because "he's ignorant." Several suggested that you must be pragmatic—that you have to pay attention to enough people to get elected. Well, I'm certainly for getting elected. But are there principles of another sort that should guide our decision about whom to include in the conversation? Which interests deserve attention and solicitude from someone who seeks to lead and heal?

*Joe #3* must be part of the conversation, and solicitude for his concerns is perfectly appropriate. That doesn't mean that we never do affirmative action when a white male bystander is affected, but the "narrow tailoring" the Supreme Court requires for government preferences, and the due care I have suggested in general, suggest that we must minimize the spillover costs of affirmative action. As well, there are clearly important dignitary reasons to make *Joe #3*'s concerns part of the conversation. It is important in both instrumental and noninstrumental terms that proponents of affirmative action endure the discipline of continually making the case for it, including trying to persuade *Joe #3* that these measures are important and are being pursued carefully. He may not be persuaded, but the conversation is nonetheless important.

*Joe #2* is also an easy case. He is a candidate for serious education efforts debunking rumors and propaganda. And the effort, while a resource drain, is necessary if we want to prevent his misinformed resentments from festering and themselves becoming a transformative experience producing racism.

*Joe #1* is the hard case. Many supporters of affirmative action want to write him off, and there's a good case for treating him as a moral outlaw. Indeed, the only obvious reason to pay attention to him is crass political concern for his vote. But there is another possibility.

Return to my death penalty example. Among its supporters, some people believe it deters crime; others believe absolutely in eye-for-an-eye retribution, whether or not it deters. Put all these supporters aside, and focus on opponents. Among these, a first group oppose executions because the evidence is that it doesn't deter, and they therefore believe it to be unjustified. A second group oppose it because it can't be administered fairly and accurately in the United States today—in part because of race. Note that these two groups do not oppose the death penalty on the basis of any absolutist moral principle about the value of human life or the nature of an ethical community. But a third group oppose the death penalty no matter what the instrumental or consequentialist calculations show, because even the most depraved murderer has moral standing as a human being. We can lock him up, but he remains a life worthy of some degree of respect. We don't write him off. We remain connected to him at some fundamental level.

On both sides of the death penalty argument, then, there are some people who focus on data, or instrumental calculations, and others who seem committed to moral or ethical judgments about our responsibilities to one another. With regard to *Joe #1*, the question is whether we consider the bigot a member of the larger community—whether we presume that he is redeemable, or in any case has some degree of moral standing. If there is a principled basis for engaging this Joe Sixpack, having nothing to do with electoral calculations, it is because we believe in the possibility of redemption.

Redemption and tolerance. My fear is that if those of us who support affirmative action and the racial-justice agenda give way to intolerance toward any person or position, then we diminish the ideal of community and tolerance. And having legitimized selective intolerance, who is most at risk of being victimized by it? America's history—and its present—make the answer painfully obvious.

• • •

Finally, we come to the question of when to end affirmative action. Thomas Sowell has noted that his review of affirmative action in several countries failed to identify a single instance in which it had been dismantled, and he doubted that its proponents would ever willingly let it end here in America.

When will affirmative action end in the United States? If we mean "end entirely and for all situations," the answer is simple: it should end when the justification for it no longer exists, when America has achieved racial justice in reality. Some critics doubt the good faith of those who promise that affirmative action is only temporary and transitional. But it is no more disingenuous or fantastic to promise that affirmative action is temporary than to promise that racial justice is achievable.

President Clinton said it well: "Mend it, don't end it." Affirmative action will remain controversial, and we should expect it to, like any policy addressing an intractable and painful problem. The cure for America's color problem surely can be no easier than the solution to problems of welfare and poverty, environmental protection, or labor-management relations. The continuing controversy—whether flames or embers—is about values and vision. What does America want to see in the mirror? What kind of communities do we want for our children? What dreams will nourish the spirits of the least among us?

We have a history of division, but for the most part it is division based on our perspectives, not our dreams. There is division between the good America and the other America, and almost every heart understands it is a division that impoverishes and, I fear, imperils us all. Faced with that peril, each generation must decide whether to dig defensive trenches or build bridges, and each of us must choose whether to participate in that decision or just let others decide for us and for our children.

I have a child. And I know what kind of America I want for him. I cannot imagine choosing to be a bystander.

# ACKNOWLEDGMENTS

First, some acknowledgments for the opportunity to serve, which made this book possible. My thanks to President Bill Clinton, Vice President Al Gore, and George Stephanopoulos, not only for accepting my services but for making the experience extraordinarily memorable and fulfilling in every respect. To George in particular, as the instigator of my involvement, all is forgiven; I seem to have survived it, and I will work for you again anytime, anyplace. (Almost.) Thanks also in this respect to Leon Panetta, Erskine Bowles, and Alice Rivlin, who not only welcomed me to the opportunity but were supportive at pivotal moments. Alexis Herman and Maggie Williams were always there for the tough times, with strength and wisdom and sympathy and energy—whatever the moment demanded. Laura Capps kept George out of my way, and Sharon Thomas's support enabled me to survive daily life in the maelstrom. Peter Yu, Carolyn Curiel, and Michael Waldman enriched the experience, lightened the burden, and gave me some sense of what it must feel like to play in a string quartet at the peak of its form. Outside the White House, I am especially indebted for the quiet but powerful contributions in support of me personally, and of our venture, to Henry Cisneros, Vernon Jordan, Tom Williamson, Deval Patrick, and the late Ron Brown.

Second, some acknowledgments for support on this writing project. At the beginning of it all, Jodie Allen gave me the opportunity to sketch my thoughts for *The Washington Post*, and Terry Donovan heard my first musings about a book, and said, "You have to do it." I must credit Victor Navasky for his sage advice, encouraging me to get an agent, and for matchmaking with the stupendously effective Chris Calhoun. I will be forever indebted to them, because Calhoun led me to Elisabeth Sifton, publisher of Hill and Wang. Saint Elisabeth also became my editor and, I hope, lifelong friend from now forward. Writing on this subject, with the earth continually quaking, was painful in many respects. Damn the cliché, but it's true: I cannot imagine having done it without her, and cannot imagine that she and her pencil can give so much to every member of her flock. Miraculous, indeed. Dorothy Robyn was patient when I whined, and cracked a loving whip when I faltered. Eugene Ludwig supported this project with the kind of no-holds-barred friendship that is one of life's great treasures. My dean, Robert Clark, is relentlessly encouraging, and sometimes to good effect. More specific to the book, I thank Susan Norton, Aaron Alt, Nicola Kean, Katrina Campbell Randolph, Jody Lissberger and Shanon Liss for their research assistance and editorial suggestions. Francis Allegra, Sarah Ingram and Zaida Coles Edley provided very helpful comments on a draft.

Finally, some acknowledgments under the broader heading of "life." I write this shortly after the tragic death of Ron Brown, most recently Secretary of Commerce. Meditating on the loss of this wonderful person has led me to appreciate belatedly how the fabric of my values, commitments, and meager talents owes its character to many people, their influences threaded through my life over the years. I, like many others, was fully aware of Ron Brown's outsize talent and contributions, but I realized only with his passing how substantial his contributions have been to me personally, and how much I depended on him at various moments to be there as an ally and a force for good. Not the least of those moments were during the Dukakis campaign's negotiations with Jesse Jackson, during the White House affirmative action review, and right now as President Clinton seeks reelection. I never told him that I considered him a mentor, an inspiration. I pray it is not too late to do so here.

And so it is not too early to acknowledge other people from whom I continue to draw strength and inspiration—reflected in this book and in my life's work generally. (In some cases the debt is personal; in others it is intellectual alone.) My thanks to friends Mary Frances Berry, Peter Edelman, Lani Guinier, Kweisi Mfume, Hugh Price, Charles Rangel, Roger Wilkins, Patricia Williams, William Julius Wilson, Andrew Young, and, most of all, Christopher F. Edley, Sr.

Ron Brown was not finished, and in that, too, his life inspires.

# INDEX

4703  17